Declaration
Statesmanship

Declaration Statesmanship

A Course in American Government

Designed for use as a one semester course in the 11th or 12th grades,
With a supplementary Book of Readings and Teachers' Manual

Richard Ferrier, Ph.D.
Andrew Seeley, Ph.D.

Fourth Edition

Authored by Richard Ferrier and Andrew Seeley

Cover design by: Caroline Green
Cover image: Declaration of Independence (1819), oil on canvas, John Trumbull (1756–1843), public domain via Wikimedia Commons.

ISBN: 978-1-5051-2269-5

Published in the United States by
TAN Books
PO Box 269
Gastonia, NC 28053
www.TANBooks.com

Printed in India

Contents

Introduction: The Declaration of America

If you ask a married couple about their marriage, "when did you get together?" that is, "when did your union really begin?". . . you might get answers as various as these:
- At the Senior Prom, when we knew we loved each other
- When he gave me the engagement ring
- Not really until the birth of our first child, when I first held the baby
- When we finally left her parents' house and had our own apartment, a year after our wedding
- When we both said, "I do"

Now there is something to be said for all these. All are in some way true. But the last one, the actual solemn vows of marriage, usually with readings from the Bible, prayers for divine aid, and the witness of friends and family, is surely the truest. You might want to consider why. We would suggest that the reason is that the union is a covenant, or as the law has it, a contract, and that the commitment is made when the couple *declares* that it is one. It is this day that they celebrate as their anniversary. They date the years of their marriage from this day. And their obligations are most especially the ones they make on this day. "Forsaking all others. . . in sickness and in health. . . till death do us part."

How old is our Republic? What day do we celebrate as its anniversary? Abraham Lincoln pointed to the answer in the Gettysburg Address, given in 1863. "Fourscore and seven years ago our fathers brought forth on this continent a new nation. . . " "Fourscore and seven," that is, eighty-seven. 1863 minus 87 equals 1776. Not the date of the Constitution, 1787. Not the outbreak of hostilities with the British, 1775. No, neither of these, but the "Glorious Fourth," as Lincoln and many others have called it. July 4th, 1776. The date of the Declaration.

The comparison of a nation to a marriage is especially strong in the case of the United States. Unlike most other nations, such as France or England, our nation came into being as a deliberate act. Before the Declaration, there were thirteen colonies. Afterwards, we were one people. We made war as one, entered into treaties as one, and made our principles known to a watching world. The Declaration states that we are "one people" who "assume. . . the separate and equal station to which the laws of nature and of nature's God entitle them."

Our union begun by the Declaration has been a great blessing. Some marriages are so successful that they become an example to other couples. We live in a nation that is an example to other nations. As ancient Rome was universally admired for its peace and stability, the United States has become a symbol of liberty and justice. When Chinese demonstrators for freedom faced the tanks in Tiananmen Square in 1989, they erected a model of a monument in New York harbor, the Statue of Liberty, to inspire them.

The Declaration of Independence, painted by John Trumbull in 1817. This depiction shows (from left to right) John Adams, Roger Sherman, Robert Livingstone, Thomas Jefferson, and Benjamin Franklin presenting the draft of the Declaration to the president of the Convention, John Hancock, with the secretary, Charles Thompson, standing at his side.

Marriages and political unions have their ups and downs. When times are tough, good friends and spiritual advisors remind couples of their solemn vows, of what they pledged to each other before their friends and their God. You might say that the founding principle of the marriage, the spirit that they try to live out day by day, is contained in those vows and the ceremony surrounding them on that special day in which the marriage was made. The same has been true in our political union.

Lincoln said, in Independence Hall, on his way to Washington D.C. to be inaugurated as President of the United States, that he "never had a feeling politically that did not spring from the sentiments embodied in the Declaration of Independence." Sixty-five years later, in that same hall, another American president, Calvin Coolidge, said:

> It was not because it was proposed to establish a new nation, but because it was proposed to establish a new nation on new principles, that July 4, 1776 has come to be regarded as one of the greatest days in history.[1]

"Publius:" left to right, James Madison, Alexander Hamilton, and John Jay

What were these new principles? We will look carefully at that question in the rest of this book. A brief answer may be found in the first of the *Federalist Papers*, a series of essays published in the newspapers of New York from 1787 to 1788. James Madison, Alexander Hamilton, and John Jay, using the pseudonym "Publius," argued in these essays for the adoption of the Constitution. In the first *Federalist* paper, Publius wrote:

---

[1] *Speech on the 150th Anniversary of the Declaration*

> ...it seems to have been reserved to the people of this country, by their conduct and example, to decide whether societies of men are really capable or not of establishing good government from reflection and choice, or whether they are forever destined to depend for their political constitutions on accident and force.

Publius meant that America would enshrine Liberty. The people would rule by their own choice. But he also meant that that choice would be reasonable. It would come from "reflection." On what would the people reflect? The answer is given early in the Declaration itself. "The Laws of Nature and of Nature's God," and the "unalienable rights" to "life, liberty, and the pursuit of happiness."

In summary, the Declaration founded America and gave it its fundamental principles. The nation so founded was seen by its founders and the whole world as a trial of the ability of a free people to establish a deliberately chosen form of government in accordance with the laws of nature and of nature's God. The basis of that government would be the authority of the people, coming from their endowment, by their Creator, with inalienable[2] rights.

The Great Seal of the United States. One Nation under God.

---

[2] "Unalienable" vs. "inalienable:" the two words mean the same thing. We have a draft in Jefferson's hand-writing with "inalienable," but John Adams' copy, the parchment copy, and the first printed copy had "unalienable." It may have been the more common spelling at the time. Unless we're quoting the document itself, we will use the accepted modern spelling, "inalienable."

Questions for Reflection

1. The Great Seal of the United States shown here may be found on the one-dollar bill. Examine the pyramid and stones, the eye, and the Roman numerals. The Latin phrases mean, "He has favored our undertaking," and "A new order of the ages." Does the seal support the claim that the American union began with the Declaration? You may want to look in an encyclopedia or other reference for ideas. Find out who designed the seal, and when it was adopted. For what purposes is it used?

2. Glance through the United States Constitution, stopping at the "Bill of Rights," i.e., the First Amendment. When did the Convention submit the Constitution to the people of the states for ratification? There are two powerful pieces of evidence in the Constitution to support the claim that the Declaration founded the union. What are they?

3. The two hundredth anniversary (bicentennial) of the Declaration was celebrated in 1976. We also celebrated the 200th anniversary of the Constitution. The first was much more spectacular, with large crowds, a fleet of tall ships, fireworks shows all over the country, and more. The latter was much lower profile. There were books and studies, editorials, academic conferences. Why the difference? Did we celebrate the year the Constitution was submitted or the year it was ratified?

A Look Backwards 1

You are not reading a history book, but a study of the meaning and power of the principles of America. Still, a bit of history is in order here. It will help us read the Declaration in the next three chapters, and it will shed a bit of light on why it happened here, in America, in 1776.

On June 10, 1776, the Second Continental Congress charged Thomas Jefferson, John Adams, Benjamin Franklin, Roger Sherman, and Robert Livingston with the task of drafting a Declaration of Independence. Congress officially declared independence on July 2, and accepted the committee's draft, with some significant alterations, on July 4.

By this time, the colonies had been engaged in armed conflict with British troops for over a year, since the famous April 1775 engagements at Lexington and Concord in Massachusetts. A Continental Army had been formed with George Washington as Commander in Chief; colonial troops had captured forts in upper New York; Americans had even attempted to seize Quebec and Montreal in Canada.

What brought about the fighting? And why did Congress take so long to declare independence?

1.1 Who Makes the Laws?
The Colonies vs. Parliament

The answer to the first question is easy in a way. Beginning in 1764, the British government, burdened with debts, including costs from the recent French and Indian War in America, had decided to raise money by placing taxes on the colonies. The colonies and mother country had benefited financially from their relationship for over a century, but the British had never tried to tax the colonies directly. Now they levied such taxes in the Revenue Act of 1764 and the Stamp Act of 1765. The British Parliament also extended the powers of the army and navy to search and seize colonial properties and to try and convict smugglers. As a further measure of enforcement, they had provided for a permanent British military presence in the colonies, and insisted that the colonial legislatures pay for the troops.

When the colonies offered fierce, united, and mostly peaceful opposition, including a boycott of British goods, the British government backed down. But it remained adamant that it had the right to make any laws for the colonies it wished. In 1766, it declared

> the King's majesty by and with the advice and consent of the lords spiritual and temporal, and commons of Great Britain, in parliament assembled, had, hath, and of right ought to have, full power and authority to make laws and statutes of sufficient force and validity to bind the colonies...

The Fight at Concord Bridge. The British Regulars, after a brief skirmish at Lexington, were turned back from Concord and lost 247 men before they regained the safety of Charleston.

This Act of Parliament, nearly identical to a 1719 Act asserting complete British sovereignty over Ireland, is known as the Declaratory Act. The Americans were pleased to be relieved of the burden of the taxes and other measures; the right to impose them they never granted. Ten years later, they were to shed their blood to vindicate their view.

Tension was renewed when Parliament insisted that the colonists buy taxed tea from the British East India Company. The colonists not only refused to pay the tax; they refused to let the ships land the tea. In Boston, colonists went so far as to board the ships and throw the tea overboard. The King and Parliament decided it was time to teach the Americans a lesson. In 1774, revealing their intention, they passed what they called the Coercive Acts. The colonists called them the Intolerable Acts. The port of Boston was to be closed until the tea was paid for, effectively shutting down Boston's economy; Massachusetts's legislature was suspended, and local council meetings were limited; American officials who didn't comply were to be tried only in England; and colonists were ordered to receive British troops into their homes.

While Massachusetts was the most directly affected by these measures, the other colonies realized that the same could easily happen to them: New York had also had its legislature suspended for resisting the Quartering Act. So twelve colonies sent representatives to what became known as the First Continental Congress. While petitioning the British government to repeal the Coercive Acts. this Congress encouraged the people of Massachusetts to form their own government and to organize a militia in order to resist the measures with force, if necessary. They laid the foundations for a united colonial government to resist the measures. They also published a declaration of their own, *The Declaration of the First Continental Congress*:

The original caption (from a London paper in 1774) reads: 'The Bostons paying the excise-man or tarring & feathering.' The 'Stamp Act' is nailed upside-down to the Liberty Tree, and the pot being held to his mouth is labeled 'Tea.'

> That the inhabitants of the English colonies in North America, by the immutable laws of nature, the principles of the English Constitution, and the several charters or compacts... are entitled to life, liberty, and property, and they have never ceded to any sovereign power whatever, a right to dispose either without their consent.

Parliament soon declared some of the colonies to be in a state of rebellion, and ordered the redcoats stationed in Boston to seize military supplies that the Massachusetts militia had stockpiled. This led to the fighting at Lexington and Concord. The Second Continental Congress met the next month, in May 1775. Besides taking charge of a coordinated continental military resistance, Congress also sent one more petition to the King. This appeal was known as the "Olive Branch Petition," so-called because of its peaceful and moderate

9

tone, and its expressions of respect for the king and the ties that bound the Americans and their British kin.

The King refused even to receive the petition. His answer was in deeds; he declared the colonies out of his protection, his Parliament prohibited trade with them and declared their vessels lawful prize and their seamen liable to impressment into the Royal Navy. In January 1776, after a group of Virginia patriots had driven the royal governor, Lord Dunsmore, out of town, the British bombarded and burned Norfolk, Virginia. Or so went the American side of the story. The British claimed that the Americans burned the town themselves, to prevent the British from obtaining supplies for use against the colonies. Dunsmore, it ought to be noted, had angered and terrified the Virginians by trying to induce their slaves and indentured servants to desert them in exchange for freedom and protection by the British forces. The offer was taken by few, but the memory of it, and the threat it posed, lived long in Southern minds, and was to show up among the charges against the king in the Declaration of Independence.

There was no dispute about a similar incident, which took place in October of 1775, at Falmouth (now Portland), Maine. Provoked by rowdy patriots, the captain of the 16-gun vessel *Canceaux* bombarded the town with heated shot, destroying it in the ensuing fire.

Order of Events I: *Prelude to the Declaration*

1763   **French and Indian War** (Seven Years War in Europe) ends, leaving Great Britain with large war debts.

1765   March: Parliament passes the **Stamp Act**, hoping to raise 60,000 pounds.

        May: **Patrick Henry** denounces the Stamp Act in the Virginia House of Burgesses

        Oct.: **Stamp Act Congress** meets in New York City with delegates from 9 colonies attending. They resolve not to import any goods affected by the tax.

1766   Feb: London merchants urge repeal of the Stamp Act.

        March: **Repeal of the Stamp Act**, but Parliament affirms its right to legislate with the **Declaratory Act**.

1767   the first of the **Townshend Revenue Acts** imposes import duties on various commodities, including tea. The act is designed to raise 40,000 pounds to pay salaries of royal governors and judges in the colonies.

1768   **Massachusetts Circular Letter** urges other colonial legislatures to resist the duties; Great Britain threatens to dissolve any assembly in sympathy with Mass.

1769   Va. responds by declaring an exclusive right to tax and agrees to boycott affected imports. The **House of Burgesses is officially dissolved** but reconvenes at the Raleigh Tavern.

1770   **Townshend Act** is repealed, except for tea tax, through efforts of Prime Minister Lord North.

1773   Apr.: **Tea Act** lowers price of tea from England, allowing East India Company to undersell American merchants.
        Dec.: **Boston Tea Party** destroys 18,000 pounds worth of tea.

1774   Spring: The **Intolerable Acts'** first piece of legislation, the Boston Port Act, closes the port of Boston.
        Sept.: **First Continental Congress** meets in Philadelphia, with all colonies but Ga. represented. They issue a "Declaration of Rights."

1775   Mar.: **Patrick Henry** makes his "Give me liberty or give me death" speech in Va. Convention.
        Apr.: **Battles of Lexington and Concord**
        May: **Second Continental Congress** convenes in Philadelphia. British reinforcements arrive in Boston.
        June 15: **George Washington** is chosen as commander of the Continental Army.
        June 17: **Battle of Bunker Hill**
        July: **Olive Branch Petition** is sent to King George by the Continental Congress.
        Oct.: **Falmouth** is bombarded and burned.
        Dec.: **The Continental Navy** is established.

1776   Jan.1: **Norfolk, Va.** is burned.
        Jan.5: New Hampshire adopts **first state constitution**.
        Jan.10: Thomas Paine publishes his pamphlet **"Common Sense."**
        June 10: Congress calls for a draft of a **Declaration of Independence**.

1.2 Hesitations: Democracy's Clouded Past

Even so, with lines drawn firmly and military action escalating, with colonies setting up their own governments, and with Congress acting as a government of the United Colonies, formal declaration of independence had to wait for over six months. This is an indication of how loath the colonists were to break with England and King George. The colonists had many ties to Great Britain. Most had family still living there. They were proud to be subjects of the British king. The colonists were generally happy with their lives, and with the peace and prosperity they enjoyed in their new land. If they separated from England and King George, then who would be their new head of state? They would have no one else with a plausible claim to be king. The colonies never even had a nobility from whom they might choose a king. Though they foresaw it only partially, a republic or democracy, some form of

The Athenian statesman Pericles, who delivered the famous *Funeral Oration* at the public funeral for all the Athenians fallen in the first year of the Peloponnesian War. He was dead himself before the war ended in the defeat and destruction of Athens. This is a Roman copy of a Greek statue made in the 5th century B.C.

popular government, was the most likely outcome of separation. And they had little desire at first to cast themselves upon the unknown waters of independence and democracy, which they associated with instability and turmoil.

A look back on the history of unlimited democracy, with which educated colonists were very familiar, would give them reason to doubt that it offered any hope of a better situation.

Liberty and Republican Governments in the Ancient World

The city state of Athens was pre-eminent among a number of democracies that flourished in the ancient world. At the height of its glory it was home to the great tragedians, Aeschylus, Sophocles, and Euripides. Socrates, the father of western philosophy, was an Athenian. The city was rich in arts and commerce, and, for a time, deployed the greatest military and naval power in the Mediterranean. Pericles was the chief Athenian leader in its glory days. This is how he described democracy in his famous *Funeral Oration*:

> Our constitution does not copy the laws of neighboring states; we are rather a pattern to others than imitators ourselves. Its administration favors the many instead of the few; this is why it is called a democracy. If we look to the laws, they afford equal justice to all in their private differences; if to social standing, advancement in public life falls to reputation for capacity,... if a man is able to serve the state, he is not hindered by the obscurity of his condition. The freedom which we enjoy in our government extends also to our ordinary life. There... we do not feel called upon to be angry with our neighbor for doing what he likes... But all this ease in our private relations does not make us lawless as citizens. Against this fear is our chief safeguard, teaching us to obey the magistrates and the laws, particularly such as regard the protection of the injured, whether they are actually on the statute book, or belong to that code which, although unwritten, yet cannot be broken without acknowledged disgrace.[1]

If our democracy is modeled on the Athenian, then Coolidge was wrong when he spoke of the newness of the principles of the Declaration (see page 3. But consider:

1. The same Athenian democracy that reared Socrates put him to death for calling into question its polytheistic gods.
2. The wealth and culture of the city was based on extensive use of slavery; slaves outnumbered free citizens.
3. Athens acquired an empire which it ruled more and more by force, culminating in an unjust aggression on the little island of Melos, whose adult male citizens were all captured and put to death for refusing to submit to the loss of their liberty.
4. Pericles himself calls democracy the rule of "the many" that is, a part, a faction of the free men, not a general popular sovereignty moderated by a written constitution setting up checks and balances to ensure the rights of holders of large properties and other minorities, like ours. This meant not only that Athenian democracy was prone to acts of tyranny over innocent foreigners like the Melians, but that it was prone

---

[1]Thucydides, *The Peloponnesian War*, Book 2

13

to what James Madison, among others, was to call "the tyranny of the majority."

5. The power and glory of the Athenians lasted only briefly, and was marred by faction, disorder, and eventually civil war, after which the city was conquered by its enemies and faded from prominence.

What was true of Athens was true of the ancient democracies generally. All had a state religion. None had adequate checks against the tyranny of the majority. All were scarred by civil conflicts and disorders. All were based on slavery and prone to injure the rights of the wealthy. In his *Politics*, Aristotle, the great political philosopher of antiquity, listed Democracy, along with Oligarchy and Tyranny, among the three forms of unjust or corrupt government. As evidenced by their treatment of the Melians and other subjects in their empire, the Athenians also did not think that freedom was the proper or natural condition of all men. That it was the proper condition of Athenians, they had no doubt. But it was not right for other men, if their subjection could be beneficial for Athens.

None of this is meant to say that the ancient monarchies were models of justice and peace. But the record of the democratic or republican government, which was also called "popular government," was sufficiently bad to lead "Publius" to write in *Federalist 10*:

> The instability, injustice, and confusion introduced into the public councils have, in truth, been the mortal diseases under which popular governments have everywhere perished; as they continue to be the favorite and fruitful topics from which the adversaries to liberty derive their most specious declamations.

Thus the facts and the judgment of such astute observers as James Madison, who was probably the author of *Federalist 10*, led sensible men to doubt the capacity of free men to govern themselves, at least as the ancient pagan city states did. Something new was needed to remove these doubts: "*novus ordo seclorum.*"

1.3   Reasons for Independence

"Did you take up arms against intolerable oppressions?"
"Oppressions? I didn't feel them."
"What, were you not oppressed by the Stamp Act?"

"I never saw one of those stamps. I certainly never paid a penny for one of them."

"Well, what then about the tea tax?"

"I never drank a drop of the stuff; the boys threw it all overboard."

"Then I suppose you had been reading Harrington or Sidney or Locke about the eternal principles of liberty?"

"Never heard of 'em. We read only the Bible, the *Catechism*, Watts' *Psalms and Hymns*, and the *Almanac*."

"Well, then, what was the matter? And what did you mean in going to the fight?"

"Young man, what we meant in going for those redcoats was this: we always had governed ourselves, and we always meant to. They didn't mean we should."

—From a conversation between Judge Mellen Chamberlain and the then-91-year-old Captain Preston, a veteran of Concord.[2]

Why did the colonists finally decide to break with Great Britain and her king? A complete explanation would be very long. Many good books have been written on the subject. (Some are named in the bibliography at the back of this book.) We only examine two of the causes here. The Americans lost faith in King George; they came to believe that he was a tyrant trying to rob them of their freedom. And they became convinced that they could do without a king. Or, to put it positively, they came to have hope in the possibility of just and stable popular government. We will look briefly at each of these factors.

The British History of Resisting Tyrants

Let's look first at the reasons the Americans did not trust the British king. The period just prior to the founding of the American colonies had witnessed the nearest thing to an unlimited monarchy that England had ever experienced. Before Henry VIII, English kings had always been limited in what they could do by their dependence on the landed aristocracy and the leaders of important towns, as well as by the independence of the Church, which could criticize their actions and impose certain penalties on them.

---

[2]Morison's *Oxford History of the American People*

King John is forced to sign the Magna Carta in the presence of his barons.

One important way in which the king was dependent on his subjects was taxation. For centuries it had been the case that, if the king wanted to institute new taxes in order to raise more money, he had to get the authorization of Parliament. Parliament was a body consisting of nobles, clergy, and representatives of important towns. If the king wanted to wage war, increase the number of his personal troops or institute new offices, he could, as long as he could fund these ventures from his personal properties or through taxes already in existence. But if he needed more money, he had to get the Parliament to agree. In time Parliament came to have a more active role in government, giving counsel to the king, proposing and discussing the merits of new laws. Even if the king didn't need to raise more money, the nobles and bishops were sufficiently independent and powerful to check royal ventures that might endanger the commonwealth over which he ruled.

The monarchs in the sixteenth century, especially Henry VIII, had broken through many of these barriers. Henry intimidated the nobles and commons in Parliament through an extensive use of trials for treason and other crimes. Those who got in his way faced loss of titles and property, imprisonment, and often death. He also subjected the bishops by having himself proclaimed head of the English Church.

When English subjects went to America in the seventeenth century, they were removed from much direct interference by the king. He remained the head of government, an office which he exercised, not very forcefully, through appointed governors in many colonies. But the role of Parliament, which included a share in making laws and approving taxation, was taken over by colonial assemblies. Over the century and a half before the Declaration of Independence, the colonial assemblies acquired more and more of a role in making laws for the colonies. Moreover, a much larger percentage of the free adult males had voting rights in America than in Britain. Accordingly, during this time, the colonists were more self-governing than their brethren who remained in England.

In the mother country, the seventeenth century witnessed two major struggles for power between the king and Parliament. Parliament won both battles, forcibly removing two kings from office. The second of these, known as the Glorious Revolution, ended with the removal of King James II. Parliament replaced him with William and Mary, making it clear that under this new regime Parliament had the greater authority.

This new relationship between king and Parliament caused a difficulty with the colonies, one that did not become evident until the middle of the eighteenth century. At that

King George III (reigned 1760 to 1820). The first Hanoverian born and bred in England, he was devout, and an affectionate husband. He read all government papers and took great interest in policy, being in effect his own prime minister.

time, Parliament began to claim an authority over the colonies even greater than the king, acting through his governors, had exercised. As we have seen, they tried to tax the colonies directly. After all, they had power to tax in Britain; should they not have power to tax in the colonies as well?

The colonists resisted this notion with all their might. Their experience, the experience of Britain over centuries, had taught them that they must have a role in deciding what taxes would be laid on them. Under the king's governors, they had this authority, as well as a major influence on all other legislation that affected them. If Parliament in Britain could make laws and pass taxes without their counsel or consent, they would have no lawful means to prevent themselves from being used for the advantage of the people in Britain. King or Parliament, it made no difference. If those directly affected by laws had no role in making them, then they would be little better than servants of distant masters.

Although the initial conflict was directly with Parliament, the actions of the king towards the end of 1775 had led some of the colonists to believe that he was encouraging, even directing Parliament, in its actions. King George had refused to hear the "Olive Branch Petition," his governors and captains had engaged in military and naval action, and concurrently, Parliament had begun to treat the Americans as open rebels. Before this time, Americans had placed their trust in, and given expressions of their loyalty to, their monarch, and complained of a corrupt and overreaching Parliament. Now, as they hesitated at the brink of independence, they were faced with the humiliating prospect of

Thomas Paine (1737–1809), author of *Common Sense*.

admitting, and professing, that they had been in error. Perhaps the king was not their friend and prop, their remaining hope for continued union with the mother country. Perhaps he was a tyrant.

In the beginning of the year 1776, an unknown young writer, brought to America by Ben Franklin, published a pamphlet called *Common Sense*. His name was Tom Paine. *Common Sense* circulated very rapidly throughout America.

In it Paine argued that not only was King George the cause of the troubles with Britain, but also that having a king at all was ungrounded in revelation and reason, and inimical to liberty. And he argued, in the most forceful and persuasive terms, that the time for independence, for separation, was now.

A few brief citations will give the taste, and the fire, of Paine's pamphlet:

—Government by Kings was first introduced into the world by the heathens, from whom the children of Israel copied the custom. It was the most preposterous invention the Devil ever set on foot for the promotion of idolatry. The heathens paid divine honors to their deceased Kings, and the Christian world hath improved on the plan by doing the same to their living ones. How impious is the title of sacred Majesty applied to a worm, who in the midst of his splendor is crumbling into the dust!

—A thirst for Absolute power is the natural disease of monarchy.

—We have it in our power to begin the world over again. A situation, similar to the present, has not happened since the days of Noah until now. The birthday of a new world is at hand, and a race of men, perhaps as numerous as all Europe contains, are to receive their portion of freedom from the event of a few months.

Within months of the publication of this pamphlet, numerous local initiatives were passed calling for independence. George Washington, commanding the Colonial forces at Boston, ceased thinking of the hostile army before him as the "Ministerial Army" and began to see it as the Royal Army, or the British Army. He wrote a friend: "A few more of such flaming arguments, as were exhibited at Falmouth and Norfolk, added to the sound doctrine and unanswerable reasoning contained in the pamphlet *Common Sense*, will not leave numbers at a loss to decide on the propriety of a separation." The pamphlet's sales were estimated as high as a hundred thousand copies, in a nation of perhaps two million readers. Rarely has a political book so met the needs of the time—a time calling for humanity, represented by the American people, to make the trial of an independent, popular government.

Liberty and Justice for All: Novus Ordo Seclorum

Men had thought for centuries that the only real political alternative to monarchy was a democracy like that of Athens. Why did the Americans come to think they could do without a king? How were they to avoid the pitfalls of ancient democracies? Again the answer is complex, and we will have to content ourselves with looking at a few of its most important aspects. Let us look at what early Americans considered to be the basis of their freedom.

In ancient Athens, democracy was the form of government for the same reason that tyranny was the form of government in other places, and even in Athens at other times. That reason was power. In a democratic society, the mob had proved itself stronger than the well-born or the rich, and so it made the laws. Consequently, it made laws to benefit itself, not the wealthy, and certainly not with any eye to non-Athenians. If the Athenian mob could beat them, it could use them.

The American colonists thought instead that all forms of government, whether monarchy or democracy or any other, should be ordered to obtaining justice, peace, and well-being for all its citizens. This was because, no matter who had the power, all were equally human beings. Their humanity gave them certain rights in any society, such as the right to move from place to place and to keep what their labor had earned them. To take away these things without their consent for the advantage of others was to violate justice. Naturally, since these fundamental rights came from being men, and not from being Englishmen or Athenians, governments, whether popular or royal, had no more right to subject other peoples than they had to subject their own people.

The idea that men had rights that came from their nature as men, rights that governments must always respect, was commonly accepted among the Americans. It was usually referred to as the "law of nature" or "natural right." The idea came from two different sources, which many people today think incompatible, but which the colonists found perfectly harmonious. One was the political philosophy of a number of English and French writers of the seventeenth and eighteenth centuries, the most prominent of whom was John Locke. These men taught that all men are equal under natural law. They also taught that this was evident to everyone who thought about the matter clearly.

The other, undoubtedly more important, source was the Bible. The Hebrew Bible, in Genesis, teaches that all men, "male and female," are created in the divine image. All men. Over and over again, the Bible condemns the injustice of rulers who ignore the plight of the powerless—widows, orphans, the poor. To do this, it teaches, is an affront to the God who made them, who promises to punish unjust rulers for their crimes.

The colonists were nearly all Christians of one sort or another, and the Bible was the most widely read book in the colonies. Even those who didn't believe all the miracles in the Bible (Thomas Jefferson and Ben Franklin are the most famous of those who held this view) thought that its moral teaching was the most enlightened ever developed, and perfectly consonant with what their minds showed them. Because their society recognized these

20

ideas and endeavored to act in accord with them, the colonists developed a confidence in their ability to make just laws even apart from the king. As King George pushed them outside of his protection, they were willing to dare that, as a people, they could provide for their safety and well being without him or any king.

Order of Events II: *English Political Liberty*

1215	King John is forced to grant the **Magna Carta**, giving power and rights to the barons of England.
1295	Edward I institutes a "**Model Parliament**," with expanded representation and a greater role in governing.
1509	**Henry VIII** becomes king. He dominates Parliament and has himself declared head of the church as well as of the secular government.
1628	**Charles I** agrees to a "Petition of Right," but subsequently ignores it. He refuses to call Parliament.
1649	Puritans support Parliament and overthrow and behead Charles I. England becomes a **commonwealth**, ruled by a committee of Parliament.
1653	Puritan leader **Oliver Cromwell** dismisses Parliament and declares himself Lord Protector, with unlimited power.
1658	After Cromwell's death, the Stuart **monarchy is restored** in Charles II.
1688 to 1689	The **Glorious Revolution**. Parliament drives out James II and invites William of Orange and Mary to rule. A Bill of Rights is passed.
1702 to 1714	The reign of **Queen Anne**. Parliament becomes the supreme power in the state. Scotland joins with England and Wales to become "Great Britain."
1714 to 1727	Reign of **George I**. He speaks no English and takes no part in government. Sir Robert Walpole, leader of the Whig Party, is considered the first prime minister.
1727 to 1760	Reign of **George II**. He likewise pays little attention to national affairs. **William Pitt the Elder, "the Great Commoner,"** is largely responsible for England's success in building up her colonial possessions.

> 1760 to 1820   **George III** comes to the throne determined to rule as well as to reign. Pitt is forced to resign. Lord North, leader of the Tory Party, becomes Prime Minister.

Questions for Reflection

1. This chapter has only been a sketch of some important events that influenced the writing of the Declaration. All the subjects mentioned merit deeper treatment. Choose one or more of the following to research more completely. (These are only suggestions; you might come up with ideas of your own to research.)
   a) The principles of England's Glorious Revolution of 1688.
   b) Taxation and representation in Britain and the American colonies.
   c) The Coercive Acts, the Stamp Act, the Boston Tea Party.
   d) Committees of Correspondence, Sons of Liberty
   e) Some of the key figures in the Revolution and their views.
      - British: William Pitt, Edmund Burke, George III, Lord North
      - American: Sam Adams, John Adams, James Otis, Patrick Henry, George Washington, George Mason, Thomas Jefferson, Tom Paine

2. To understand better the views of Americans on democracy and its problems, look at what is said in *Federalist Papers 9 & 10* about the history of democracy and the problem of faction (these are both in the *Book of Readings*).

3. Using the material from this chapter and any other research you have done, write an essay or a dialogue in which you raise and answer objections to declaring independence. (For a good example of political dialogue, read Thucydides' account of the debate about the fate of the Melians, "The Melian Dialogue" in *The Peloponnesian Wars*, Book V. This is available on-line and also in the *Book of Readings*)

Chapter 1 Review Questions

1. Use the material in this chapter to put the following events in order; write the date (year and month if possible) for each.

   a) Continental Congress approves Declaration of Independence
   b) British government first imposes taxes on American colonies
   c) Continental Congress declares independence
   d) British Parliament declares right to make laws for American colonies
   e) Battles of Lexington and Concord
   f) Coercive Acts ("Intolerable Acts")
   g) Falmouth, Maine, burned
   h) Boston Tea Party
   i) First Continental Congress meets
   j) Boston Massacre
   k) "Olive Branch Petition"

2. What three authorities did the First Continental Congress cite as entitling them 'to life, liberty and property'?

3. Name three Acts in which Parliament asserted its right to make laws for the colonies.

4. Turn to page 13. We note five facts that indicate differences between the principles of Athenian democracy and our own. The following statements from famous American documents show the contrast. Match each quotation below with one of the points on page 13.

   a) "From the disorders that disfigure the annals of those [Greek and Italian] republics the advocates of despotism have drawn arguments, not only against the forms of republican government, but against the very principles of civil liberty."
   b) "[Governments derive] their just powers from the consent of the governed."
   c) "Congress shall make no law respecting an establishment of religion nor prohibiting the free exercise thereof, or abridging the freedom of speech."

    d) "All men are created equal [and are] endowed by their Creator with certain unalienable rights."

    e) "That among these are life, liberty and the pursuit of happiness."

5. What was Parliament? Name two duties that Parliament exercised under the king.

6. How did the "Glorious Revolution" of 1688 lead to difficulties between Britain and the American colonies?

7. Write a brief quotation from Thomas Paine's *Common Sense* that argues that:

    a) monarchy is not supported by the Bible.

    b) monarchy is inimical to liberty.

8. Fill in the blanks:

    a) In Athens, democracy was based on _____; American colonists thought that democracy should be based on _____.

    b) Two sources that taught Americans about the laws of nature were _____ and _____.

Paper Topic 1:

On page 14, Capt. Preston summed up why the Americans rebelled: "We always had governed ourselves, and we always meant to. They didn't mean we should." Write a short paper (2–3 pages) giving reasons to support Capt. Preston's statement.

In CONGRESS, July 4, 1776.

The unanimous Declaration of the thirteen united States of America.

When in the Course of human events, it becomes necessary for one people to dissolve the political bands which have connected them with another, and to assume among the powers of the earth, the separate and equal station to which the Laws of Nature and of Nature's God entitle them, a decent respect to the opinions of mankind requires that they should declare the causes which impel them to the separation.

We hold these truths to be self-evident, that all men are created equal, that they are endowed by their Creator with certain unalienable Rights, that among these are Life, Liberty and the pursuit of Happiness.—That to secure these rights, Governments are instituted among Men, deriving their just powers from the consent of the governed,—That whenever any Form of Government becomes destructive of these ends, it is the Right of the People to alter or to abolish it, and to institute new Government, laying its foundation on such principles and organizing its powers in such form, as to them shall seem most likely to effect their Safety and Happiness. Prudence, indeed, will dictate that Governments long established should not be changed for light and transient causes; and accordingly all experience hath shewn, that mankind are more disposed to suffer, while evils are sufferable, than to right themselves by abolishing the forms to which they are accustomed. But when a long train of abuses and usurpations, pursuing invariably the same Object evinces a design to reduce them under absolute Despotism, it is their right, it is their duty, to throw off such Government, and to provide new Guards for their future security.—Such has been the patient sufferance of these Colonies; and such is now the necessity which constrains them to alter their former Systems of Government. The history of the present King of Great Britain is a history of repeated injuries and usurpations, all having in direct object the establishment of an absolute Tyranny over these States. To prove this, let Facts be submitted to a candid world.

He has refused his Assent to Laws, the most wholesome and necessary for the public good.

He has forbidden his Governors to pass Laws of immediate and pressing importance, unless suspended in their operation till his Assent should be obtained; and when so suspended, he has utterly neglected to attend to them.

He has refused to pass other Laws for the accommodation of large districts of people, unless those people would relinquish the right of Representation in the Legislature, a right inestimable to them and formidable to tyrants only.

He has called together legislative bodies at places unusual, uncomfortable, and distant from the depository of their public Records, for the sole purpose of fatiguing them into compliance with his measures.

He has dissolved Representative Houses repeatedly, for opposing with manly firmness his invasions on the rights of the people.

He has refused for a long time, after such dissolutions, to cause others to be elected; whereby the Legislative powers, incapable of Annihilation, have returned to the People at large for their exercise; the State remaining in the mean time exposed to all the dangers of invasion from without, and convulsions within.

He has endeavoured to prevent the population of these States; for that purpose obstructing the Laws for Naturalization of Foreigners; refusing to pass others to encourage their migrations hither, and raising the conditions of new Appropriations of Lands.

He has obstructed the Administration of Justice, by refusing his Assent to Laws for establishing Judiciary powers.

He has made Judges dependent on his Will alone, for the tenure of their offices, and the amount and payment of their salaries.

He has erected a multitude of New Offices, and sent hither swarms of Officers to harrass our people, and eat out their substance.

He has kept among us, in times of peace, Standing Armies without the Consent of our legislatures.

He has affected to render the Military independent of and superior to the Civil power.

He has combined with others to subject us to a jurisdiction foreign to our constitution, and unacknowledged by our laws; giving his Assent to their Acts of pretended Legislation:

For Quartering large bodies of armed troops among us:

For protecting them, by a mock Trial, from punishment for any Murders which they should commit on the Inhabitants of these States:

For cutting off our Trade with all parts of the world:

For imposing Taxes on us without our Consent:

For depriving us in many cases, of the benefits of Trial by jury:

For transporting us beyond Seas to be tried for pretended offences:

For abolishing the free System of English Laws in a neighbouring Province, establishing therein an Arbitrary government, and enlarging its Boundaries so as to render it at once an example and fit instrument for introducing the same absolute rule into these Colonies:

For taking away our Charters, abolishing our most valuable Laws, and altering fundamentally the Forms of our Governments:

For suspending our own Legislatures, and declaring themselves invested with power to legislate for us in all cases whatsoever.

He has abdicated Government here, by declaring us out of his Protection and waging War against us.

He has plundered our seas, ravaged our Coasts, burnt our towns, and destroyed the lives of our people.

He is at this time transporting large Armies of foreign Mercenaries to compleat the works of death, desolation and tyranny, already begun with circumstances of Cruelty & perfidy scarcely paralleled in the most barbarous ages, and totally unworthy the Head of a civilized nation.

He has constrained our fellow Citizens taken Captive on the high Seas to bear Arms against their Country, to become the executioners of their friends and Brethren, or to fall themselves by their Hands.

He has excited domestic insurrections amongst us, and has endeavoured to bring on the inhabitants of our frontiers, the merciless Indian Savages, whose known rule of warfare, is an undistinguished destruction of all ages, sexes and conditions.

In every stage of these Oppressions We have Petitioned for Redress in the most humble terms: Our repeated Petitions have been answered only by repeated injury. A Prince, whose character is thus marked by every act which may define a Tyrant, is unfit to be the ruler of a free people.

Nor have We been wanting in attentions to our British brethren. We have warned them from time to time of attempts by their legislature to extend an unwarrantable jurisdiction over us. We have reminded them of the circumstances of our emigration and settlement here. We have appealed to their native justice and magnanimity, and we have conjured them by the ties of our common kindred to disavow these usurpations, which, would inevitably interrupt our connections and correspondence. They too have been deaf to the voice of justice and of consanguinity. We must, therefore, acquiesce in the necessity, which denounces our Separation, and hold them, as we hold the rest of mankind, Enemies in War, in Peace Friends.

We, therefore, the Representatives of the united States of America, in General Congress, Assembled, appealing to the Supreme Judge of the world for the rectitude of our intentions, do, in the Name, and by Authority of the good People of these Colonies, solemnly publish and declare, That these United Colonies are, and of Right ought to be Free and Independent States; that they are Absolved from all Allegiance to the British Crown, and that all political connection between them and the State of Great Britain, is and ought to be totally dissolved; and that as Free and Independent States, they have full Power to levy War, conclude Peace, contract Alliances, establish Commerce, and to do all other Acts and Things which Independent States may of right do. And for the support of this Declaration, with a firm reliance on the protection of divine Providence, we mutually pledge to each other our Lives, our Fortunes and our sacred Honor.

John Hancock

Button Gwinnett
Lyman Hall
Geo Walton.

Wm Hooper
Joseph Hewes,
John Penn

Edward Rutledge.

Thos Heyward Junr.
Thomas Lynch Junr.
Arthur Middleton

Samuel Chase
Wm Paca
Thos Stone
Charles Carroll of Carrollton

George Wythe
Richard Henry Lee
Th Jefferson
Benja Harrison
Thos Nelson jr.
Francis Lightfoot Lee
Carter Braxton

Robt Morris
Benjamin Rush
Benja Franklin
John Morton
Geo Clymer
Jas Smith.
Geo Taylor
James Wilson
Geo. Ross
Caesar Rodney
Geo Read
Tho M:Kean

Wm Floyd
Phil Livingston
Frans Lewis
Lewis Morris

Richd Stockton
Jno Witherspoon
Fras Hopkinson
John Hart
Abra Clark

Josiah Bartlett
Wm Whipple
Saml Adams
John Adams
Robt Treat Paine
Elbridge Gerry
Step Hopkins
William Ellery
Roger Sherman
Samel Huntington
Wm Williams
Oliver Wolcott
Matthew Thornton

The Declaration Itself   2

This is the shortest chapter in this book. The text for it is almost entirely the Declaration itself.

The Declaration of Independence of the Thirteen Colonies
In CONGRESS, July 4, 1776
The unanimous Declaration of the thirteen United States of America,

When in the Course of human events, it becomes necessary for one people to dissolve the political bands which have connected them with another, and to assume among the powers of the earth, the separate and equal station to which the Laws of Nature and of Nature's God entitle them, a decent respect to the opinions of mankind requires that they should declare the causes which impel them to the separation.

We hold these truths to be self-evident, that all men are created equal, that they are endowed by their Creator with certain

Reading the Declaration of Independence from the east balcony of the State House in Boston, 1776.

unalienable Rights, that among these are Life, Liberty, and the pursuit of Happiness. That to secure these rights, Governments are instituted among Men, deriving their just powers from the consent of the governed. That whenever any Form of Government becomes destructive of these ends, it is the Right of the People to alter or to abolish it, and to institute new Government, laying its foundation on such principles and organizing its powers in such form, as to them shall seem most likely to effect their Safety and Happiness.

Prudence, indeed, will dictate that Governments long established should not be changed for light and transient causes; and accordingly all experience hath shewn, that mankind are more disposed to suffer, while evils are sufferable, than to right themselves by abolishing the forms to which they are accustomed.

But when a long train of abuses and usurpations, pursuing invariably the same object evinces a design to reduce them under absolute Despotism, it is their right, it is their duty, to throw off such Government, and to provide new Guards for their future security.

Such has been the patient sufferance of these Colonies; and such is now the necessity which constrains them to alter their former Systems of Government. The history of the present King of Great Britain is a history of repeated injuries and usurpations, all having in direct object the establishment of an absolute Tyranny over these States. To prove this, let Facts be submitted to a candid world.

"He...has endeavoured to bring on the inhabitants of our frontiers, the merciless Indian Savages..." Memories of early atrocities, like the Jamestown Massacre of 1622 (depicted here), gave the colonists a fear of the Native Americans, which had been renewed when the French used their Iroquois allies to attack outposts in the recent French and Indian Wars.

He has refused his Assent to Laws, the most wholesome and necessary for the public good.

He has forbidden his Governors to pass Laws of immediate and pressing importance, unless suspended in their operation till his Assent should be obtained, and when so suspended, he has utterly neglected to attend to them.

He has refused to pass other Laws for the accommodation of large districts of people, unless those people would relinquish the right of Representation in the Legislature, a right inestimable to them and formidable to tyrants only.

He has called together legislative bodies at places unusual, uncomfortable, and distant from the depository of their public Records, for the sole purpose of fatiguing them into compliance with his measures.

He has dissolved Representative Houses repeatedly, for opposing with manly firmness his invasions on the rights of the people.

He has refused for a long time, after such dissolutions, to cause others to be elected; whereby the Legislative powers, incapable of Annihilation, have returned to the People at large for their exercise; the State remaining in the meantime exposed to all the dangers of invasion from without, and convulsions within.

He has endeavoured to prevent the population of these States; for that purpose obstructing the Laws for Naturalization of Foreigners; refusing to pass others to encourage their migrations hither, and raising the conditions of new Appropriations of Lands.

He has obstructed the Administration of Justice, by refusing his Assent to Laws for establishing Judiciary powers.

He has made Judges dependent on his Will alone, for the tenure of their offices, and the amount and payment of their salaries.

He has erected a multitude of New Offices, and sent hither swarms of Officers to harass our people, and eat out their substance.

"For quartering large bodies of armed troops among us..." Hessian troops commandeering a private home.

He has kept among us, in times of peace, Standing Armies, without the consent of our legislatures.

He has affected to render the Military independent of and superior to the Civil power.

He has combined with others to subject us to a jurisdiction foreign to our constitution and unacknowledged by our laws; giving his Assent to their Acts of pretended Legislation:

For quartering large bodies of armed troops among us:

For protecting them by a mock Trial from punishment for any Murders which they should commit on the Inhabitants of these States:

For cutting off our Trade with all parts of the world:

For imposing Taxes on us without our Consent:

For depriving us in many cases of the benefits of Trial by Jury:

For transporting us beyond Seas to be tried for pretended offences:

For abolishing the free System of English Laws in a neighbouring Province, establishing therein an Arbitrary government, and enlarging its Boundaries so as to render it at once an example and fit instrument for introducing the same absolute rule into these Colonies:

For taking away our Charters, abolishing our most valuable Laws and altering fundamentally the Forms of our Governments:

For suspending our own Legislatures, and declaring themselves invested with power to legislate for us in all cases whatsoever.

He has abdicated Government here by declaring us out of his Protection and waging War against us.

He has plundered our seas, ravaged our Coasts, burnt our towns, and destroyed the lives of our people.

He is at this time transporting large Armies of foreign Mercenaries to complete the works of death, desolation and tyranny, already begun with circumstances of cruelty and perfidy scarcely paralleled in the most barbarous ages, and totally unworthy the Head of a civilized nation.

"He has constrained our fellow Citizens taken Captive on the high Seas to bear Arms against their Country..." The impressment of American seamen (even when justified, on the grounds that they had deserted from the British Navy) was an affront and humiliation.

He has constrained our fellow Citizens taken Captive on the high Seas to bear Arms against their Country, to become the executioners of their friends and Brethren, or to fall themselves by their Hands.

He has excited domestic insurrections amongst us, and has endeavoured to bring on the inhabitants of our frontiers, the merciless Indian

Savages, whose known rule of warfare is an undistinguished destruction of all ages, sexes and conditions.

In every stage of these Oppressions We have Petitioned for Redress in the most humble terms. Our repeated Petitions have been answered only by repeated injury. A Prince, whose character is thus marked by every act which may define a Tyrant, is unfit to be the ruler of a free people.

Nor have We been wanting in attentions to our British brethren.

We have warned them from time to time of attempts by their legislature to extend an unwarrantable jurisdiction over us.

We have reminded them of the circumstances of our emigration and settlement here.

We have appealed to their native justice and magnanimity, and

"For cutting off our Trade with all parts of the world..." This cartoon on the plight of Boston with its port closed appeared in a London newspaper on Nov. 19, 1774, shortly after the Boston Tea Party.

we have conjured them by the ties of our common kindred to disavow these usurpations, which would inevitably interrupt our connections and correspondence.

They too have been deaf to the voice of justice and of consanguinity. We must, therefore, acquiesce in the necessity, which denounces our Separation, and hold them, as we hold the rest of mankind, Enemies in War, in Peace Friends.

WE, THEREFORE, the Representatives of the UNITED STATES OF AMERICA, in General Congress, Assembled, appealing to the Supreme Judge of the world for the rectitude of our intentions, do, in the Name, and by the authority of the good People of these Colonies, solemnly publish and declare,

That these United Colonies are, and of Right ought to be FREE AND INDEPENDENT STATES; that they are Absolved from all Allegiance to the British Crown, and that all political connection between them and the State of Great Britain is and ought to be totally dissolved; and that as Free and Independent States, they have full Power to levy War, conclude Peace, contract Alliances, establish Commerce, and to do all other Acts and Things which Independent States may of right do.

And for the support of this Declaration, with a firm reliance on the protection of divine Providence, we mutually pledge to each other our Lives, our Fortunes, and our sacred Honor.

Order of Events III: *Facts About the Declaration*

June 7, 1776	Richard Henry Lee of Va. moves in the Continental Congress that "these United Colonies are, and of right ought to be, free and independent States."
June 11, 1776	Congress names John Adams (Mass.), Benjamin Franklin (Pa.), Thomas Jefferson (Va.), Robert Livingston (N.Y.), and Roger Sherman (Conn.) to the committee to draft a declaration. The committee selects Jefferson to do the writing.
July 2, 1776	Congress approves the Lee resolution of June 7.
July 4, 1776	After discussion and amendments, Congress adopts the final draft in Independence Hall in Philadelphia, the New York delegation abstaining. John Hancock, President of Congress, signs "by order and in behalf of Congress." Charles Thomson, secretary of Congress, attests his signature.
July 9, 1776	General Washington, already encamped on York Island, receives a copy of the Declaration, and has it read to the troops on parade that evening.
July 19, 1776	The New York delegation reports that it favors the Declaration. Congress orders that a copy be made on parchment.
Aug. 2, 1776	Fifty members of Congress sign the document. It is in the silence following this solemn ceremony that Ben Franklin remarks, "Gentlemen, we must now all hang together, or we shall most assuredly hang separately."

The original parchment was successfully hidden from the British when they raided Washington, D.C. during the War of 1812. It was kept in the Library of Congress from 1921 to 1952, when it was moved to the National Archives Building in Washington, where it is now kept.

Questions for Reflection

1. Write a summary or outline of the Declaration. To begin, give your outline three chief divisions, with the middle division as the longest. Be sure you present the parts that are clearly meant to be arguments as arguments. An argument or proof is more than a list of opinions, it tries to convince by showing how one thought, idea, or fact logically follows from another.

2. Having it by heart:

   > And these words which I command you this day shall be upon your heart; and you shall teach them diligently to your children and shall talk of them when you sit in your house, and when you walk by the way, and when you lie down, and when you rise. ——Deuteronomy 6:6–7

   In Laura Ingalls Wilder's *Little Town on the Prairie*, there is a chapter called "Fourth of July." A man says in that chapter, "It's the Fourth of July, and on this day somebody's got to read the Declaration of Independence. It looks like I'm elected, so hold your hats boys; I'm going to read it." The next sentence reads: "Laura and Carrie knew the Declaration by heart, of course, but it gave them a solemn, glorious feeling to hear the words." They knew it by heart, "of course." It turns out to be easier, and much more worthwhile, than many of us think now-a-days. The purpose of this exercise is an easy one: learn it by heart. An easy version of this project, is to memorize the first five paragraphs and the closing material, omitting the list of charges against the king.

3. God is referred to several times in the Declaration. Find all the references. How are these references made; that is, what aspects of God are used to name him?

4. The long middle section of the Declaration contains a list of complaints against the British King, George III. You are probably familiar with the threefold division of branches in the American Constitu-

tion: Legislative, Executive, and Judicial. Number the charges and list which of the complaints correspond to each branch. You should be able to see from the complaints what Congress thought the proper business of the branches was. Using the historical background in chapter 1, can you give a few details of what acts or events some of these complaints were directed against?

5. In 1954, Dumas Malone, a prominent scholar, wrote a book called *The Story of the Declaration of Independence*. The last chapter of that book is called, "What it means now." Malone gave a summary like the one you were called upon to write in the first exercise above:

> By birth all men are equal, not in ability or condition, for that has been untrue in all the ages of which we have any record, but in the possession of fundamental rights. Life, liberty, and the pursuit of happiness are mentioned in the great Charter; but more important than any list is the 'truth' that men possess these rights, not because of race or creed or station, but because they are human beings. Here is the eternal answer to bigotry and intolerance of any and every sort.
>
> Government and every other form of public control is a means to human well-being, not an end in itself. Man is not made for the state, but the state for man, and it derives its just powers only from the consent of the governed. In extreme cases, like the one in 1776, this 'truth' justifies political revolution, and in all cases it provides the criterion by which any government or institution should be judged. No sort of rule can justly rest on power alone, and here is the eternal answer to all forms of tyranny over the persons, the property, and the minds of men.

Malone's summary leaves out the list of complaints that explains why the colonists were justified in their revolution. What else does he omit? Why do you think he puts "truth" in quotation marks? What do you think of the way he treats what he calls the "list," namely, life, liberty, and the pursuit of happiness? Defend your summary against Malone's.

The Roots of American Liberty 3

The ideas behind the Declaration were not new with Jefferson. He denied that anything he said was new to the American mind. What he drafted, and Congress amended and adopted in the Declaration, Americans had been thinking for a long time. In this chapter, we will explore some of the sources of these common American opinions.

3.1 Written on the Heart: The Witness of the Bible

> Then God said, "Let us make man in our image, after our likeness; ... "
> So God created man in his own image, in the image of God created
> he him; male and female he created them.   —Genesis 1:26–27

> For what can be known about God is plain to them, because God
> has shown it to them. ... When gentiles who have not the law do
> by nature what the law requires, they are a law to themselves, even
> though they do not have the law. They show that what the law
> requires is written in their hearts, while their conscience also bears
> witness...   —Romans 1:19–2:15

> We hold these truths to be self evident, that all men are created
> equal...   —Declaration of Independence

The roots of the Declaration's self-evident truths go back a long way. They are both Biblical and rational, and the Bible itself claims that they are known by reason as well as by faith. The Hebrew Bible teaches in Genesis that men, "male and female," are in the divine image. All men. For centuries that was taken by believers, Jewish, Catholic, Orthodox, and Protestant, to mean that our free will and reason are a sharing in the divine nature; that we are, though decidedly not gods, godlike in our ability to think and act in accordance with our reason.

The reasonable plan for human life, often called the natural law or the law of nature, is, according to St. Paul, written in our hearts. We know by reason, by the image of God in us, that we are men and that men are not beasts. We know that there are some things that we may do to beasts that we may not do to each other, and that there are others that we must do for each other that we are not obligated to do for the beasts. In other words, we find a ground for both rights and duties in our common humanity, which is a gift of the Creator. As the Declaration assumes, this truth is taught both by reason and faith. The same Bible that proposes it for our belief asserts that it may be known to our minds and is written on our hearts.

Calvin Coolidge was President in 1926, the 150th anniversary of the Declaration of Independence.

These ideas were put in succinct form by President Coolidge in an address in 1924:

> The position which the individual holds in the conception of American institutions is higher than that ever before attained anywhere else on earth. It is acknowledged and proclaimed that he has sovereign powers.
>
> It is declared that he is endowed with inalienable rights which no majority, however great, and no power of the Government, however broad, can ever be justified in violating. The principle of equality is recognized. It follows inevitably from belief in the brotherhood of man through the fatherhood of God.

Coolidge spoke those words to a Roman Catholic audience. Listen to what he said to a Jewish group the following year:

> I remember to have read somewhere, I think in the writings of the historian Lecky, the observation that 'Hebrew mortar cemented the foundations of American democracy.' Lecky had in mind this very influence of the Bible in drawing together the feelings and sympathies of the widely scattered communities.

Later in the speech he added,

> Every inheritance of the Jewish people, every teaching of their secular history, and religious experience, draws them powerfully to the side of charity, liberty, and progress.

Coolidge was himself Protestant, a serious and devout Congregationalist. Most of the inhabitants of the colonies before the revolution were Protestants of one sect or another. Coolidge said this of the ministers and other clergy of that time: "The sturdy old divines of those days found the Bible the chief source of illumination for their arguments in support of the patriot cause. They knew the Book."

Colonial preaching

Readings

Those "sturdy old divines" were men convicted both of the liberating truths of the Gospel and of the God-given rights of man. Let's see what they said.

Our first excerpt is taken from an essay by John Wise of Massachusetts. Wise was a Congregationalist, born in Roxbury in 1652. The essay, *A Vindication of the Government of the New England Churches*, was published in 1717. Although the work as a whole is about church government, in particular defending the Congregationalist version of church order, we have chosen a portion on human nature and the natural law or law of nature.

> 1. The Prime Immunity in Mans State, is that he is most properly the Subject of the Law of Nature. He is the Favourite Animal on Earth; in that this Part of Gods Image, viz. Reason, is Congenial with

his Nature, wherein by a Law Immutable, Instamped upon his Frame, God has provided a Rule for Men in all their Actions, obliging each one to the performance of that which is Right, not only as to Justice, but likewise as to all other Moral Virtues, the which is nothing but the Dictate of Right Reason founded in the Soul of Man....

2. The Second Great Immunity of Man is an Original Liberty Instampt upon his Rational Nature. He that intrudes upon this Liberty, Violates the Law of Nature...

3. The Third Capital Immunity belonging to Mans Nature, is an equality amongst Men; Which is not to be denied by the Law of Nature, till Man has Resigned himself with all his Rights for the sake of a Civil State; and then his Personal Liberty and Equality is to be cherished, and preserved to the highest degree, as will consist with all just distinctions amongst Men of Honour, and shall be agreeable with the public Good. ... [and so] it would be the greatest absurdity to believe, that Nature actually Invests the Wise with a Sovereignty over the weak; or with a Right of forcing them against their Wills; for that no Sovereignty can be Established, unless some Human Deed, or Covenant Precede: Nor does Natural fitness for Government make a Man presently Governor over another; for that as Ulpian says, by a Natural Right all Men are born free; and Nature having set all Men upon a Level and made them Equals, no Servitude or Subjection can be conceived without In-equality, and this cannot be made without Usurpation or Force in others, or voluntary Compliance in those who Resign their freedom, and give away their degree of Natural Being. And thus we come to consider Man in a Civil State of Being...

The first Human Subject and Original of Civil Power is the People. For as they have a Power every Man over himself in a Natural State, so upon a Combination they can and do bequeath this Power unto others—and settle it according as their united discretion shall Determine. For that this is very plain, that when the Subject of Sovereign Power is quite Extinct, that Power returns to the People again. And when they are free, they may set up what species of Government they please; or if they rather incline to it, they may subside into a State of Natural Being, if it be plainly for the best.[1]

The next selection is from Samuel West, another New England Congregationalist. West delivered the sermon, from which we quote, to the Council and House of Representatives of Massachusetts, in 1776.

---

[1] Taken from Gerald N. Grob and Robert N. Beck, eds., *American Ideas*

... [T]he Deity has also invested us with moral powers and faculties, by which we are enabled to discern the difference between right and wrong, truth and falsehood, good and evil; hence the approbation of mind that arises upon doing a good action, and the remorse of conscience which we experience when we counteract the moral sense and do that which is evil. This proves that, in what is commonly called a state of nature, we are the subjects of the divine law and government; that the Deity is our supreme magistrate, who has written his law in our hearts, and will reward or punish us according as we obey or disobey his commands...

... [t]he authority of a tyrant is of itself null and void; for as no man can have a right to act contrary to the law of nature, it is impossible that any individual, or even the greatest number of men, can confer a right upon another of which they themselves are not possessed; i.e., no body of men can justly and lawfully authorize any person to tyrannize over and enslave his fellow creatures, or do anything contrary to equity and goodness. As magistrates have no authority but what they derive from the people, whenever they act contrary to the common good, and pursue measures destructive of the peace and safety of the community, they forfeit their right to govern the people.[2]

Next, we offer a short selection from a sermon given in Boston in 1774 with the Royal Governor of Massachusetts, General Thomas Gage, in the audience. Gage had been appointed, and given large numbers of redcoats, to put down the incipient rebellion in Massachusetts. The preacher, Gad Hitchcock, fearlessly spoke as follows:

[I]n a state of nature men are equal, exactly on a par in regard to authority; each one is a law to himself, having the law of God, the sole rule of conduct, written on his heart...

No individual has any authority, or right to attempt to exercise any, over the rest of the human species, however he may be supposed to surpass them in wisdom and sagacity...

And as its [i.e., political power's] origin is from the people, who have not only a right, but are bound in duty, for the preservation of the property and liberty of the whole society, to lodge it in such hands as they judge best qualified to answer to its intention; so when

---

[2]From Hyneman and Lutz's *American Political Writing during the Founding Era*

it is misapplied to other purposes, and the public, as it always will, receives damage from the abuse, they have the same original right, grounded on the same fundamental reasons, and are equally bound in duty to resume it, and transfer it to others.[3]

Finally, here is an excerpt from a lecture given by a clergyman and educator, the only ordained minister to sign the declaration, John Witherspoon. Witherspoon served as President of the College of New Jersey, or, as we know it now, Princeton University.

[R]ights are alienable and inalienable. The first we may, according to justice and prudence, surrender or give up by our own act; the others we may not. A man may give away his own goods, lands, money. There are several things which he cannot give away, as a right

Rev. John Witherspoon, a Presbyterian minister and a signer of the Declaration.

over his own knowledge, thoughts, etc. Others which he ought not, as a right to judge for himself in all matters of religion, his right to self-preservation, provision, etc.[4]

Catholic Witness: Government By Consent

Though the vast majority of Wise's countrymen were Protestants, it may not be out of place to note the Catholic antecedents of some elements of his thought. Besides the long tradition of reading the passage from Romans as pointing to a natural law accessible to human reason, the Declaration principle of governments deriving their authority from the people had been put very forcefully by Cardinal Robert Bellarmine in the 17th Century:

Note, secondly, that this power [the power of government, or political power] resides...immediately in the whole state, for this power is by Divine law, but Divine law gives this power to no particular man, therefore, Divine law gives this power to the collected body.

---

[3]Ibid.

[4]Taken from Grob and Beck, eds., *American Ideas*

> Furthermore, in the absence of positive law, there is no good reason
> why, in a multitude of equals, one rather than another should dominate.
> Therefore, power belongs to the collected body.[5]

When King James I of England began to assert the contrary of this position, that he ruled by God's appointment, or "divine right," the great Spanish Jesuit, Francisco Suárez, wrote in reply that James's view was, "new and singular, invented to exaggerate the temporal...power," and that Bellarmine's views were, "the ancient, commonly accepted, and true teaching."

If you think about it, it is only reasonable that readers of a sacred book teaching that all men have dignity in the same way, and from the same Giver, and that all men may be saved by His grace, should find in it the seeds of a political teaching offering political happiness based on the free consent of the equal men who form their own government in accord with the His natural law. Of course, these were only seeds until the wonderful year 1776. Our founding fathers made them sprout, and in this work they were aided by other sources, especially the arguments of political thinkers like John Locke, as well as their own experience in self-government. We will turn to the philosophers in the next part of this chapter.

We have argued in this section that the religious sources of the Declaration stretch far into the past, finally to the beginning of the Bible itself. Of course, the scriptural texts need to be read and understood, that is, interpreted. In Colonial America, that interpretation was exemplified by what we read from John Wise and the other preachers. It is by no means the case that all readers of Scripture were in agreement on the principles of civil government then, any more than they are now. But it is not unfair to say, with President Coolidge, that, "in the great outline of its principles, the Declaration was the result of the religious teachings of the preceding period."

Questions for Reflection

1. Consider the text of Romans 13:1–8 or 1 Peter 2:13–16: "There is no authority except from God..." Can you see that the hearers of these sermons have some reason, from Scripture, to doubt the argument for a right to revolution? If you want to see how that passage was interpreted as *supporting* a right of revolution in 1750, read the sermon *A Discourse Concerning Unlimited Submission*

---

[5] *De Laicis*, ch. 6

and Non-Resistance to the Higher Powers by Jonathan Mayhew, delivered in 1750. (This can be found in the *Book of Readings*.)

2. President Coolidge, in his great 150th Anniversary speech in honor of the Declaration, claimed that the three central ideas of the Declaration could all be found in John Wise and the other colonial preachers. Coolidge identified these ideas as: "1) the doctrine that all men are created equal, 2) that they are endowed with certain inalienable rights, and 3) that therefore the source of the just powers of government must be derived from the consent of the governed." Find these ideas in the texts quoted in this chapter.

3. Are you surprised at the explicitly political content of the writings of these clergymen? Do you think it would be well received in our times? How would you defend, or criticize, such a role of religious ministers in political discourse? Does Scripture, or the tradition of some religious bodies, support such intervention in "secular" affairs?

4. This is not really a question, but... weren't you struck by the "old-fashioned" language of John Wise? He wrote about two generations before the other preachers we cited, and you can tell something is happening to the way men write, and presumably speak, over that time. It's easy enough to figure what he means by "instampt," but you won't find that word in a modern novel or newspaper, and you might have to use a large dictionary, or some intelligent guessing, to decide what Wise means by "Immunity." You surely found his capitalization and spelling more archaic than Witherspoon's and the others'. Throughout this book, we will keep the older spelling and punctuation in our original citations, partly because it's simply fun to see it, and partly because we want you to feel the changes in language and style that really did happen in the English—or should we say, "American"—language.

5. Perhaps the most important question of all: Are these authors, mostly preachers and teachers, right? Is there a law written on the heart? We writers of this book do not tell you so on our authority, though we believe it ourselves. The two chief witnesses are Holy Scripture, for those who believe, and the evidence of each human being's own heart. Do you find such a law within? Who can answer that but you?

3.2   The Witness of the Philosophers

Near the end of his life, Thomas Jefferson wrote to Henry Lee to explain how he came to draft the Declaration:

> When forced, therefore, to resort to arms for redress, an appeal to the tribunal of the world was deemed proper for our justification. This was the object of the Declaration of Independence. Not to find out new principles, or new arguments, never before thought of, not merely to say things which had never been said before; but to place before mankind the common sense of the subject, in terms so plain and firm as to command their assent, and to justify ourselves in the independent stand we are compelled to take. Neither aiming at originality of principle or sentiment, nor yet copied from any particular and previous writing, it was intended to be an expression of the American mind, and to give to that expression the proper tone and spirit called for by the occasion. All its authority rests then on the harmonizing sentiments of the day, whether expressed in conversation, in letters, printed essays, or in the elementary books of public right, as Aristotle, Cicero, Locke, Sidney, etc.

Much of that "harmonizing sentiment," as we have seen above, came from the Bible and the sermons of the day. What about the testimony of reason, especially the witness of the "elementary books of public right?" We will follow Jefferson's own lead in his letter to Henry Lee, and look at some of the ideas that Americans would have borrowed from their philosophical tradition, using the authors Jefferson himself indicated.

Aristotle: Nature and Reason

Aristotle heads the list. He was a student of Plato, a Greek, writing in the fourth century B.C. His writings cover the whole range of human curiosity and wonder, from biology to logic, from the psychology of dreams to the art of poetry, and for our purposes, from nature (or as he called it, the science of physics) to politics and ethics. His practical judgment was so impressive that King Philip II of Macedon gave him the task of tutoring his son and heir. That young student is now known as "Alexander the Great." His philosophical work was so masterly that St. Thomas Aquinas, the great medieval theologian, calls him simply, "the Philosopher," while Dante, in his *Divine Comedy*, gives him the title, "the master of those who know."

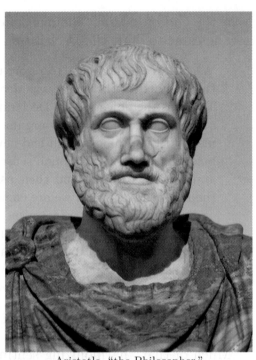

Aristotle, "the Philosopher."

It is to Aristotle that we owe the idea of 'species' in biology. A species is a kind of creature, marked by a 'specific difference,' which sets it apart from all other similar plants or animals. Now man is a member of the animal kingdom, similar to other animals in many ways. What is his 'specific difference?' According to Aristotle, (and can a better answer be given even today?) the answer is, "man is the animal that speaks and thinks," or as we say, the rational animal.

But in his ethical and political writing, Aristotle went further. He asked a question big with consequence. To what end does man have this ability to think? What had nature in mind for him in giving him this capacity? His answer was that men, by their reason, could find out the way to live and to live well. He held that men live best in a society with other men. So, he also defined man as a 'social or political animal.' Here are his exact words, from his book on political theory, called, *Politics*:

> Nature, as we often say, makes nothing in vain, and man is the only
> animal whom she has endowed with the gift of speech. And whereas

mere voice [that is, an animal sound, like a hawk's cry] is but an indication of pleasure and pain, and is therefore to be found in other animals (for their nature attains to the perception of pleasure and pain and the intimation of them to one another, and no further), the power of speech is intended to set forth the expedient and inexpedient, and therefore likewise the just and the unjust. And it is a characteristic of man that he alone has any sense of good and evil, of just and unjust, and the like, and the association of living beings who have this sense makes a family and a political community.[6]

So one principle from Aristotle is that all men are endowed with a common nature. This common nature allows them to think and speak, and makes them naturally want to live together for their own happiness.

The idea that all classes of men should participate in government also comes from Aristotle. In the 'mixed' form of government the majority, men of ordinary means, and the minority, owners of large properties, check each other's tendency to inflict injustice. He called such a mixed government, 'polity' or 'constitutional government,' and he suggested that it was the best achievable form of political organization. Aristotle considered communist or socialist systems, but rejected them on the sensible grounds that property owned by everyone is cared for by no one. He rejected absolute monarchy on the grounds that it would only be just for one man to rule if that man were so superior as to be a god among men, a condition not generally met with in human experience.

Two other principles that Jefferson may have taken from Aristotle are found in the *Ethics*, Aristotle's book on happiness and the good life. One is that there is something "just by nature." That is, justice is not the same thing as whatever men have set up as their laws. The legislator is measured by something not of his own making, something given in the nature of things, especially in human nature. The other idea Jefferson takes from Aristotle is that happiness, the thing at which all men aim, is not pleasure or glory or power, but, "activity of soul in accordance with virtue." He meant by this that the person who lives in accordance with reason and the moral virtues like courage and justice and self-control, which are the highest things in human nature, and who does so with a suitable share of this world's goods throughout his life, is truly happy.

---

[6] *Politics*, Book 1, ch. 2

Cicero: Equality and the Natural Law

Cicero was one of the greatest men in the Roman Republic, an orator, philosopher, and statesman, and finally a martyr to the cause of liberty when he was condemned to death by the junta known as the 'Second Triumvirate,' in 43 B.C. Cicero, like Aristotle, taught that there is higher law that stands above any man-made law, one that lawmakers have a sacred obligation to obey:

Cicero was a Roman statesman of the first century B.C.

> True law is right reason, harmonious with nature, diffused among all, constant, eternal... It is a sacred obligation not to attempt to legislate in contradiction to this law; nor may it be derogated from nor abrogated. Indeed by neither the Senate nor the people can we be released from this law; nor does it require any but yourself to be its expositor or interpreter. Nor is it one law at Rome and another at Athens; one now and another at a late time; but one eternal and unchangeable law binding all nations through all time.[7]

It is striking that Cicero thought that none but ourselves need be the interpreter of the natural law. That is because he, like St. Paul a century later, found it written on the human heart, or as Cicero himself would probably have put it, etched in the human mind. Because all men have equal access to the natural law, all men should be equal under that law. Cicero takes the Aristotelian discovery of the common human nature, ascribed to our being rational, and draws from it the Declaration principle of human equality. Thus we find him writing in his *De Legibus (On the Laws)*:

---

[7] *De Republica*, cited in Lactantius, *Divinae Institutiones*

> There is no one thing so like or equal to one another as in every
> instance man is to man. And if the corruption of custom and the
> variation of opinion did not induce an imbecility of minds and turn
> them aside from the course of nature, no one would more resemble
> himself than all men would resemble all men. Therefore, whatever
> definition we give to man will be applicable to the entire human race.

Edwin S. Corwin, a great historian of the Constitution at Princeton
University when future U.S. President Woodrow Wilson was head of the
University, wrote of the quotation from Cicero above: "... [Equality] is the
inescapable consequence of Cicero's notion of the constancy of the distinctive
attributes of human nature, those which supply the foundation of natural
law." Corwin goes on to say:

> The notion of popular sovereignty, of a social contract, and of a
> contract between governors and governed are all foreshadowed by
> Cicero with greater or less distinctness. The notion of a state of
> nature, on the other hand, is missing, being supplied by Seneca and
> the early Church Fathers.[8]

Jefferson did not mention Seneca to Henry Lee, and he was most likely
not widely read in the 'early Church Fathers,' but he did know the work
of John Locke, as did most literate and politically aware Americans and
Britons of his day.

Locke: Natural Right and the State of Nature

John Locke holds a place among the most important philosophers of the
western tradition. Like Aristotle, he thought and wrote on ethics, education,
physics, and the soul. Locke was friends with the pioneering chemist Robert
Boyle, and an avid reader of René Descartes and Isaac Newton. Like Aristotle,
he played a role in the political life of his day, though where Aristotle was
a tutor to a young statesman, Locke was more of an advisor to mature
politicians and a civil servant himself. His chief writings are his *Letter on
Toleration*, *Essay Concerning Human Understanding*, and *Two Treatises of
Government*. Jefferson no doubt had the *Second Treatise of Government* in
mind when he wrote to Lee.

The *Second Treatise* opens with a definition of "political power," its
source and its ends. It closes with two chapters on tyranny and the right of

---

[8]Edwin S. Corwin's *The 'Higher Law' Background of American Constitutional Law*

47

rebellion. Political power he defines as "a right of making laws with penalties of death, and consequently all less penalties, for the regulating and preserving of property..." This power implies the legal use of force, and so an executive function, both for domestic order and for protection from "foreign injury." Though he adds that this is "only for the public good," his primary emphasis seems to be on private property.

Where does the right to make laws and use force come from? According to Locke, we must look back to "the state of nature," that is, a real or imagined time before men had any government at all. In this state all men enjoy "perfect freedom to order their actions and dispose of their possessions and persons as they see fit, *within the bounds of the law of nature...*" [italics added]. Locke adds that the state of nature is a "state also of equality" echoing Cicero when he remarks that there is "nothing more evident than that creatures of the

John Locke (1632–1704)

same species and rank, promiscuously born to the same advantages of nature and the use of the same faculties, should also be equal amongst one another without subordination or subjection..."

Americans can see at once the seeds of what Jefferson would write 100 years later for the Continental Congress: men are created equal, and there are laws of nature that govern them. Locke takes special pains in chapter 2 to insist that the "perfect freedom" of the state of nature does not mean that anyone can do anything:

> The state of nature has a law of nature to govern it... and reason, which is that law, teaches all mankind who will but consult it that, being all equal and independent, no one ought to harm another in his life, liberty, or possessions.

But men are not always observant of the law of nature, or of the dictates of reason generally. Who will enforce the law of nature? In the state of nature, there is no government beyond each individual man. Therefore, the power of the sword, or the executive power, lies in each and every person. Now Locke was a shrewd observer of human behavior. He saw as well as anyone the bias that our natural love of ourselves produces in every human being. So he could not fail to note that leaving the execution of the law to every individual would lead to conflict. A neutral person, a disinterested party, was clearly needed to ensure that justice was done. In short, there was a need for government, or what he had called "political power." But this person is not designated by any obvious signs or marks, nor has God made plain who he is. He is needed, but he is not established by nature. Therefore he and the other magistrates, and ultimately the laws, must be grounded upon the consent of the equal men who form the civil society. Locke puts the whole argument succinctly in chapter 8:

> Men being, as has been said, by nature all free, equal, and independent, no one can be put out of this estate and subjected to the political power of another without his own consent. The only way whereby any one divests himself of his natural liberty and puts on the bonds of civil society is by agreeing with other men to join and unite into a community for their comfortable, safe, and peaceable living one amongst another, in a secure enjoyment of their properties and a greater security against any that are not of it... When any number of men have so consented to make one community or government, they are thereby presently incorporated and make one body politic wherein the majority have a right to act and conclude the rest.

Locke was also enough of a realist to anticipate circumstances in which any government, even a republican one, might turn to tyranny. He devoted the entirety of chapter 18 to the question of tyranny. There he remarks:

> It is a mistake to think this fault is proper only to monarchies; other forms of government are liable to it as well as that. For whenever the power that is put in any hands for the government of the people and the preservation of their properties is applied to other ends, and made use of to impoverish, harass, or subdue them to the arbitrary and irregular commands of those that have it, there it presently becomes tyranny, whether those that use it are one or many.

Locke is very direct and forceful on what may and should be done when tyranny is being established. First, it is the government's fault, and not the people's. Second, the people shall be the judge of whether it is coming to pass. They need not wait until it has been thoroughly established. Third, the people should wait until "a long train of actions show the councils [of the government] all tending that way," i.e., towards tyranny. And fourth, that when this comes to pass, "the people are at liberty to provide for themselves by erecting a new legislative, differing from the other by the change of persons or form, or both, as they shall find it most for their safety and good..."

Locke was sounding a new theme in declaring the right to rebellion. His critics called it a dangerous teaching. Most political thinkers before Locke had been more concerned to discourage men from rebelling, than to defend a right to rebel. Civil war and revolution are terrible things, full of the most extreme sufferings and loss of life and property.

But, replied Locke, there are good reasons to think that a people conscious of its right to rebel will be no more inclined to exercise it than one taught not to. In the first place, it is not abstract principle only, but also the experience of misery that leads men to turn on their masters. The victims of Soviet tyranny, both in Eastern Europe and in the Soviet Empire, were not taught that they had a natural right to rebel, but at length they did. Perhaps if they had cherished such a teaching, and proclaimed it publicly, the very possibility of communist tyranny would not have been so great. Further, from the point of view of the governors, who have no desire to be disgraced, cast from power, and even put to death, their first and best defense against civil war is to govern well.

Locke makes both of these arguments to show that his teaching does not lead to frequent rebellion. He also makes another, in chapter 19, using words which are closely followed in the Declaration:

> Great mistakes in the ruling part, many wrong and inconvenient laws, and all the slips of human frailty will be born by the people without mutiny or murmur. But if a long train of abuses, prevarications, and artifices, all tending the same way, make the design visible to the people, and they cannot but feel what they lie under and see whither they are going... it is not to be wondered that they should rouse themselves and endeavor to put the rule into such hands which may secure to them the ends for which government was at first erected.

Algernon Sidney: The Whig Martyr

Algernon Sydney (1623–1683)

The reputation of the fourth of Jefferson's cited authorities, Algernon Sidney, does not stand so high as the other three, who are in nearly everyone's list of the greats of our civilization. Sidney was a passionate and partisan British Whig, active in Parliament and other government service, who was charged with treason in connection with a conspiracy to assassinate King Charles II (the so-called 'Rye House Plot') and executed in 1683. Sidney's *Discourses Concerning Government*, published in 1698, has been described by Donald Lutz, a 20th century historian, as "especially interesting, since he combines reason and revelation in his analysis, and thus shows how easily the Declaration can be an expression of earlier, biblically based American constitutional thought." Another historian, Bernard Bailyn, says that the American Revolutionary writers "above all...referred to the doctrines of Algernon Sidney, that 'martyr to civil liberty' whose *Discourses*...became a textbook of revolution in America."

Two quotations from the *Discourses* may give a taste of Sidney's thought, which is, in most important points, like Locke's:

> Man cannot continue in the perpetual and entire fruition of the Liberty that God hath given him. The Liberty of one is thwarted by that of another; and whilst they are equal, none will yield to any, otherwise than by a general consent. This is the ground of all just governments.
>
> ...'tis evident in Scripture God hath ordained Powers; but God hath given them to no particular Person, because by nature all men are equal; therefore he has given Power to the People or multitude. (Algernon Sidney paraphrasing Bellarmine)

51

It was Sidney, himself far from being a Catholic, and indeed not obviously of any religious sect of any kind, who cited the Jesuits Bellarmine and Suárez, thus bringing their arguments to a wide English and American audience composed almost entirely of Protestants. And we know that Thomas Jefferson, among others, was paying attention. The Library of Congress owns Jefferson's copy of a book titled *Patriarcha*, by the "Divine Right of Kings" theorist, Robert Filmer. Filmer was an archenemy of the English Whigs, and hence of both Sidney and Locke. Jefferson heavily annotated his copy, marking these sentences, among others. They are Filmer's summary of Bellarmine's ideas. (Filmer listed them before going on to attack them.)

- Secular or civil power is instituted by man.
- It is in the people unless they bestow it upon a prince.
- The Divine Law hath given this power to no particular man.
- It depends on the consent of the people to ordain over them a king, council, or other magistrates.
- If there be lawful cause, the people may change the kingdom into an aristocracy or a democracy.

The great David Hume, who *is* of the rank of Cicero and Locke, said of Sidney that he "had maintained principles, favorable indeed to liberty, but such as the best and most dutiful subjects in all ages have been known to embrace; the original contract, the source of power from a consent of the people, the lawfulness of resisting tyrants, the preference of liberty to the government of a single person." If we add to Hume's list the insistence on the natural equality of men as coming from God, together with the law of nature to govern men, we shall have in Sidney's works a concise list of the key propositions Jefferson had recourse to in framing the Declaration.

William Blackstone (1723–1780), Charles Montesquieu (1689–1755), and David Hume (1711–1776)

Jefferson did not tell Lee of all the authors that influenced his and his countrymen's thought in 1776. Surely he could have mentioned William Blackstone, the great English jurist, and the French political philosopher, Charles Montesquieu; the former for the natural law, the latter for the excellence of 'mixed government' and the separation of powers. Plutarch, Livy, and other authors from classical antiquity were part of the story, too. And of course, the Bible. The key point is that our founders saw these authors, both philosophical and sacred, as pointing to a common teaching, of human rights and natural law, of the dignity of man and of the political life, and of the possibility of just, free, republican government, based upon the consent of the governed. And with this in mind they made their Declaration, their revolution, and us.

Order of Events IV: *Roots of Liberty*

The Bible	men are made in the divine image
	men have free will and reason
	men have rights and duties
Pericles (c. 430 BC)	Democracy, rule of the many, proper for free men
Plato (c. 360 BC)	liberty without law leads to tyranny
Aristotle (c. 330 BC)	all men have a common nature
	polity (mixed government) is best
	a thing can be just "by nature"
	happiness is living in accord with reason and virtue
Cicero (c. 50 BC)	natural law can be interpreted by each man
	equality of men
Livy (c. 10 AD)	republics grow great through virtue
Seneca (c. 50 AD)	"state of nature"
Plutarch (c. 100 AD)	virtues and vices of powerful leaders
Robert Bellarmine and **Francisco Suárez** (c. 1610)	civil power is instituted by man
	God gives this power to no particular man
	rule requires the consent of the people
	people have the right to alter their government
Robert Filmer (c. 1650)	divine right of kings
Algernon Sydney (c. 1680)	government by consent
	cited Bellarmine and Suárez
John Locke (c. 1690)	political power is to protect property
	government is based on consent of the governed

right to rebel against tyranny

Charles Montesquieu excellence of mixed government
(c. 1750) separation of powers

David Hume original contract
(c. 1760) consent of the people
lawfulness of resisting tyrants
liberty preferable to rule by one

Questions for Reflection

6. Do you think there is a tension between Locke's emphasis on property and Aristotle's idea that happiness is found in action in accordance with virtue? Are there virtues that are connected to the acquisition and protection of property? What is the role of government in fostering these virtues?

7. Obviously men are not equal in every way...in strength, or age, or wisdom, or wealth. What do the thinkers that Jefferson cited take to be the fundamental equality of men? Do you agree with them?

8. Older authors like Plato, Aristotle, and St. Thomas Aquinas describe tyranny as the rule of one man not aimed at the common, or public, good. They often go on to say that this happens when a bad man becomes king and puts his desire for wealth or pleasure, for example, over his reason and sense of justice. Locke is explicit in holding that tyranny can be found in a body of men who have political power as well as in a monarchy. Is Locke's wider use of the term more or less reasonable? You might want to read chapter 18 of the *Second Treatise* to help you give an answer.

9. Evidence of the influence of classical thought on early Americans can be found on the map. Here are four instances: Athens, Georgia; Spartansburg, South Carolina; Utica, New York; and Cicero, Illinois. You might have fun looking for others. Nearly all such names will be from the ancient republican tradition, very few from a monarchial or imperial one.

10. You may have met Cicero as a minor character in Shakespeare's *Julius Caesar*. Shakespeare himself drew largely from *Plutarch's Lives* for the facts in that play. If you want to know more about Cicero the man, try reading Plutarch; that's what your revolutionary forbears did; Plutarch was widely owned and read in America at

the time of the Revolution, and for many years thereafter. And he's a fun read.

11. An excellent discussion of the issues raised in our review of the philosophers and the Biblical foundation may be found in Gary Amos's *Defending the Declaration*. His citations from Blackstone fill a gap in the argument presented here. You may wish to read Locke and the other authors mentioned in this part of our text. One chapter (chapter VI) of Locke's *Second Treatise on Government* is included in our *Book of Readings*, but all of it is worth reading, and we have particularly noted chapters II, VIII, XVIII and XIX. A somewhat more demanding scholarly treatment may be found in Paul Rahe's magisterial three volume *Republics, Ancient and Modern*, Vol. 3, "Prologue: Novus Ordo Seclorum," and Ch. 6, "Virtue in the Modern Republic".

Of course, there is no substitute for reading the great old books themselves. Book One of Aristotle's *Ethics* is deep and thought provoking (excerpts from this are found in the *Book of Readings*), but also accessible to any serious reader, as is the *Second Treatise* of Locke. If you read the second chapter of the *Treatise*, you will find Locke citing arguments from the great Anglican political thinker, Richard Hooker. You might do a bit of historical research on Hooker and the tradition from which he comes. Amos's book could help get you started here.

Another recent book of great interest on these matters is *Written on the Heart: the Case for Natural Law* by J. Budziszewski.

12. Another historical question you might wish to pursue is the party system in English politics. We mentioned that Sidney was an ardent Whig. Who were the Whigs, and what did they stand for? Do you know anything about the "Glorious Revolution" of 1688? Or how it was regarded in America at the time of our Revolution?

Chapter 3 Review Questions

1. On page 35, we says, "...the Bible claims that [the Declaration's self-evident truths] are known by reason as well as by faith." What

does "known by reason" mean?

2. What is meant by 'natural law' or the 'law of nature'?

3. What is the difference between a right and a duty?

4. What are the three "great immunities" identified by John Wise?

5. What reason does Wise give to support his claim that "no Sovereignty can be Established, unless some Human Deed, or Covenant Precede"?

6. Samuel West says, "...[t]he authority of a tyrant is null and void." What two statements does he make to argue for this claim?

7. How does John Witherspoon distinguish alienable from unalienable rights?

8. What does Aristotle identify as man's specific difference?

9. What does Aristotle mean by defining man as a "social or political animal"?

10. What did Aristotle consider the best achievable form of political organization?

11. Who is the truly happy man according to Aristotle?

12. Identify two doctrines that Jefferson might have learned from Cicero.

13. What is the definition of political power according to Locke? What is its purpose?

14. According to Locke, how are political communities formed? Why are they formed in this way?

15. Name three Declaration principles David Hume found in the writing of Algernon Sydney.

Thinking Through the Declaration 4

In this chapter, we will look carefully at the details and language of the Declaration. We will assume that the Congress, the drafters, and the signers made sense. They knew what they wanted to declare, and they did so with precision. After all, if men are capable of ruling themselves by reason, they must also be able to communicate their thoughts clearly to one another so that what each thinks can become known to the other. This means that we will be paying attention to particular words and arguments, and that we will not say, as many do, that one thing is true "for me" and another "for you."

4.1 Independence, Revolution, and Prudence

Independence

Let's start at the beginning, with the first paragraph. "When in the course of human events, it becomes necessary for one people to dissolve the political bands..." We note in the first place that Congress is arguing for separation. The resulting war was called the War of Independence, and July 4th is called "Independence Day." America was separating from Great Britain. This meant that we would no longer form one political society with what they later call, "our British brethren." It meant that we would become independent.

The founders held that this separation was "necessary," and that they were compelled to it by causes outside themselves. "Necessary" here does not mean that "there was nothing they could do about it," as, for example, it must be that a part is always less than the whole, or that when a triangle is right-angled, then the square on the hypotenuse is equal to the squares on the other two sides, or that water must flow downhill. The necessity that they had in mind was moral necessity. When a young man says, "I had to answer my country's call," or a witness admits, "I was compelled to say what I knew about the charges," he or she is acknowledging the force of moral necessity. Perhaps I would much rather stay home with my family or at my job or school. Perhaps I grieve that my testimony will convict a friend or relative. Nonetheless, I must do it. It is a duty. I may be reluctant, but I must do what is right.

Congress was indeed reluctant to separate from "our British brethren." Ties of blood—"consanguinity... ties of our common kindred"—are cited in the concluding paragraphs of the Declaration. But, that same passage goes on to say, "We must, therefore, acquiesce in the necessity which denounces our separation..."

The Horse America Throwing His Master. A British cartoon published in 1779. The figure looking on in the background represents France.

Their claim, consequently, was that the separation from the British government, and hence the British people, was their duty.

Moreover, since separation, or dissolving political bands, sometimes called rebelling, is generally and reasonably held to be a dangerous if not desperate action, they also felt a duty to explain their reasons. And not only to the British, but to "the opinions of mankind." They called this duty a "decent respect."

The word "decent" is noteworthy. A decent person feels himself measured by a standard. He is also capable of feeling shame for his words and deeds, should they fall short of that standard. He cares about what others think of him. A decent respect for the opinions of others implies that the others, too, are decent, or capable of decency, and hence have dignity. These "others" are all our fellow human beings. Thus the founders bore witness to that common human dignity which would ground their own independence. That dignity has a source, namely the "laws of Nature and of Nature's God." We have seen in previous chapters that they drew their belief in, and their knowledge of, those laws from Scripture and from the arguments of such men as John Wise, William Blackstone, and John Locke.

But this source of our common dignity has another consequence. If men have the power and right of separation because they are "made in the image and likeness of God," then when they have good reason, genuine moral

58

necessity, they may also form a new people and take their stand among "the powers of the earth." That is, they may form a new political community by the right invested in them by their Creator.

Revolution

The second paragraph moves from our right of separation to inalienable rights, and next on to our hopes for a new order of government It gives the general reasons that would justify revolution. To assert a right does not make its exercise right. I may have a right to free speech, but that doesn't mean I should, by speaking, betray a confidence, slander my fellow man, or inform on a fellow citizen.

The Declaration spells out what God and nature have given us in terms of inalienable rights. "Unalienable" (or in the modern spelling, "inalienable"), means not able to be given away. The first of these inalienable rights is the right to life. Because God has made us, we cannot rightly destroy our lives, His workmanship. Next, because He

The "Pine Tree Flag," used by the Continental Navy and the Massachusetts state navy. Note the association of piety with liberty.

has made us reasonable and equal, we cannot give away our right and our liberty to use that reason in living well and in aiming at our happiness. These, then, are the inalienable rights that the declaration says governments are to secure: life, liberty, and the pursuit of happiness.

"Pursuit of Happiness" was consciously chosen by Jefferson and the Congress to be inserted in place of "property," which was the term found after liberty in Locke's *Second Treatise*. There are two good reasons for this change. One, there is no inalienable right to property in the ordinary sense of the word. Property rights are precisely 'alienated' every time we freely sell or buy something. Better would be a right *to acquire* property, by labor or other honest means. This indeed could be fundamental and inalienable, because it is grounded in our human nature. When George Mason drafted the Virginia *Declaration of Rights*, he acknowledged the force of this reasoning by including among the "inherent rights" of man "the means of acquiring and possessing property." But by speaking of a right to "acquire," we would be already in the realm of "pursuits."

59

This leads us to the second reason. We pursue other things than property, often at the expense of property. Is property, especially in the sense of items able to be bought and sold, the sum total of the things that we think are ours, or for which we labor? Surely not. For example, we will spend money to defend our reputation, to please a friend, to help the poor, to learn a skill, to acquire knowledge, to honor God. We are happy if we succeed. The more inclusive and nobler term, "happiness," and not happiness itself, but the pursuit of it, was the founders' choice, and we think it a wise one.

Since governments exist by human consent to secure these rights, if any government becomes destructive of them, the people may and, if possible, should, rebel. What then? If the rebellion succeeds, they may and should form a new government better than the tyrannical one they have abolished. What will make it better? How shall the new government be judged? The answer to the first question can be as simple as a change of the persons who rule. Get the bad old king out and replace him with a new one. Or it could be as complex as forming new structures of government and society. Let us call this complex answer, "political revolution."

Political revolutions have a nasty habit of turning into bloodbaths, with the new regime often no better, or even worse, than the old one. The boldness of the Declaration may be seen in its avowal of the possibility of a political revolution. The colonists declared that they had the right to "alter or abolish" the form of government, and to lay the foundations for a new government, "on such principles, and organizing its powers in such form as to them shall seem most likely to effect their safety and happiness." This gives us the grounds for judging the new government. Is it likely to insure safety and promote happiness?

Of course, the Declaration was primarily concerned with independence. Although it gave the principles on the basis of which Americans would erect their fundamental laws, it set up no structure of government. The Congress that adopted it was a kind of emergency "committee of the whole" for the American people, but the Declaration itself does not propose articles of confederation or a constitution. In looking to the Declaration for such a structure, we must be content with the spirit, not the letter, of constitutional law. We can see a most important part of that spirit in the part of the Declaration that we are now analyzing.

John Locke's theory of government emphasized its role in protecting individual rights against injustice, primarily a negative function, while neglecting its positive role in attaining good things. In other words, he is strong on rights, but weak on ends, especially virtue and the good life, which includes but goes beyond the acquisition of property. To this day Americans find it easier to discover and fight for rights than to praise virtues and proclaim duties. The most famous early flag of the revolution had a rattlesnake with thirteen rattles and the words, "Don't Tread on Me." We were, and are, jealous for our rights. This can lead to unending squabbling, with each person trying to get his own rights and not noticing he is treading on those of others. And even consulting our rights with due concern for others doesn't say much about what we are to do with our lives, liberties, and property once we have recognized or secured them.

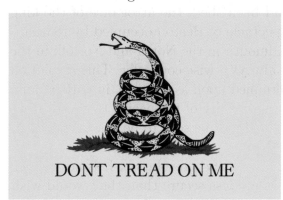

DONT TREAD ON ME

The original "Rattlesnake Flag," designed by Colonel Christopher Gadsden of South Carolina in 1775. Rather than 13 stripes in the background, there are 13 rattles on the tail. It is one of the first flags of the country, pre-dating the "Stars and Stripes."

The older political theory, inherited from the Greek and Roman thinkers and from our religious heritage, spoke of ends. Laws were for the sake of virtue and justice, that men might live well. It is to the credit of the founders that they point us in this direction in the Declaration. They do it by speaking in this second paragraph of the rights listed earlier as the "ends" of government, and by replacing "pursuit of happiness," a right, with happiness itself, an end. It is, we may securely state, self-evident that happiness is not a *right*. Men can and must pursue it, and they have a right to do so, but the degree to which they achieve it will depend on many things not in their power. It will also depend on one very great thing that largely is in their power, especially in a democratic republic: Good government.

Prudence

"Prudence, indeed, will dictate that governments long established should not be changed for light and transient causes..." What is prudence? Why does the Declaration consider its dictates before making its list of charges against the king and finally declaring independence?

In order to act well, men, as reasonable creatures, must also think well. Thinking well about what is to be done goes by the name of "practical wisdom" or "prudence." It includes a sense for what is good and right, and an ability to choose the best ways to accomplish it. Sometimes it means patiently waiting and not acting, because there is no decent or safe way to achieve what would otherwise be desirable. In our western tradition, practical wisdom is often called simply wisdom, and both the Greek philosophers and the Hebrew Bible praise the wisdom that directs the community as higher than the wisdom of a private man. Political prudence they call almost 'god-like.' The man who has it, and who has power, is the statesman.

There is an obvious reason for those who were about to take the bold step of separating and even revolutionizing to pause and give wisdom her due. Passions were high; blood had been shed; the arrogance of the king was plain to the colonists in the spectacle of Boston occupied by redcoats, no stirring of sails in its harbor; Falmouth in the North and Norfolk in the South burning. But passion is not always a wise counselor. This revolution was to be deliberate, as coolly determined upon as possible, in part because it was being made in the name of the capacity of the people to govern itself. It was essential that the Declaration be, and be seen to be, the work, not of a mob, but of an assembly of rational men reasoning together.

Prudence makes it more difficult to justify a revolution. It is not enough for the patriots to show their rights are less secure than they would wish. They must prove that the king shows in his words and deeds a tendency that makes the act of revolution not only the right of the colonists but also their duty. These words and deeds will be published and the tendency explained in the list of grievances that follows, but the list makes for dry reading compared to the great general ideas of the first two paragraphs of the Declaration. To read it with understanding requires that you be something of a lawyer and an historian now... perhaps a journalist or regular reader of newspapers then. You might even say that it requires a share of statesmanship.

Questions for Reflection

1. *Sturdy old words.* Some of the words used in the Declaration are uncommon, or used in a sense uncommon in today's English. "Unalienable," for instance. A bit of dictionary work may be in order for contemporary readers. When looking up a word, try to find the roots of the term. For example, "democracy" comes from two Greek words, one for the people, *demos*, and one for ruling, *kratein*. Another good way to get the sense of a word in Jefferson's time is to check

out how it is used in a familiar text, like Shakespeare or above all the King James Bible. Try this with "happiness." (You might start with Psalms 144:15.) Below is a sample of words worth considering:
  - happiness (contrast with happiness as a feeling)
  - denounce (try to get this one from context and the root)
  - bands
  - prudence (contrast with the slang term, "prude")
  - assume
  - endowed
  - unalienable (check the root)
  - ends
  - transient
  - light
  - usurpations
  - evinces
  - despotism
  - people (note how it is not always the plural of "person")
  - men (note how it means human beings, male and female)

2. *Revolutions.* We have argued in this part that the founders were prudent to consider that revolutions are not lightly to be undertaken. You might do a little reading on the two most famous revolutions that followed ours, the French and Russian revolutions. Consider what kind of regimes they led to, and the use of terror in each. Jefferson and the Congress may have been thinking of the civil and religious wars in France and England in the two centuries prior to the Declaration. Your teacher may wish to assign a short research paper on any of these historical events, or even on the very recent "Arab Spring."

4.2 A Long Train of Abuses

The longest and central part of the Declaration is our next object of study. In it the founders give the reasons that impelled them to independence and indicate some of the considerations that should direct the formation of the new government. In thinking through this list, you will want to remember some of the history that we set out in chapter 1.

Tyranny, the Branches of Government, and the Seeds of a Constitution

There are twenty-seven specific complaints against the British King, followed by a conclusion that the king is a tyrant, and his government deaf to the colonists' pleas, and accordingly, the separation is necessary. The first seven all include the term, "laws," or in the case of the fourth and fifth, "representative houses," and "legislative power," i.e., the bodies and authority by which laws are made. You might think that the grounds for or independence would normally be that the people suffers under bad laws. Look carefully at these seven complaints. All of them have to do with blocking the passage of laws aimed at "the public good."

A Summary of the Legislative Abuses

1. "He has refused his assent to Laws... necessary for the public good."
2. "He has forbidden his Governors to pass Laws... till his Assent should be obtained; and has neglected to attend to them."
3. "He has refused to pass other Laws for... people unless [they] would relinquish the right of Representation."
4. "He has called together legislative bodies at places unusual... for the sole purpose of fatiguing them into compliance.
5. "He has dissolved Representative Houses... for opposing invasions on the rights of the people."
6. "He has refused for a long time, after such dissolutions, to cause others to be elected; whereby the Legislative powers, incapable of Annihilation, have returned to the People at large for their excercise..."
7. "He has endeavoured to prevent the population of these States... obstructing the Laws for the Naturalization of Foreigners."

The full text of the sixth charge against the king is especially noteworthy. The law-making power is there said to be "incapable of annihilation." The thought is that men are entitled to government by God and nature, and that the power to make laws is delegated to the legislative body. When the action and even the existence of that body is threatened, the power returns to its origin, the people. Law-making is so fundamental to humanity that the authority to make law cannot be destroyed.

A Summary of Judicial Abuses

8. "He has obstructed the Administration of Justice by refusing his Assent to Laws for establishing Judiciary Powers."

9. "He has made the Judges dependent on his Will alone..."

From law-making the list moves on to judging. Here too the charge is not that the king imposed bad judges, but that he refused the people its fundamental right to *have* judges, and to have them be independent. In particular, judges must be free from pressure from the executive, but the king has made them "dependent on his will alone." We begin to see in this list of charges

Self government. Patrick Henry addressing the Virginia House of Burgesses in 1765.

the outlines of the branches of government that will be established in the American Constitution. The king is said to have blocked the exercise of the legislative and judicial branches, and to have interfered with the independence of the judicial. He has usurped powers that ought to be exercised by others. A little more than a decade later, Publius will say of such usurpation:

> The accumulation of all powers, legislative, executive, and judiciary, in the same hands, whether of one, a few, or many, and whether hereditary, self-appointed, or elective, may justly be pronounced the very definition of tyranny.[1]

A Summary of Executive Abuses

10. "He has erected a multitude of New Offices...to harass our people, and eat out our substance."

11. "He has kept among us in times of peace, Standing Armies..."

12. "He has affected to render the Military...superior to the Civil Power."

13. "He has...subject[ed] us to a jurisdiction foreign to our constitution; giving his Assent to their acts of pretended legislation:

   14. "For quartering large bodies of armed troops among us..."

   15. "For protecting them, by a Mock Trial, from Punishment..."

---

[1] *Federalist 47*

16. "For cutting off our Trade..."
17. "For imposing Taxes on us without our Consent"
18. "For depriving us...of Trial by Jury"
19. "For transporting us beyond the Seas to be tried..."
20. "For abolishing...English Laws in a neighboring Province"
21. "For taking away our Charters, abolishing...Laws, and altering Forms of our Governments."
22. "For suspending our own Legislatures..."
23. "He has abdicated Government here, by declaring us out of his Protection and waging War against us"
24. "He has plundered our seas..., burnt our towns..."
25. "He is...transporting armies of foreign mercenaries..."
26. "He has constrained our fellow citizens taken captive on the High Seas to bear arms against their Country..."
27. "He has excited domestic insurrections...and has endeavoured to bring on the inhabitants ..., the merciless Indian Savages..."

All the remaining charges, our numbers 10 through 27, are about abuses of the executive power. Although numbers 14 through 21 are acts of Parliament, of legislation, they are here because they are the consequences of 13, by which the king has interfered with the proper distribution of power and so allowed this "pretended legislation." Almost all the rest have to do with military policy, which will be the first responsibility of the executive in the new Constitution. One (11) concerns the excessive cost and inconvenience of the military forces, and another (10) the unneeded increase of bureaucracy and attendant costs.

Anyone who complains about something must have in mind the opposite state of affairs, a good and just one, to serve as a standard. When it comes to the complaints of the Declaration, that standard is evidently one in which the structure of government respects the different functions and lines of division between the branches. When our ancestors came to erect such a structure, first in the Articles of Confederation, and next in the Constitution, they took their bearings in large measure from the principles laid down in the Declaration. They had outlined the features of tyranny in King George, and they acted to prevent tyranny for themselves and us in the Constitution.

That is why they said, in the preamble to the Constitution, that the people were acting to "secure the blessings of liberty to ourselves and our posterity."

Questions for Reflection

3. Using the earlier part of this book and other resources, try to find the particular historical events that the Congress was referring to in some of the charges. You will find an excellent link at www.founding.com. But don't stop there. You might read Jefferson's *Summary View of the Rights of British America* (found in the *Book of Readings*). Of particular importance among the political acts of the British Government is the "Prohibitory Act" of December 22, 1775. Write a short essay, or prepare a talk, in which you argue that the charges in the Declaration are true.

4. Take a look at the British side of the controversy. Pretend you are a lawyer or a statesman arguing against the conclusion of the charges. There is almost always something to be said for both sides in any human controversy. You could look at Thomas Hutchinson's "Strictures upon the Declaration of the Congress at Philadelphia," (in the *Book of Readings*.) What would it mean for us today if some of the charges were overstated? In particular, what would it mean for the theory of governmental structure hinted at in the Declaration? Does the rightness of that structure depend on the historical facts that Congress cited?

5. What were the "domestic insurrections" mentioned in the last charge? Does your answer cause you to doubt the intentions of Congress, especially as to their commitment to the proposition that "all men are created equal?" Think about this with regard to prudence.

6. The standard of good government that the king violated was not limited to a proper separation of the branches. Governments must be well organized to do good things. You can get an idea of some of those good things from the list of charges. One of particular relevance today is that population increase is a desirable thing. An obvious one is that the civil authority should keep the peace and protect the lives of the citizens. Can you find a few more? Do you think the ones you found are still among the ends of the American government, and that our current political arguments refer to them?

4.3 Words of Power, and the Power behind the Words

After the deep principles of the opening section and the painful details of the central part, the close comes with a sense of solemn necessity. Here, "the representatives of the UNITED STATES OF AMERICA," (the capital letters are in the original) acting "in the name of the good people of these colonies. . . declare That these United Colonies are, and of right ought to be, FREE AND INDEPENDENT STATES."

They knew, of course, that this meant war with England, and that no one could be sure who would win that war, or whether any of them would survive it with his life or liberty. They were sure that, as representatives of the people, of the good people, of the colonies, they had the right and the duty to declare independence, and that their declaration made it a fact. Much earlier in this book we compared the Declaration to a marriage. This is where that comparison is most plain. You are married when you *say*, "I do." We became independent when, after due deliberation and decent notification of mankind, we *said* we were. That is why we celebrate the Fourth of July, and it is also probably why the new name, "UNITED STATES OF AMERICA," was printed in the original all in capital letters.

Another way of saying this is that genuine declarations are a special kind of language, like vows or contracts. They not only express our thoughts or desires, as when we say "It's warm today," or "I'd like a sandwich." They make what they say real, as in a marriage vow. They are words of power, almost like the words in Genesis that God said in creating. He spoke, "and it was so." The Declaration says that the colonies "*are*, and of right ought to be, FREE," that "all political connection between them and the state of Great Britain *is*, and ought to be, totally dissolved." It says that "as Free and Independent States, [we] have full power to levy war, conclude peace, contract alliances, establish commerce, and to do all other things which Independent States may of right do."

Congress declared these things conscious of the people's right to have them so. But it did not think might makes right. The colonies ". . . are, and of right *ought to be*, FREE AND INDEPENDENT. . ." The tie to Britain "is and *ought to be*, totally dissolved." And most important, Congress appealed "to the Supreme Judge of the world for the rectitude of our intentions. . ." It was His law that entitled us to independence in the opening of the Declaration. It was His judgment (and not that of men, to which we owe, indeed, a decent respect) by which we would be judged. And it is His supervising power, "divine Providence," upon which our founders relied in the war that all expected would follow their declaration.

War would come. The signers knew it, and they knew that their own lives and liberty would be at risk. Some would in fact lose their property or their lives in the revolution. That they were willing to take the risk is a sign that, though government may be founded on rights to things we desire, like life and property, men living the political life keep an eye on something higher. Life itself, Aristotle taught long ago, is for the sake of the good life, and a noble man will risk many material goods for his honor, the sign of a life well lived. The founders thought it was an honor, even a sacred thing, to share in a common struggle for liberty, and so they closed the Declaration with those two words: "sacred Honor."

Questions for Reflection

7. *Might and Right.* In declaring the right of the people to revolt, did the founders throw open the door to all ? Consider:

   a) Take the argument about the marriage vows a bit further. The couple has the right to have its words make the marriage, but not simply from their will. What if one of the partners is already married to someone else? What if one is underage—say twelve years old? Do his or her words continue to have the power to make them wedded? Do the words of two males or two females have such a power?

   b) Now think about the right to revolution and independence. Does the fact that the Congress has the authority to represent the people give it the right to overthrow the king under any circumstances, or only under certain ones? What does the Declaration have to say on this point? Discuss this in the light of the expression "Supreme Judge of the world."

   c) What will your answers to the first two sections mean about the possibility of revolution against the new government set up after the defeat of King George? This will be a life and death issue for Americans when a portion of the nation declares its independence in 1860, and has recourse to arms to vindicate that rebellion. Could such a rebellion come up at any time in the future? How ought men to think and act about such a possibility?

8. *Honor and politics.* In a certain way, it was easier for the founders to see that they were serving in a high cause, an honorable one, in the Revolution, than it is for us to see that we are doing something similar in performing our civic duty today. More seems to be demanded of a man to stand up to a line of British Grenadiers than to decide rightly on a school bond issue, or to obey the zoning laws of his county. What else might lead us to deny the honorable character of public service in our times?

9. *More on the Honor of the Revolutionary Cause.* It was not the risk alone, or the fact that battles would ensue, that gave the founding its noble or honorable character. Politics itself, rightly pursued, is honorable. The ancient Romans used to call the public life "cursus honororum" the path of honors. The following quotations, from Abraham Lincoln, Alexander Hamilton, and David Ramsay (a member of the Continental Congress who also wrote a history of the Revolution), illustrate the extent to which the founding of America elevated men's thoughts and kindled in their hearts a noble love of fame and virtue.

> [a member of Congress] is to be regarded not only as a legislator, but as the founder of an empire. A man of virtue and ability, dignified with so precious a trust, would rejoice that fortune had given him birth at a time, and placed him in circumstances so favorable for promoting human happiness. He would esteem it not more the duty, than the privilege and ornament of his office, to do good to mankind; from this commanding eminence, he would look down with contempt upon every mean or interested pursuit. (Alexander Hamilton, *Federalist 3*, 1778)

> In the years 1775 and 1776, the country, being suddenly thrown into a situation that needed the ability of all its sons, these generally took their places, each according to the bent of his inclination. As they generally pursued their objects with ardor, a vast expansion of the human mind speedily followed...It seemed as if the war not only required, but created talents...

> ...Men whose minds were warmed with the love of liberty, and whose abilities were improved by daily exercise, and sharpened with a laudable ambition to serve their distressed country, spoke, wrote, and acted, with an energy far surpassing

all expectations which could be reasonably founded on their previous acquirements. (David Ramsay, *The History of the American Revolution*, 1793)

Then, all that sought celebrity and fame and distinction expected to find them in the success of that experiment. Their all was staked upon it:—their destiny was inseparably linked with it. Their ambition aspired to display before an aspiring world a practical demonstration of the truth of a proposition, which had hitherto been considered, at best not better, than problematical; namely, the capacity of a people to govern themselves. If they succeeded, they were to be immortalized; their names were to be transferred to counties and cities, and rivers and mountains; and to be revered and sung, and toasted through all time. If they failed, they were to be called knaves and fools, and fanatics for a fleeting hour; then to sink and be forgotten. They succeeded. The experiment is successful; and thousands have won their deathless names in making it so. (Abraham Lincoln, *"Address before the Young Men's Lyceum of Springfield"*, 1838)

Ramsay, Hamilton, and Lincoln point us towards the conclusion we have been arguing for in this entire chapter: the Declaration opens a way to a political life not only based on the rational capacity of mankind, but ending in high and noble political action. We will show later that Americans have risen to this challenge by returning to the principles of the Declaration in times of crisis. What of our own times? It might prove useful to discuss or write a brief essay on this question.

Chapter 4 Review Questions

1. What does the Declaration mean by calling separation from Britain a "necessity"?
2. According to the Declaration, why do we have unalienable rights to life, liberty, and the pursuit of happiness?
3. What is a 'political revolution'?

4. "[Locke] is strong on rights, but weak on ends." (page 60) Compare this statement about Locke with the Declaration.
5. Why does the Declaration consider the dictates of prudence before declaring independence?
6. Why does the Declaration state that the "legislative powers [are] incapable of annihilation'?

Paper Topic 2:

Write a short paper (2–3 pages) on the following question: Does the Declaration's justification of the American revolution undermine the moral right of a free nation to suppress rebellion within it? (See Questions for Reflection 7, page 69)

American Constitutions 5

> ... That whenever any Form of Government becomes destructive of
> these ends, it is the Right of the People to alter or to abolish it, and
> to institute new Government, laying its foundation on such principles
> and organizing its powers in such form, as to them shall seem most
> likely to effect their Safety and Happiness.

Through the Declaration of Independence, the united colonies had abolished their old form of government under the king. But they also had to institute a new government that would bring about their safety and happiness in a manner consistent with the principles of the Declaration. Although separation was the more momentous and daring, forming a new government was necessarily much harder. As noted in the next sentence in the Declaration, the founders were well aware of the difficulty of this labor. Perhaps the new form will fail even more miserably than the old. But actions of king and Parliament had forced them to try and see whether they could not do better.

The Continental Congress had already acted to establish the new government before it had officially declared their old one defunct. At the same time it authorized Jefferson to draft the Declaration, it also established a committee to draft articles that would establish the form of government. Within a few days of accepting the Declaration, the Congress was presented with a draft of what were called "Articles of Confederation." Because of the difficulties of the matter and the press of the war, which it had to oversee, it was over a year before the Continental Congress accepted the articles and presented them to the states. Most of the states ratified the articles within a year, by the end of 1778, though only in 1781 did the last state agree to them.

The Articles of Confederation and the state constitutions that were developed in the same period represented the first stage in the great experiment of republican government. Nothing like them had ever been attempted before. Written constitutions that detailed what a government could and could not do, how it must go about its business, who should do what, had hardly ever been attempted outside of America, and never to the extent that the Americans now proposed. Most societies of men had worked according to custom or laws that arose from particular situations or conflicts. To sit down, discuss, and then deliberately decide what manner of government would most likely bring about safety and happiness was rare. To do this in the name of the people, and then to submit the result to them for their approval, was radical.

Americans, however, had already had more experience at constitution making than anyone else in history. From the time of the first settlers, Americans in small groups had been compacting with each other to form societies, and then forming governments to rule over them. They had experience with what worked and didn't work. They even had experience of confederation, that is, of joining smaller societies together to achieve better the ends of government. Even with all this experience, however, their many failures made them feel how difficult their project was. The fifteen-year period from 1776 to 1791 saw states propose constitutions once, twice, even three times, as they discovered fundamental flaws in the governments that arose. Given the difficulty, it is amazing that in the most novel of their experiments, a united government for all the states, only two attempts produced the wonder that is our Constitution.

In the present chapter, we will look closely at both attempts, the Articles of Confederation and the Constitution, to see what made them fitting forms of government for a people committed to Declaration principles. Besides this text, the reader should have and consult the two constitutional documents as he reads what follows.

5.1 The Articles of Confederation

Probably the most striking aspect of the Articles, especially for those familiar with the Constitution, can be summed up in the word "confederation." What exactly does that mean? Article II indicates that states remain independent; Article III describes confederation as "a firm league of friendship." Are the states forming, not one government, but an alliance like NATO?

The immediate answer to the latter question is, "No." By means of the Declaration of Independence, the Americans, through their representatives, had asserted their independence as "a people," not "peoples"; they declared the independence of the "united Colonies," not simply of the colonies. By

declaring their independence commonly, through a common body—the Continental Congress—and a common document—the Declaration—the Americans also formed themselves as a people.

This fact is abundantly confirmed in the Articles. The Articles were proposed by Congress to the states in 1777, which is called in that proposal "the Second Year of the Independence of America," and it was essentially ratified "in the third year of the independence of America." In these words, the Articles recognize that "America" was formed as a people by their decision to make their declaration of independence a common act. The official title of the document is "Articles of Confederation and perpetual Union" between the thirteen states. The last article, Article XIII, forcefully claims that the states must abide by all the decisions made according to the Articles by the common Congress of the states. It then adds with great significance, "and the Union shall be perpetual." However much or little the independent states committed to their common government, they committed it forever. They had already determined that their safety and happiness, their ties of blood, language, culture, and ideals, should make them a people, and they meant to abide by that act forever.

As an act of perpetual Union, the Articles differ essentially from any treaty or compact between fully independent nations. Alliances and leagues are usually established for limited, renewable terms. Decisions made according to them must be confirmed by the proper governing power of each state, which may at any time decide to withdraw from the league. Under the Articles, the United States bound themselves in perpetuity to a form of government that could only be altered by the United States in Congress, with the concurrence of every state. A single state, though it retained considerable sovereignty and independence under the Articles, could not alter or abolish the national government on its own.

The intention to form a government suited to a united people is found particularly in Article IV, according to which a "free inhabitant" of any state shares fully in the "privileges and immunities of free citizens" whenever he is in any other state. No American would be prevented from relocating anywhere in the United States. Any contract that he had formed in one state would be recognized by all the other states. This act would "secure and perpetuate mutual friendship and intercourse among the people of the different States of the Union..." It would solidify their sense of themselves as a people, as Americans. It was this sense of unity as a people that, more than anything else, would ensure the perpetual existence of the new nation.

Why, then, the strong emphasis on the independence and sovereignty of the states? As was mentioned earlier, for Americans, deliberately forming governments was not a new enterprise. During the first century of colonization, a multitude of new civil and church governments were formed by groups of colonists. The process was different in different places, but it occurred everywhere. This process often involved confederation, especially in the New England colonies.

New England was settled by small groups of adventurous, resolute men. When they arrived, they quickly formed themselves into a community under a common compact and government. A number of towns were started in different areas, which began and for a time remained independent of each other. It wasn't long, however, before the inhabitants of these towns realized that many benefits were to be gained from joining together. While they valued their independence, and didn't always entirely like or agree with the views of the men in neighboring towns, they understood that they were unable to secure certain important aspects of their "safety and happiness" alone. So they formed a new compact, a larger society. In this way, the united colonies of Massachusetts, Connecticut, and the "Rhode Island and Providence Plantations" were formed.

In forming these larger societies, the townspeople did not abandon their town governments. While realizing that certain important ends could only be obtained by uniting with other towns, they also believed that their town communities were adequate for most of the purposes of daily life. They thought a united government would serve a few definite tasks well, but not most of the tasks of government. So they deliberately limited the authority of the new governments, retaining most powers and duties for the smaller town governments.

The Americans brought this same notion of limited confederations to the formation of a national government. Although the colonies had led mostly separate lives for their first 150 years, the crisis with Britain had quickly convinced them of the need to be and remain united. Certain crucial aspects of their safety and happiness depended on their perpetual union. But by no means all. Just as they were content with town or other local governments for most of the affairs of life, so they were content with their colonial or state governments for most of the functions that they had fulfilled up to that time. So the union was to be a federation, with the national government strictly limited with regard to what it would be responsible for doing. Article II makes this

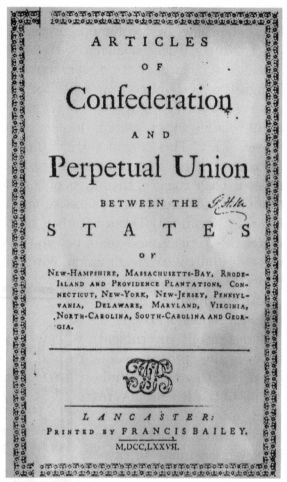

abundantly clear by retaining to the states their complete independence in matters not expressly assigned to the united government.

What were the matters more competently addressed by the United States than by the states separately? It is striking that the powers given to the United States in the Articles are those very acts that the Declaration explicitly states characterize independent nations. In its last paragraph, having dissolved the bonds joining them to the British crown and people, the Declaration claims for the united colonies, that:

> ... as Free and Independent States, they have Full Power to levy War, conclude Peace, contract Alliances, establish Commerce, and to do all other Acts and Things which Independent States may of right do.

These acts all have in common that they occur between societies of peoples that are not pollitically united, i.e., that do not submit to common government. Because of this, they must regulate their affairs, not according to laws established by a common government, but according to agreements: peace treaties, defensive alliances, trade agreements. The authority to enter into such agreements or to declare war if necessary is expressly given to the Congress of the United States (Article IX) and is expressly denied to the states (Article VI). Single states are not to act as "Free and Independent States" either with respect to foreign nations like France, nor with respect to each other. They cannot enter into compacts among themselves without the consent of the United States. Their right to maintain a standing army is limited. Their coinage, the means of commerce, is subject to the determination of the Congress. States must submit disputes with other states to the federal government. Taken together, all this leads to a simple conclusion: under the Articles, and years before the Constitution, the United States was essentially a sovereign union, not an alliance or mere confederation of perfectly sovereign states.

Although the Articles bound together the people of America in one government, they finally proved inadequate to the task. While giving to the federal government the ends appropriate to it, the states feared to give it powers adequate to carry out its missions. The federal government could apportion taxes, but could not collect

A political cartoon created by Benjamin Franklin in 1774. (The "N.E." stands for New England.)

them. That was left up to the states. It could regulate coinage, but had no power to enforce its regulations. It could negotiate treaties with other nations, but could not compel states and individuals to live up to them. It had no courts to judge violators of its laws. It was nearly impossible even for it to come to any decision: in matters of any importance, the consent of nine states, each with a single vote, was needed to act. Given the diversity of the new states, such agreement was all too often impossible.

Yet the Articles, for all their weakness, were an important first attempt at forming a government consistent with the Declaration.

Questions for Reflection

1. You might want to read Publius's criticism of the Articles, in *The Federalist Papers*, especially numbers *15–23*. Also, Donald Lutz's book, *The Origins of American Constitutionalism*, explores in detail the history of confederation and constitutional government in America. A fine account of these matters, with special emphasis on the state constitutions, may be found in Morison's *Oxford History of the American People*, pages 270–281.

5.2 Preamble to the Constitution

> ... the American Constitution is, so far as I can see, the most wonderful work ever struck off at a given time by the brain and purpose of man.
> (British Prime Minister W.E. Gladstone, 1878)

The Constitution of the United States is unique in the history of the world, the providential product of a group of outstanding statesman, who in themselves contained the genius of a great people and of the Western political experience of 2000 years. It has lasted for over two centuries, and is still admired and drawn on by statesmen around the world for its wisdom. This chapter on the Constitution does not pretend to plumb its depths. Many books have been written on the subject, a number of which are referenced in the back of this book for those who want to understand it better.

What we want to accomplish here is to fulfill something of the promise we made in the beginning of the book, where it was claimed that, as the Law of Moses can't be understood apart from the covenant of Abraham, which is its spirit, so the Constitution is only properly understood in the light of the principles laid down in the Declaration.

Considered in itself, the Constitution appears to be something of a mechanical or technical manual: "how to elect Representatives," "how to elect Senators," "how to admit new states," "Congress can do certain enumerated things; it cannot do other things," etc. But the Constitution doesn't stand by itself; it comes after and presupposes the Declaration, as we hope to show.

The Constitution begins with a short paragraph, or long sentence, as famous as the opening paragraphs of the Declaration. "We the People of the United States..." This paragraph is known as the "Preamble." A quick reading breaks it into three parts, explaining Who is doing What and Why. The second of these parts, the "in order to" section, is the longest, consisting of six separate goals to be attained by the Constitution.

Why did the framers of the Constitution bother to enumerate these goals? Before we look at each particular goal, let us note something fundamental: just as the founders had a duty to explain to themselves and to the world the reason why they were separating from England, so they had a duty to explain to themselves and others exactly why they were giving the national government the particular structure they detailed.

As we have seen, the founders understood the importance of prudence. In any venture, the prudent man looks to clearly understood goals. These goals make sense of all the choices he makes on his way to attaining them. They also prevent him, as long as he keeps them clearly in mind, from making serious mistakes. A doctor has to keep clearly in mind his goal of helping the patient recover. He cannot rely simply on the procedures he learned in medical school, because they might fail in any particular case. A standard procedure applied to a particular patient may be harmful and not helpful. The measure is not the procedure, but health.

Political decisions, judgments, and interpretations are even less subject to mindless, automatic procedure. In order to use the Constitution effectively, its framers realized that legislators, officers, and judges would have to keep in mind the goals for which it was intended. The Preamble is their attempt to express its goals in as concise a formula as possible. As one early influential commentator on the Constitution wrote:

> [The Preamble's] true office is to expound the nature and extent and application of the powers actually conferred by the Constitution, and not substantively to create them.[1]

In this section, we will look at the ends stated in the Preamble.

In Order to Form a More Perfect Union

> ...Whereas experience hath evinced that there are defects in the present Confederation...Resolved that in the opinion of Congress it is expedient that on the second Monday in May next a Convention of delegates who shall have been appointed by the several states be

---

[1]Court Justice Joseph Story, in 1833

held at Philadelphia for the sole and express purpose of revising the Articles of Confederation and reporting to Congress and the several legislatures such alterations and provisions therein as shall... render the federal constitution adequate to the exigencies of Government and the preservation of our Union.

—Resolution of Congress, Feb. 21, 1787

By February 1787, it had become abundantly clear that the Congress established under the Articles of Confederation was failing as a governing body. In the resolution calling for a convention to revise the Articles, Congress implied what was in fact the case: the continued existence of the Union was in danger, because the constitution (the Articles) was inadequate to the needs ("exigencies") of the national Government. The problem was not to be found primarily in the role assigned to it under the Articles, but in the means to perform its assigned tasks effectively. While desiring to live under one government, the states had feared to entrust adequate power to that government. Having just rid themselves of one tyrant and tyrannical legislature in King George and Parliament, they did not want to run the risk of having another closer to home.

"E Pluribus Unum" appears on our currency, as well as on the Great Seal. It translates to "out of many, one."

In his letter presenting the proposed Constitution to Congress, George Washington, President of the Convention, recognizes this fear as the source of the difficulties:

> The friends of our country have long seen and desired, that the power of making war, peace, and treaties, of levying money and regulating commerce, and the correspondent executive and judicial authorities should be fully and effectually vested in the general government of the Union; but the impropriety of delegating such extensive trust to one body of men is evident—Hence results the necessity of a different organization.

In the beginning of this sentence, Washington enumerates the powers that should belong to a general government. He includes the four mentioned in the Declaration, and adds that of taxation or "levying money." As we saw, all of these powers were assigned by the Articles to the general government, although the power of taxation consisted simply in a levy against the states. The difficulties are suggested in the next few phrases. The Articles did not provide a means of enforcing Congress's laws ("executive authority"), or of trying and convicting violators ("judicial authority"). For these reasons, as well as

"George Washington Addressing the Constitutional Convention," painting by Junius Brutus Stearns, 1856

its inability to tax individual persons directly, the Congress was ineffective. The powers, although given on paper, were not "fully and effectually" given. Washington then alludes to the fear that prevented the states from establishing such an effective government. He locates the root of that fear in the Articles' decision to vest all national power in "a single body of men," the Congress. This suggests one of the most important features of the new Constitution, the separation of powers. "Hence results the necessity of a different organization."

After mentioning the great obstacles posed by the different particular interests of the states, Washington continues in the letter to inform the Congress of what the Constitutional Convention believed was at stake:

> In all our deliberations on this subject we kept steadily in our view, that which appears to us the greatest interest of every true American, the consolidation of our Union, in which is involved our prosperity, felicity, safety, perhaps our national existence. This important consideration, seriously and deeply impressed on our minds, led each State in the Convention to be less rigid on points of inferior magnitude, than might have been otherwise expected...

The immediate goal of the Constitution is the "consolidation" of the Union. By making the national government strong enough to execute its functions, the Constitution, it was hoped, would strengthen the Union among the states. By so doing, the prosperity, "felicity" (happiness) and safety of all Americans would be enhanced. If the Union were not strengthened, the Convention feared that the nation might cease to exist, as the states, with no effective limit to their power, began to act as "Free and Independent States" with regard to each other.

An important way in which the Constitution forms a "more perfect union" is contained in the Preamble itself. Unlike the Articles of Confederation, which were established by the states, the Constitution is established by "the People." Of course, the states only acted in virtue of the power granted them by their respective peoples, and so even the Articles were indirectly an act of the people of the United States. But the Constitution, in its Preamble, claims itself to be a direct act of "the People of the United States." It was to be ratified by special conventions called in each state for the purpose of accepting the Constitution. That means that the authority given the federal compact came from the people in the several states, not their legislatures. One of the questions at the end of this section will ask you to reflect further on this interesting fact.

Given their view of the powers government needed to be effective, it was crucial to the framers that the Constitution emanate directly from the people. The new government would have the power to tax directly. It would have the power to enforce its laws on recalcitrant individuals and even states. It would be able to judge and imprison offenders against its laws. Its laws would be the "supreme law of the land," having precedence over state laws. Such authority over individuals and states could only come directly from the people.

Establish Justice

One great difficulty confronting a student of the Preamble is that its terms are very general. "Justice" is a prime example. It is a term that means somewhat different things to different people. Can one find a meaning that

Justice. What do the balance and sword represent?

would be common enough to be accepted, but not so vague as to be useless?

Perhaps we can, especially if we think back on the Declaration's distinction between peoples that are independent of each other and those that are bound together. Independent peoples or states act together by means of alliances or treaties. In case of serious differences, they must either come to

83

an agreement or go to war with each other. Smaller, weaker nations depend for their existence on the goodwill of the more powerful nations.

Within a nation, however, disputes between individuals or communities are settled in courts. Judges and juries make judgments according to established laws. Disturbers of the peace are arrested and punished by officers who act according to the laws. The small and the weak are now protected by the laws.

Justice, then, implies the rule of law. The rule of law is a guarantee that judgments will be applied impartially, and hence the image of Justice is often of a goddess who is blind-folded. Remember also that there is a law higher than the laws made by governments, the natural law. The laws of the state are expected to be in accord with this innate knowledge of what is fair or balanced.

Thinking along these lines, we can see that "to establish justice" describes the whole effort of the Constitution. A more perfect union demands a stronger, more effective government. But that government must use its strength to rule according to law, not to carry out the current passions of those who wield that power. The very act of establishing a Constitution, which is a set of laws specifying the scope and procedures of exercising power, is an act of establishing justice, or the rule of law. Perhaps that is why the same word, "establish," is used in the Preamble in reference to both "justice" and "this Constitution."

Domestic Tranquility & Defense

By creating the powers of an effective national government limited by law, the Constitution itself goes a long way toward strengthening the Union and establishing justice. Officials appointed according to the Constitution will be able bring about the next two ends mentioned in the Preamble.

The greatest danger to life, liberty, and property comes from men who will use force to seize them from each other. These might be other men living in society who refuse to live according to law, or they might be other peoples formed in their own societies. A fundamental role of any government is to ensure that in neither case is force allowed to triumph. By organizing the power of the people as a whole, the government can take effective measures to keep the peace at home and defend itself against enemies abroad.

In regard to these ends, it is worth reminding ourselves that the Preamble does not create any powers; it only defines the purpose of the powers granted

West pediment (front) of the Supreme Court building. The central figure is Justice, with the scales on her lap, flanked by Order (holding the "fasces") and Authority (with the sword). The inscription proclaims, "Equal Justice Under Law."

to the national government in the body of the Constitution. With regard to the common defense, the national government has preeminent jurisdiction. It can raise troops necessary for war, and it can assume command of the state militias when necessary. With regard to domestic peace, on the other hand, power is retained by the states unless a case can be made for a national law to be enacted. Murder, robbery, and such crimes do not ordinarily involve the federal government.

The General Welfare

"Welfare" is a term that today usually refers to federal and state government programs that provide financial support to those in need. That is definitely not the sense the word has here. "Welfare" here means "well being." We have seen similar terms used throughout the texts we have been considering—"happiness," "felicity," "prosperity." Clearly, our founders realized that men wish not only to live, but to live well. And they thought that men formed societies because they make both living and good living possible. So beyond the safety of its citizens ("domestic tranquility" and "common defense"), the government formed by the Constitution is to act to promote the happiness of its citizens.

Of course, this end is limited by the powers enumerated in the Consti-

tution. The government, for instance, can't eliminate state governments in
order to bring about happiness. Nor can it act in favor of one state over
another. In order to indicate this, "welfare" is qualified by the term "general,"
(meaning in this context, 'of the whole.') The federal government receives
powers to act in those matters where the people's welfare can best be served
by acting altogether for goods that benefit the whole nation.

The Blessings of Liberty

If we look at Article I, Section 8, where powers are specified which are to
promote the "general welfare," we see that many concern the material prosperity of the nation. A common government that could regulate commerce,
establish a uniform currency, and grant patents to inventors would provide
excellent opportunities for private citizens and corporations to develop the
abundant natural resources of the nation for the ultimate benefit of all.

Does the national government have no concern about higher goods?
The Preamble points beyond material concerns in its last purpose phrase
"secure the blessings of liberty to ourselves and our posterity." What are the
blessings of liberty? If liberty means the power and right to act according
to one's choices, then the blessings of liberty include all that proceed from
the free choice and cooperation of private men: religion, education, the fine
arts, friendship. Unlike the Europeans, most Americans had come to the
conclusion that these goods were better attained by free, private associations
than by government patronage or regulation. Government was necessary in
part to make secure the freedom of its citizens to pursue these goals.

The Union itself, whose maintenance is the chief end of the Constitution,
enhanced liberty. The prospect for individuals to achieve happiness is far
greater in an extended society. Citizens of Virginia could attend the fine
universities in Massachusetts without passports—Robert E. Lee, for example,
would send one of his sons to Harvard. Citizens of Connecticut could move
to South Carolina if that society were more to their taste. National churches
or other organizations could be formed, with greater power to achieve their
goals than a relatively small society such as Rhode Island or even Virginia
would permit. By facilitating harmony and friendship among the states, the
federal government would secure and enhance the liberty of its citizens.

Finally, we should note that the government should secure the "blessings"
of liberty. Freedom makes the greatest goods possible, but it also can be
abused. The founders were under no illusion about the evils that can and

86

sometimes do result from a free society. But freedom is not desired for the sake of these evils, nor even solely for its own sake, sweet though the savor of liberty is. Freedom is also, and perhaps chiefly, desirable because of the good things that it alone can produce. The government is to make secure liberty for the sake of the blessings. To the extent that a free man uses his freedom to the harm of others, the government is to resist him.

The federal government has undergone tremendous changes over the course of its existence. Eighteenth century Americans would undoubtedly be shocked at the function it plays in our society today. Some of its metamorphosis has come about through amendments, such as the Fourteenth, Sixteenth, and Seventeenth Amendments. More changes have come through adapting the existing Constitution to the perceived needs of different times. Some changes have undoubtedly bettered our nation; some have probably made it worse. In order to judge properly those changes, and to make good decisions in the circumstances we face today, statesmen must understand the spirit of the laws. Absent the light of the spirit, the people wander in the dark.

Questions for Reflection

2. The first Congress formed by the Constitution faced tremendous financial difficulties arising from the war and from mismanagement under the Articles. Alexander Hamilton proposed rectifying the situation by the creation of a Bank of the United States. Congress passed legislation enacting the proposal. Look in the Constitution proper to see under what provision Congress would be acting. Would anything in the Preamble have a bearing on the question? You might need to consult some history books for help.

3. The same Congress considered another proposal of Hamilton's— construction of canals in various states to help promote commerce— and Hamilton claimed Congress was authorized to do this because it would promote the general welfare. James Madison objected that Congress could justify any action if it understood general welfare so broadly. Congress rejected the proposal. Consider Article I, Section 8. Was Hamilton right? Was Madison?

4. The Convention took great pains to choose the exact words that would convey their meaning. In the light of this consideration, go back and find the verbs in each of the clauses of the Preamble. "Form,

establish, etc." Why did the convention choose the verbs they did for the various ends "union, justice, etc."?

5. In arguing for the fundamental role of the American people in authorizing the Constitution, we noted that, though the states did not ratify through their legislatures, neither was there a national plebiscite or national convention for that purpose. There remains, therefore, some residue of the old sovereignty of the states in the ratification process. And, more importantly, there is a real division of sovereignty between the states and the national government in the American constitutional order. How this works out precisely is a matter for deep reflection and even controversy, and we do not mean to settle the question in this book. The inquiring student is urged to read and meditate on *Federalist 39, 40* and *43*, especially the end of *43*, and to read Daniel Webster's *Second Reply to Hayne*, written in 1830. For the position contrary to Webster's, consult *Declaration of the Immediate Causes Which Induce and Justify the Secession of South Carolina from the Federal Union*. (Both the Webster and the "Declaration" are in the *Book of Readings*.)

5.3   The Structure Established in the Constitution

Before we explore the mechanics of the government, let's recall what was said about proper government in the Declaration.

1. Receiving their authority from the consent of the governed, governments have for their ends the safety and happiness of the people. Their safety consists in the defense of their natural rights to life, liberty, and the pursuit of happiness, Their happiness extends beyond property, to include fulfillment of duty, honor, and justice.
2. Governments are judged, first by their fidelity to natural law ("the laws of Nature and of Nature's God") respecting all men, secondly by their effectiveness in attaining the happiness and safety of the people.
3. In the Declaration, the colonists compacted themselves as one people, recognizing that their safety and happiness depended on their national unity.
4. The importance of prudence in all political decisions is emphasized.
5. There is a clear separation of legislative, executive, and judicial powers.

Now let's turn to the government established by the Constitution. There is a fundamental principle behind it that helps to explain, at least in part, many of its features: Because governments exist for the good of a free people, the people, to the extent that they can, must be in charge. In the Preamble, we saw that the people intend to secure their safety, their liberty, and their happiness through the Constitution. The experience of the British and American peoples had led them to realize the importance of having those whose interests or goods are involved be the source of this deliberation and choice. After all, who is more likely to take care of what is yours than you? So the Constitution involves the people directly in governing.

Article I establishes that one part of the legislative body, the House of Representatives, will be directly elected by the people. Article Two establishes that the President shall be chosen by electors appointed "in such manner as the legislature of [each state] may direct." If the people want to directly vote for President, they can. The House of Representatives and the President have the

U.S. House of Representatives, 1920

most direct effect on the people, the House being the source of all taxation, the President having the executive power, "the power of the sword."

In the original wording of the Constitution, other important governmental bodies are *indirectly* appointed by the people. Senators are appointed by their state legislature, which is itself elected by the people; while the President, with the Senate, appoints justices to the federal courts. While all these are ultimately answerable to the people, they stand at some distance from them, their longer terms (six years for senators, life tenure for the justices) ensuring some insulation from popular will. How is this consistent with the principle that the people should rule?

We have seen earlier that Americans were well aware of the disastrous consequences of popular rule in ancient times. Most men are prone to quick judgments, especially when they are affected by their passions—fear, greed, jealousy, vengeance, or even pity, sympathy, or love. Quick judgments often lead to great errors. (Remember King Herod and John the Baptist, or King Midas and his touch.) This is especially true when they don't have all the facts. Imagine hearing a breathless report on the radio of a vile crime. It is

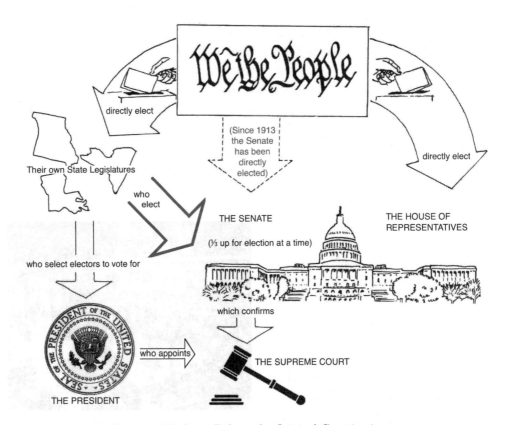

Direct and Indirect Rule in the Original Constitution.

human nature to want the person accused to be punished at once. But we don't know all the facts. It could turn out that the person wasn't guilty, or there were mitigating circumstances. That is why such matters are settled in courts, and not by having buttons on our remote controls that will allow us to say whether the person should be convicted and punished or not.

While the founders firmly believed that they could rule themselves, they knew that important decisions take time, time to let passions cool, to discover the facts, to discuss the matter with friends or trusted counselors. In other words, important decisions must be the result of prudent deliberation. The crucial importance of the need for deliberation was a major factor in the decision to have a representative government rather than a direct democracy. Most of us don't have the time or inclination to deliberate properly about all the affairs of government. So we appoint certain people to act on our behalf, in much the same way as we might appoint a lawyer to argue for us in court. A small number of experienced men, devoted to the work of governing, makes for effective deliberation.

The need for deliberation also explains in part why the Constitution separated the legislature into a House and Senate, and separates the law-making branch from both the executive and the judicial branches. All three functions are needed for government to be successful. Laws must be passed, then carried out, with offenders judged and punished. Further, each branch can affect the other in its own sphere; the President can veto legislation, the Congress can refuse to confirm judges, the courts can declare legislation unconstitutional. This means that under the Constitution, change will take time. The more serious the change, the longer it will take. In order for serious changes in governmental practice to take place, all three branches have to work together. If all three powers are united in a monarch, all one has to do is convince the king that something should be done, and it is done.

Detail of the tally sheet of the March 4, 1865 Electoral College vote. The names are Abraham Lincoln of Illinois and George B. McClellan of New Jersey.

Under the Constitution, even if a majority of the people elect enough representatives to get the House to pass a law, it can't change the Senate all at once. If the law is radical and uncertain, it will have to be moderated to get the Senate to agree, or else the people will have to show by their election of state legislators (who used to appoint the senators) in the next few elections that they continue to want the change. The people will also have to elect a president who will not veto the measure, or else get two thirds of both houses of Congress to override the veto. All of these measures gain time, which is crucial to successful deliberation. If the change is not for the good of the people, then they generally won't continue to want it for the time required to make it. We can easily imagine what the Constitution's framers would think of senators, presidents, or even representatives who make their decisions according to the latest opinion poll.

The Constitutional structure also tries to ensure that changes are for the good of the whole people, and not just of one segment which might have a majority. Each state has an equal number of votes in the United States Senate. The Electoral College system forces the President to win a majority of electors from the states rather than a majority of the popular vote. These measures and others ensured that a more single-minded section of the country, say the Northeast or the South or the Coastal states, has to convince the rest of the country that what it wants is good for everyone. These regional checks built into the Constitution have played an important role in keeping our country united.

So far we have seen how the Constitution allows the people to use government structures in a deliberate manner to bring about the general welfare. How does it protect liberty? Most importantly, it places rule in the hands of the people as whole. No greater protection for freedom can be found than by placing power in the hands of those who would be most affected by its loss. The separation of powers strengthens popular authority by placing hindrances in the paths of ambitious men who might want to take it away. Notice, for instance, that the President begins his term by swearing to "preserve, protect and defend the Constitution of the United States." The President is authorized by this to resist any attempts on the parts of the other branches to violate the

That Trojan Horse Trick Won't Work Now

When the Supreme Court threw out parts of FDR's "New Deal" program, he proposed appointing up to 6 additional justices, "packing" the court to get a majority, but he was prevented by Congress, which confirms appointments.

Constitution and seize power from the people. Although ordinarily we think of the Supreme Court as the body that determines what the Constitution means, the President and Congress have a solemn duty to resist the court when it tries to usurp powers not given to it in the Constitution. Andrew Jackson and Abraham Lincoln both resisted Courts that they thought had exceeded their proper roles. The chart on the next page shows some of these checks on government power.

Specific guarantees of liberty are also built into the Constitution. Although they don't stand out like the Bill of Rights, they have been very important in maintaining peace and freedom in our country. For instance, the definition of treason (Article III, section 3) is strictly limited. Only

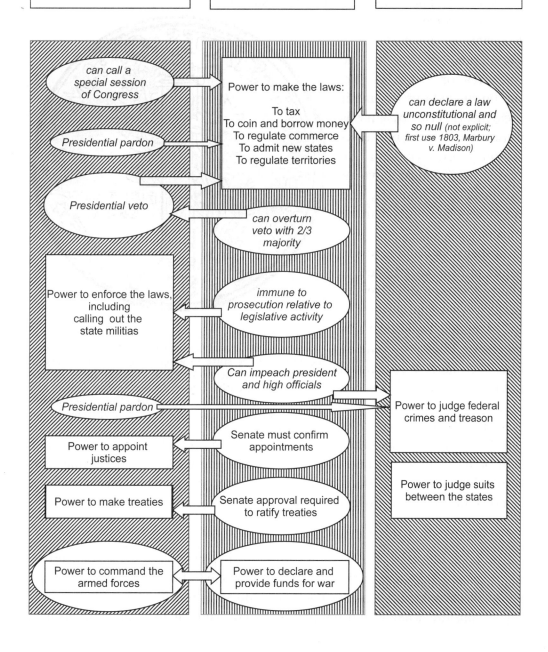

actual aid to a national enemy can be considered treason. Ambitious rulers have often used accusations of treason as a way to get rid of political enemies and terrify the populace. Any statements, even private conversations, in which the sovereign's decisions were criticized, were used as grounds for punishment. The Constitution forbids such tyrannical acts.

Other safeguards include taxation in proportion to population, ensuring that no one area or group of people be singled out for unfair treatment. Trial by jury is guaranteed. Religious tests for office are forbidden. All of the states must have republican governments, and no titles of nobility can be granted.

Finally, as Publius was to argue in *Federalist 10* and *51*, the very extent and diversity of occupation and interest in an extended republic helps to ensure liberty by placing checks on narrow or regional commercial and political factions. Compromise, collaboration, and appeals to reason

The "fasces," seen here on the dime, is a symbol from the Roman Republic. The bundle of sticks bound together shows strength through union, the axe in the center shows the power of the state to execute justice. That the axe is bound within the sticks shows that the many should restrain the executive power. When, in the days of the ancient republic, the fasces was carried in parade within the City of Rome, the axe was not included. Why do you think this was?

will be needed to make the wheels of legislation and administration turn; it will be hard, in a vast and diverse political community, for designing men and self-interested factions to have their way when others are watching, jealous for their own liberty and interest.

Questions for Reflection

6. Look for other specific limitations on the power of the federal government. Take any of the measures mentioned above or that you have discovered and consider how they safeguard our freedom. You might consider what would happen if the government were not limited in

these ways.

7. What are the chief ways in which the power of the federal government was weaker under the Articles of Confederation than it is under the Constitution? Does the Declaration imply or assert that excessive weakness in government is contrary to the ends of safety and happiness? If so, where?

8. Consider one of the four major parts of government—the House, Senate, President, or Judiciary. What specific powers does the Constitution grant it? How does its having and using those powers promote the safety and happiness of the people and how does it serve the ends mentioned in the Preamble? Review the list of criticisms the Declaration makes against King George. Can this list be better understood in the light of the branches of government the founders established in the Constitution?

9. Consider the guarantee of "a republican form of government" to the states in Article IV, section 4. What do you think is meant by "republican" in this section? Does it limit the sovereignty of the people in a state to prohibit them from choosing a non-republican form? Could a mere league or treaty between sovereign nations include such a guarantee?

5.4 The Bill of Rights

As Americans, we are justly proud of our Constitution, which has been a bulwark of our freedom for two centuries. Through the structures it established, it has guaranteed popular government by bringing to it a stability unknown to previous history. However, when Americans think of safeguards to liberty, we often think of something not originally in the Constitution, namely the Bill of Rights, the first ten amendments to the Constitution. With their guarantees of freedom of religion and of the press, of bearing arms, of due process, and so on, it is no wonder that we would consider them a bulwark against governmental and majority tyranny.

Although, as we have seen, the Constitution contains some determinate restrictions on the federal government, the Constitutional Convention deliberately refrained from including a bill of rights in the original document. The most severe criticism of the Constitution was occasioned by this omission. Indeed, the lack of a bill of rights endangered ratification in a number of states. The intensity of this criticism led to promises that a bill of rights would be included after ratification, by way of amendment. And this promise was kept. The first ten amendments are a powerful sign that the Constitution is really an act of the people, not of the Convention.

Why did the Convention, so wise in many ways, not include a bill of rights in the Constitution? The best defense of their decision was given by Publius in *Federalist 84*. "I go farther and affirm that... bills of rights are not only unnecessary in the proposed Constitution, but would even be dangerous." Publius argued that they are unnecessary because, under the Constitution, the rule of the people was guaranteed. No better safeguard to liberty can be found than the people themselves. Even advocates of a bill of rights agreed that no substitute could be found for the exertion of the popular will in defense of the people's liberties. A bill would simply make it easier for the people to tell when its liberties were in danger. As Richard Henry Lee put it,

Richard Henry Lee (1732–1794) was a delegate to the Continental Congress from Virginia, and made the motion to declare independence from Great Britain.

"... They become visible boundaries, constantly seen by all, and any transgression of them is immediately discovered: they serve as sentinels for the people at all times, and especially in those unavoidable intervals of inattention."

But why would a bill of rights be dangerous to liberty? With remarkable foresight, Publius explained the danger. Those clamoring for a bill of rights had a false notion of the Constitution. Through the Constitution, the people grant certain, definite powers to the federal government. If the people does not explicitly grant the power, the government does not have it. The government is like a lawyer, whose actions on behalf of his client are limited to what is explicitly authorized by the client. A lawyer doesn't need to be told that he can't sign your checks, unless he has been granted some power over your money. Tell your lawyer, in writing, that he can't sign your checks, and he might argue that you implied he could use your credit card! You didn't tell him he *couldn't*, after all. Explicit limits on a power imply that such a power exists, indeed has been granted. In Publius's words, "They [bills of rights] would contain various exceptions to powers which are not granted; and, on this very account, would afford a colorable pretext to claim more than were granted. For why declare that things shall not be done which there is no power to do?"

The first Congress tried to overcome the danger through what became the Ninth and Tenth Amendments. It is as though, once the first eight articles of the Bill of Rights were drafted, two more were added precisely to meet the arguments of *Federalist 84*. The Tenth Amendment makes explicit the limited nature of the authority of the federal government. It has only those powers that the people delegate to it, and it can only perform those functions it has been authorized and empowered by the people to perform. All other powers are left in the hands of the people or the states. This amendment is crucial to maintaining freedom because it denies unlimited federal power, not only for ill, but even for good. We don't expect or want the federal government to remedy all evil. Maybe my neighbor's music is too loud, but I don't necessarily want the FBI to ensure that he turns down the volume. The power any government has to do good is also a power that can be used for evil, and given the nature of men, often will. The FBI might come knocking at my door next time.

The Ninth Amendment is crucial for similar reasons. But where the Tenth limits government powers, the Ninth retains popular rights. "The enumeration in the Constitution, of certain rights, shall not be construed to deny or disparage others retained by the people." The Constitution is not the source of our fundamental rights. As we have seen from the Declaration, the source of our rights is found in a much higher authority than the Constitution. They come from our nature as men, created in the image of God. The rights to life, liberty, and pursuit of happiness are not mentioned in the Constitution, but they still exist, as the Constitution itself presupposes them.

In spite of the precautions in the Ninth and Tenth Amendments, some of Publius's fears have come to pass. Today, many of us look to government, especially the federal government, to solve all our problems. What, we ask, is the President, or the Congress, going to do to direct the economy, or education? What are they going to do about greed, violent crime, drugs, offensive television programs, smoking, unhealthy foods, etc.? If there is a good to be done, or a wrong to be righted, we unreflectively expect the federal government to do it, whether the power to do such things is found in the Constitution or not. Maybe we make an idol of the federal government, imagining that if a good can done, the Constitution must have given it the power to do it.

The Bill of Rights has played a two-fold role in this evolution. One we have just noted. It was meant to check these developments, but did so only imperfectly. In spite of the Ninth and Tenth Amendments, the political branches of the federal government, the legislative and the executive, have tended to assume powers and duties not granted in the Constitution.

The other role played by the Bill has been, and remains to this day, deeply controversial. The Supreme Court has used the first eight amendments, and other amendments passed after the Bill of Rights, to block countless acts of Congress, state legislatures, popular initiatives, and city governments. Since the Supreme Court is a federal organ, this has meant the extension of federal authority over state and local authority. Since the judiciary is the least accountable branch, it has constituted, even at the federal level, a veto over the popular will, as expressed by elected representatives. Accordingly, it has been the means of forcing changes on an unwilling society. Some of these changes have been for the better. When state governments and other local sources of authority refuse to right notable injustices, such as slavery or segregation, then the people will find a champion somewhere. Slavery was ended by war and amendment, but segregation was struck down by the courts. Some changes at the state and local level, in the mode of election of state and municipal governments, in the role of religion in public schools, in the authority of local school boards and local police forces, and many other matters, have been instances of the federal courts applying the words of the Bill of Rights to matters the framers may well have meant to be left to the states and the people.

Given the tremendous impact the Bill of Rights has had in our day, perhaps the Declaration of Independence is most immediately important in helping us to understand those amendments properly. Let us look at a few of them, and see how Declaration principles preclude the most extreme of today's interpretations. We begin with religion and civil society, and hence with the First Amendment.

East pediment of the Supreme Court building, Hermon A. McNeil's "Justice the Guardian of Liberty," is intended to be a symbolic representation of the Eastern civilizations from which our laws were derived, personified by the three great lawgivers: Moses, Confucius, and Solon.

The First Amendment

It is worth noting that the First Amendment yokes two things, which could have required separate amendments. The First Amendment prohibits Congress from establishing any religion and from restraining the free exercise of religion. And it forbids Congress from abridging the rights of free speech, a free press, and free public assembly. These latter are all political rights, and specific to a regime in which sovereignty rests in the people. To vote well, to give reasoned consent, a citizen must be able to assemble with others, he must have access to a free press, and such a citizen must be able to speak freely in public. By coupling promotion of a soul's freedom to worship God as it sees fit with promotion of a citizen's free political judgment, the amendment seems to hint that the two operate in tandem in securing the blessings of liberty. In this light it is worth wondering whether in the framers' view you could have political liberty without religion and religious liberty.

In the last fifty years, however, the First Amendment has been used to ease God out of public life in many ways. Christmas displays are banished

99

from public property; prayers in public schools, or before the football games their teams play, are forbidden; laws regulating risky and peculiar sexual behavior or other activity are overturned, apparently on the grounds that the preferred, safe, and sane conduct is in conformity with religion; charities and voluntary associations, like the Boy Scouts, find difficulty in co-operating with government agencies because they stand for a moral code in accord with religious tradition. Most recently, religious institutions find themselves forced to participate, in matters of health care and family policy, in activities contrary to their faith. The thinking on which these policies and judgments are based seems to be that the First Amendment, understood as requiring an absolute "separation of church and state," forbids deference to the Creator in American public life.

Little of this would have happened had we read the Constitution in the light of the Declaration. If, as the Declaration plainly states, our fundamental rights come from God, then there is no way that He can be excluded from public life, or that religion, which teaches the respect for God and consequently our rights, can be treated as a public enemy. To do so is to undermine the very basis of our society and guarantee of our liberties.

Thinking from the Declaration, we can better understand what the amendment really means to prevent. In their former countries Americans knew the horrors of wars fought by those so sure they knew which church was the true one that they were ready, nay eager, to destroy those they could not persuade. The First Amendment prevents Congress from supporting one church against another, and from punishing anyone for not believing or worshiping as a majority might think they should. The Episcopalians cannot be favored over the Catholics, the Presbyterians over the Jews. The amendment does not, however, prevent Congress from honoring or otherwise encouraging religion generally. "In God We Trust" proclaim our dollars; our armed services are supplied with chaplains at public expense; sessions of the Supreme Court begin with the words, "God save this honorable court!" There are disputable matters in this field, and men of goodwill may reasonably differ about them. But the First Amendment certainly was not intended to prevent a statue of Moses holding the Ten Commandments from being displayed in a courthouse, or a public school teacher from handing out to his students extracts from American statesmen in which the religious roots of republican liberty are stressed. A republic founded on self-evident truths that include the divine source of rights cannot enshrine a right to exclude God altogether from the public square.

The Second Amendment

The Second Amendment protects the right of the people to keep and bear arms. Why did Americans see this as crucial? First, they thought the individual, in his natural right of self-government, also enjoyed a right to self-defense. This implied a right to be armed. Second, as the Declaration sees so clearly, a government itself can become tyrannical, and when it does, the people have a right to abolish it. But how can a people exercise that right if they have no arms? The American Revolution would never have succeeded if the multitude of citizens had not been well armed and well able to use those arms.

A depiction of the minuteman harrying the British troops retreating from Lexington and Concord.

More however was needed, and the Second Amendment shows it when it speaks of "bearing arms," which means carrying them in public; above all when it speaks of militias. The Americans never would have succeeded if they had not been regulated in militias. The "minutemen" were ordinary, but armed, citizens, ready at a moment's notice from their elected leaders to resist in a body the armies of the king. They were a tolerably "well regulated militia." The Second Amendment exists to sustain the practical possibility of precisely such a just rebellion, and to instill fear in potential tyrants. We must admit that allowing ordinary citizens to have weapons might be dangerous. But the framers thought that allowing the government to command a standing army while at the same time disarming its citizens would surely invite tyranny.

The Fourth through Eighth Amendments

Amendments Four through Eight protect citizens against abuses of legal and police powers. Government officials cannot invade or spy on the lives of ordinary citizens without having some definite, particular reason to suspect them of a crime. Citizens are entitled to a speedy, fair trial by a jury. Punishments and fines are not to be cruel, unusual, or arbitrary.

We can lose our rights by criminal activity, but only when guilt has been determined through a careful, public, legal process. In undoubtedly the most controversial interpretation of the Bill of Rights in our century, the Supreme Court determined in *Roe v. Wade* that these amendments, together with an open-ended reading of the unenumerated rights of the Ninth Amendment, guarantee a mother's right to kill her unborn child. The Declaration's assertion of the fundamental right to life militates against such a reading of the meaning of the Constitution. The Preamble itself points to legal duties towards, and rights of, the unborn when it speaks of securing the "Blessings of Liberty to ourselves and our posterity." Surely the first of "our posterity" is the innocent, but unborn, child in the womb. Moreover, the Declaration asserts that our fundamental rights, including the right to life, come from God. Can these fundamental rights be taken away without violation of the higher law that makes all our human laws possible?

President Truman addressing a joint session of Congress

Conclusion

We can see by now that the Constitution as a whole was the product of prudent men. They saw clearly the goals they wanted to achieve, and they drew from their experience and the experience of the ages to establish a practical and effective instrument of popular rule and national unity. The Constitution is a great instrument of a free people.

But in order for us to use the Constitution properly, we have to keep before us the goals that it is meant to achieve. These are most clearly stated in the Declaration of Independence: to maintain the rights to life, liberty, and the pursuit of happiness; to promote the safety and happiness of the people. The Constitution presupposes these goals. It does not determine what things are just and right and good; it merely provides the means to bring them about, especially by making it possible for the people to exercise effective authority.

Over the years, justices, presidents, senators, and representatives have all had to try to use this great instrument in different ways. They have used its powers from day to day, struggled to interpret it in very different situations from that of the founders, and have adapted it by numerous amendments when it seemed to be inadequate. Through it all, the American people have had to judge these efforts, giving their blessing or reacting in outrage. Often, people would read the Constitution apart from the Declaration, as though it were the sole foundation of our country. In the most important decisions, this inevitably fails. When we forget to read the Constitution as the instrument of a people of the Declaration, we make many grave mistakes. We will consider some of these in the next chapter.

Questions for Reflection

10. The First Amendment is explicit in restricting Congress. It says nothing about the states. What would you do, as a judge on the court in 1795, about a complaint that a state, say Massachusetts, had established a religion, not nationally, but in that state? Could a community, first informally, then as a town or city in a state, establish a religion, or require jurors or school board members to have a belief in God, or in a particular creed? Did any of the states have established religions in the founding period? Should they have them, then or at any time? Who should decide this?

11. One state, Virginia, faced the question of religious establishment in a

political contest that involved the "Father of the Constitution" himself, James Madison. Read Madison's "Memorial and Remonstrance" (in the *Book of Readings*) to see what one important founder thought about these matters.

Chapter 5 Review Questions

1. Identify at least two aspects of the Articles of Confederation that indicate that the Union was more than an alliance.
2. Why do the Articles insist that the states remain independent?
3. According to the Articles, which body has "full Power to levy War, conclude Peace, contract Alliances, establish Commerce"?
4. What does Washington imply was the chief mistake Congress made in the governmental structure set up under the Articles, and why did Americans make that mistake?
5. What does Washington identify as "the greatest interest of every true American" and the immediate goal of the Constitution?
6. Who established the Constitution? How does this compare to the agents of the Articles?
7. How does the Constitution "establish Justice"?
8. The Declaration of Independence states that people form governments to "effect their safety and happiness." Which parts of the Preamble to the Constitution show it is established for the safety of the people? For their happiness?
9. What, in general, are the "Blessings of Liberty"?
10. What branches of the federal government are most directly connected to the people? Why?
11. *Federalist 59* says: "the abuse of liberty is a greater danger than the abuse of power." How would this explain the following aspects of the Constitution?
    a) Representative government rather than direct democracy
    b) Election of Senators by state legislatures
    c) Separation of the powers of government into legislative, executive, and judicial branches
12. How does the Constitution attempt to ensure that government works for the good of the whole people?

13. According to Richard Henry Lee, what is the purpose of the Bill of Rights?
14. Why might the Bill of Rights be dangerous to liberty? How did the first Congress act to overcome this danger?
15. How does the Declaration of Independence help us avoid erroneous interpretations of the First Amendment?
16. What is the purpose of the Second Amendment?

Paper Topic 3:

Write a paper of 4 to 5 pages on the following topic: Choosing one the four major parts of government—the House, Senate, President, or Judiciary—discuss in what way the major powers granted to it by the Constitution would promote the people's safety and happiness without endangering their liberty. (See Questions for Reflection 8, page 95)

The Stain of Slavery 6

...He has waged cruel war against human nature itself, violating its most sacred rights of life and liberty in the persons of a distant people who never offended him, captivating & carrying them into slavery in another hemisphere, or to incur miserable death in their transportation thither.

—Jefferson, first draft of the Declaration of Independence, 1776

...And can the liberties of a nation be thought secure when we have removed their only firm basis, a conviction in the minds of the people that these liberties are of the gift of God? That they are not to be violated but with his wrath? Indeed, I tremble for my country when I reflect that God is just: that his justice cannot sleep for ever: that considering numbers, nature, and natural means only, a revolution of the wheel of fortune, an exchange of situation, is among possible events: that it may become probable by supernatural interference! The Almighty has no attribute which can take side with us in such a contest...I think a change is already perceptible, since the origin of the present revolution. The spirit of the master is abating, that of the slave rising from the dust, his condition mollifying, the way I hope preparing, under the auspices of heaven, for a total emancipation, and that this is disposed, in the order of events, to be with the consent of the masters, rather than by their extirpation.

—Jefferson, *Notes on the State of Virginia*, 1782

The American Republic, born in 1776 and confirmed in the Constitution of 1787, sparked the wonder and interest of the world. It was to be the test of self-government based on equal natural rights. The founders had declared that, "all men are created equal." Yet many of them, Jefferson included, held their fellow men in bondage, in slavery. Their Constitution counted each slave at the rate of three-fifths of a free person in apportioning taxes and representatives to the lower house of Congress. It required that "[a] person held to service or labor [i.e., a slave,] in one state, escaping into another...shall be delivered up on claim of the party to whom such service or labor may be due." It promised not to interfere with "the migration or importation of such persons as the States now existing shall think proper to admit [i.e., slaves] prior to the year 1808."

The Spirit of the Declaration and Slavery

What were the founders thinking, and why did they act as they did? Were they so blinded by race prejudice as to believe the black men and women they held in slavery were not human beings? This second question admits of an easy answer. They knew that blacks were men. Jefferson's original draft of the Declaration, quoted above, goes on to denounce the king as "determined to keep open a market where MEN should be bought and sold..." The parts of the Constitution that recognize the institution of slavery and grant certain

Property? A wood engraving of handcuffed and shackled slaves passing the U.S. Capitol, depicts a scene circa 1819.

protections to the slave owner consistently refer to the slave as a "person," and what beast or mere article of property, what indeed but a human being or something higher than a human being has ever been called a person? The language of the Constitution does not even bear the words slave or slavery, as though, as Lincoln was to remark later, the framers did not wish to stain the purity of the Federal Constitution with the ugly name of an unjust institution. Alexander Hamilton, writing to John Jay in 1779, urged the emancipation of those black slaves who had served in the Continental Army (and there were many of them) in these words, "...the dictates of humanity and true policy equally interest me in favor of this unfortunate class of men." It is needless to insist on this point further. Evidence abounds that the men of the founding generation, whatever they may have thought about social equality or differences in natural talents, universally recognized that their black slaves were men.

How, then, could they justify their actions, especially the constitutional provisions that protected the slave owners? How persuasive was that justification? And what does it mean for us in understanding America, its history, and its principles?

6.1   The Declaration Principle of Equality

Before we go on to try to answer the questions raised above, we should look at how the generation that fought for independence, the generation of the Declaration, dealt with slavery in America. It is a stirring but incomplete tale of progress and partial victory, but also of exhaustion and defeat. It shows the power of ideas, but also the need for perseverance and wise statesmanship. Lack of that perseverance ushered in the crisis of the "house divided," and the bloodshed of the Civil War. But without the success that was attained, Jefferson's brooding remarks about divine retribution for injustice would have fortold an even more tragic outcome.

As with the revolutionary movement itself, so with the question of slavery, we would do well to look first to the churches and sermons of the day to discover the motives and ideas that were leading Americans to dream of and fight for liberty for the slaves. Congregationalist Levi Hart, writing in 1774, put the case in the fervid rhetoric of the day. "What have the unhappy Africans," he wrote in a sermon delivered in Farmington, Connecticut, "committed against the inhabitants of the British colonies and islands in the West Indies to authorize us to seize them and transport them a thousand leagues into a strange land, and enslave them for life?... What inconsistence and self-contradiction is this!... When, O when shall the happy day come, that Americans shall be consistently engaged in the cause of liberty?" Baptist preacher John Allen called the keeping of African slaves an "iniquitous and disgraceful practice." Samuel Hopkins, another Congregationalist minister, who had once been a slaveholder himself, pointedly declared that the charges of tyranny and slavery that their fellow colonists had levied against the king were "lighter than a feather compared to their [the slaves'] heavy doom, and may be called liberty and happiness when contrasted with the most abject slavery and unutterable wretchedness to which they are subjected."

Such ideas, widely promulgated in pamphlets and sermons, were not

"They ordered the first woman to lay down her child and mount the auction block; she refused to give up her little one and clung to it as long as she could, while the cruel lash was applied to her back for disobedience... There was each speculator with his hand-cuffs to bind his victims after the sale; ... the Christian portion of the slaves asked permission to kneel in prayer on the ground before they were separated."

—from the autobiography of Henry Bibb, an American slave.

without effect. Before the revolution, Massachusetts' legislature had twice voted to abolish the slave trade, only to be thwarted by the royal governor's veto. Momentum built during and after the revolution. Even before independence, in April of 1776, Congress voted that "no slaves be imported into any of the thirteen colonies." Local action in New Hampshire and Massachusetts effectively ended slavery in those states in the 1780s. Pennsylvania passed a gradual emancipation law in 1780. Jefferson himself introduced a proposal for abolition in the Virginia legislature in 1778, and in 1784, he drafted legislation for the Congress that would have banned slavery in all the territories of the United States, including the "Southwest" i.e., the areas that would become the states of Alabama, Mississippi, Tennessee, and Kentucky. The measure failed by just one vote. Even the slave states of the deep South had all abolished the slave trade, though not slavery itself, by 1798.

The Northwest Ordinance is a striking witness to the moral authority of Declaration principles in the national government. In 1787, still under the Articles of Confederation, Congress passed this ordinance for the government of the Northwest Territory, forbidding slavery in these lands which would subsequently become the states of Ohio, Indiana, Illinois, Michigan, and Wisconsin. Unlike the Southwest Territory, which was ceded to the national government by slaveholding states on the condition that slavery be permitted, the Northwest was essentially under the tutelage of the national government. Congress, free to act, enacted freedom.

Slave vs. Free: 1787

The states here labeled "free" were achieving that status slowly and some would not be entirely free until the 1840s.

Two centuries and more after these events, we tend to view the slavery question through the lens of the Civil War, as a sectional issue only, pitting North against South. True though it was that slavery was concentrated in the Southern states, it is important to remember that all thirteen of the original states were slave states at the outbreak of the revolution. Abolition anywhere, North or South, entailed struggle and sacrifice, sometimes of the greater part of one's own wealth. So did voluntary release from slavery, a practice known as "manumission." Even so, by the time of the 1810 census, slavery was abolished or on the road to abolition in the majority of the 13 original states, and over 100,000 former slaves were free men in the South, more than the nearly 80,000 in the North. Taken together, free blacks, North and South, amounted to about one eighth of the black population counted in that census.

None of this progress towards freedom would have happened without the force of the moral and religious convictions of the Americans of the revolutionary period, that is, without their adherence to the principles of the Declaration. Twentieth century historian Bernard Bailyn, in his book on the origins of the American Revolution, puts it this way: "[slavery] had been subjected to severe pressure as a result of the extension of Revolutionary ideas, and it bore the marks ever after. As long as the institution lasted, the burden of proof would lie with its advocates to show why the statement 'all men are created equal' did not mean precisely what it said: all men, 'white or black.' "

The logic of Bailyn's conclusion is sound only if we grant the Declaration's self-evident truth that it cites. As a political fact, it is sound only if statesmen take that truth as their pole star, and teach and proclaim it to citizens who also find it written in their hearts. Something was amiss in one or both of these conditions as the founding generation grew old and died. The southward-moving trend of abolition stopped, north of the Potomac River. No more states voluntarily ended the practice of human bondage after New Jersey's legislation of 1804. A weary Jefferson, no longer the sanguine young man who wrote the *Notes on the State of Virginia*, wrote in his eighty-third year:

> The revolution in public opinion which this cause [ending slavery] requires, is not to be expected in a day, or perhaps in an age; but time, which outlives all things, will outlive this evil also. My sentiments have been forty years before the public. Had I repeated them forty times, they would only have become the more stale and threadbare. Although I shall not live to see them consummated, they will not die

with me; but living or dying, they will ever be in my most fervent
prayer. This is written for yourself and not for the public...[1]

Six weeks and three days later, on July 4th, 1826, Thomas Jefferson died.

6.2   Prudence: Saving the Union

Let us review what we have concluded and what we want to ask. The
founders knew perfectly well that black slaves were men. They knew that
the institution of slavery contradicted the spirit of the Declaration. The
generation of the Revolution abolished slavery in the North, and in the
territory that the nation controlled. It outlawed the slave trade as soon as
the Constitution allowed, in 1808. But it also gave constitutional guarantees
to the right of property in slaves, including the distasteful duty of hunting
down and returning escaped slaves. And in the South, where the bulk of the
slaves lived, it failed to outlaw the practice.

What then were the founders thinking? A direct answer would be simple:
to save the Union. A longer form of that answer would be: to preserve the
principles of the Declaration, and act with prudence in the hope that the
evil, if contained, would diminish and die.

In the previous section we have argued that slavery was in principle a
problem for the American nation as a whole. Among the reasons we gave
were that *all* the states were originally slave states, and that the national
legislative body, Congress, with Jefferson himself voting "aye," had passed the
ban on slavery in the Northwest Ordinance. And of paramount importance,
the basis for rejection of human slavery is the equality of men as a gift of
God, a founding truth of the republic.

As a matter of practical politics, however, there was a strongly sectional
color to the issue, one that it would have been unwise and even irresponsible
for Madison and the other members of the Constitutional Convention to
ignore. There was some trouble in ending slavery in Massachusetts, where
the slave owners were few and the Declaration principles strong. It was
much harder to do in New York; the Tories had been strong there, and the
wealth represented by the more numerous slaves was considerable. Virginia,
led by the redoubtable Jefferson, at least considered the question. In the
lower South, especially South Carolina and to a lesser degree Georgia, the

---

[1] Jefferson to James Heaton, Monticello, May 20, 1826

113

task was practically impossible. More than half the human population of South Carolina consisted of black slaves, and Georgia, which had prohibited slavery up to 1751, was a rich agricultural frontier by 1787, filling up with plantation wealth and the attendant slaves, numbering about two-fifths of the total inhabitants as early as 1780.

PICKING COTTON

Slaves on a large plantation.

Individuals could manumit their slaves, and many, including George Washington in his will, did so. But emancipation, even gradual emancipation, would not occur by the voluntary act of the states. In 1776, according to Jefferson, the charge against the king of "[waging] cruel war against human nature itself" in perpetuating the slave trade had to be dropped from the Declaration, "in complaisance to S. Carolina and Georgia, who had never attempted to restrain the importation of slaves, and who on the contrary still wished to continue it."

By the time of the Constitutional Convention, not only would South Carolina refuse to emancipate its own slaves, it would not, according to its delegates, John Rutledge and Charles Pinckney, join the Union if the slave trade was permanently abolished, or if there was no fugitive slave law. Pinckney declared in the Convention that, "South Carolina can never receive the plan if it prohibits the slave trade," while Rutledge openly avowed that

114

"humanity and religion have nothing to do with this question—interest alone is the governing principle with Nations—The true question at present is whether the Southern States shall or shall not be parties to the Union." The more moderate Hugh Williamson of North Carolina, himself on record as opposed to slavery in principle, declared that "the S. States could not be members of the Union if the clause [forbidding Congress from banning the slave trade] should be rejected."

We should remember what Publius said in the first issues of the *Federalist*, that the world was watching their experiment in republican government to decide the question of whether men could govern themselves

John Rutledge (1739–1800), later the first governor of South Carolina and second Chief Justice of the Supreme Court

by "reflection and choice," and that the "prosperity of America depended on its Union." The Convention was called to meet an emergency. The Articles were inept, and thus the Union, and with it the great experiment, was in danger. If there was no Union, Madison and the convention judged, there would be no durable and safe republican regime in the new world, and mankind would be the loser. Compromise was necessary, or there would be no "*novus ordo seclorum.*"

6.3 Compromise and Hope

South Carolina's delegate Pinckney, who was a patriot and had been a general in the Revolutionary War, wanted a strong Union, too. He might not have made good on his threats. In the event, he and his Southern brethren

115

accepted a compromise and ratified the Constitution. The Southerners got a postponement of the national ban on the slave trade until 1808, and they got the fugitive slave clause. They did *not* get the term "legally" used to describe "persons held to service or labor." Those in the Convention who held to the natural law doctrine insisted that what was inherently unjust must never be termed "legal."

The slave states also won a major point on the issue of representation of their slave population in Congress and in electoral votes for the presidency. It seemed natural to many, most of all the enemies of slavery, that slaves should not be counted in calculating the states' shares in a Congress representing free citizens. Gouverneur Morris, of Pennsylvania, whose sentiments on slavery may be judged from his calling it in the Convention debates, "a nefarious institution," opposed counting slaves at all, on the grounds that it would give "encouragement to the slave trade." Counting "all other persons" (note again how the Constitution recoils from even the words, 'slave' or 'slavery') as three-fifths of free persons was a concession to the South, which wanted the slaves to "stand on an equality with the whites," as Pinckney put

Charles Cotesworth Pinckney (1746–1825). As a prisoner of war during the Revolution, he played a major role in maintaining the troops' loyalty to the Patriots' cause. During this time, he famously said, "If I had a vein that did not beat with the love of my Country, I myself would open it. If I had a drop of blood that could flow dishonourable, I myself would let it out."

it, in setting the states' representation and taxation. Free blacks were, of course, counted as free persons, although they did not usually have the vote.

Pinckney wanted, but did not obtain, an explicit statement that Congress could not abolish slavery. The Constitution was silent on this point until the Thirteenth Amendment directly outlawed the "nefarious institution" in 1865, after the Civil War. Benjamin Franklin seems to have thought the power to abolish slavery did exist in the Constitution. At least, that is a reasonable

116

inference from his last great public act, in 1790. On February twelfth of that year, a petition arrived in the House of Representatives, under the signature of Franklin, asking Congress to "take such measures in their wisdom, as the powers with which they are invested will authorize, for promoting the abolition of slavery. . . " The petition argued that Congress had power over slavery from the "general welfare" clause of the Constitution. The petition was received by the House, over protests from Georgia and South Carolina, which did not even want it read or noticed, and a vigorous debate ensued. Fearing the dissolution of the Union in its infancy, the House, under the influence of James Madison, passed a report denying any federal power over slavery. The vote was 29–25. This effectively ended any abolition efforts by the national government until the Civil War, though some anti-slavery Congressmen argued in the debates over the admission of Missouri in 1819 and 1820 that the commerce clause did give Congress such power over a state. But the anti-slavery congressmen of 1820 never had the votes to put the interpretation to the test, and Abraham Lincoln himself did not make such a claim in the controversy over slavery before the Civil War.

The anti-slavery men at the Convention thought that they had won enough in these compromises to guarantee the slow decline and eventual end of slavery. They had seen it outlawed in some of their own states, and they looked forward to the abolition of the trade. Without importation of slaves, they thought the free population would increase much faster than the slaves and that it would become as possible for Georgia or South Carolina to abolish it as it had been for New York or Connecticut in their day. They thought that the limited lands suitable for plantation agriculture, and the absence of slavery in the Northwest Territory, together with its lack of respectability even in the

Frederick Douglass (1818–1895). In 1838 he escaped from slavery and became a well-known anti-slavery orator and author.

117

South—men were unwilling to end it, but even more unwilling to praise it or deem it moral—would cause it to wither and die.

We now have the answer to the question at the beginning of this chapter. The founders accepted the compromises out of prudence, while they endeavored to sustain the founding principles, resolving to wait patiently in hope of the consummation of those principles.

Questions for Reflection

1. At the end of the second *Federalist*, Publius wrote, "...whenever the dissolution of the Union arrives, America will have reason to exclaim, in the words of the poet: 'Farewell! A long farewell to all my greatness.'" To establish the importance of the Union was the chief object of the first 22 of the papers, especially of the first ten. Reflect on these questions on your own:

   Could America have enjoyed peace and prosperity in several distinct confederacies better than in one Union? Suppose that South Carolina and Georgia had formed a distinct republic in 1790. Would it have been in their interest to reach a military and diplomatic understanding with Great Britain? What might the War of 1812 have looked like with British naval forces based in Charlestown harbor? Would a disunited America have had a greater or a lesser chance of being drawn into the Napoleonic Wars, which convulsed Europe for the first decade and a half of the 19th century?

   You might also want to compare our experience with that of Latin America, which made its own democratic revolution in the first part of the 19th century. Find out how many times those republics have gone to war with each other since achieving their independence.

   Even if the foreign affairs of the disunited Americans may have suffered, perhaps their domestic happiness would have been greater. Are small republics more free and prosperous? What do you think? After discussing this or writing about it, take a look at Publius's arguments on the same question. *Federalist 10* (found in the *Book of Readings*), is especially interesting in this regard, and may surprise you by its reasoning.

2. Madison said at the Constitutional Convention, "the real difference of interests lay, not between the large and small, but between the Northern and Southern states. The institution of slavery and its

consequences formed the line of discrimination [i.e., of difference in these interests]." We have argued above that slavery was a national question. Does Madison's judgment contradict our argument? How could Madison not have foreseen, at the time of the Convention, the sectional controversy that was to come to a head in the Civil War?

3. If the Northwest Ordinance had not banned slavery from Indiana and Ohio, do you think slavery would have become legal in those regions as they became states? What sort of evidence would bear on your answer? You might consider moral, legal, religious, economic, and geographical reasons; then look at Lincoln's Peoria speech (it's in the *Book of Readings*) and see how he handled it. What would have happened to the persuasive power of those making the moral argument if the federal government, having passed the ordinance, had later rescinded it? Or if the Supreme Court had declared it invalid?

4. Which of the inalienable rights named in the Declaration did slavery violate? If you say, "liberty, at least," would the abolition of slavery end the violation of that right, or does liberty include such matters as voting, freedom to travel, jury duty, and militia service? You might want to look at the Fourteenth Amendment to the Constitution, and ask why it was thought necessary or desirable given that the Thirteenth Amendment had prohibited slavery. The relation between the right to liberty and the right to citizenship is covered in an interesting section of Thomas G. West's recent book, *Vindicating the Founders*, pages 25–28.

5. In the founders' minds, slavery was an evil, but an evil that they inherited from their ancestors. What are the moral obligations of statesmen in dealing with such evils? Comment on the following passage from Sabato and O'Connor's contemporary textbook, *American Government: Roots and Reform*: "Whereas earlier the Declaration of Independence had so eloquently proclaimed that 'all men are created equal,' the delegates to the Constitutional Convention put political expediency before the immorality of slavery."

6. Frederick Douglass, the great black orator, writer, and statesman, said this about the Constitution: "Liberty and Slavery—opposite as Heaven and Hell—are both in the Constitution." What did Douglass have in mind? Cite the appropriate portions of the Constitution. You

119

might enjoy doing a little reading on Douglass. His *Autobiography* is well worth reading.

7. One of the puzzling things about the founders' hopes is that they thought that without importation, the slave population would not increase very much. This judgment was in error. You might wish to speculate on what economic or social assumptions led them to make this mistake. Consider the awful fact that the child of slave parents was a capital asset to the owner. Consider, too, the great increase in lands open to cultivation, Northern and Southern, in the first half of the 19th century.

8. It is a teaching of both classical and Judeo-Christian morality that doing unjust things harms not only the victim, but also the doer. Comment on this passage from Madison, from his remarks at the Convention:

> The poor despise labor when performed by slaves... They [slaves] produce the most pernicious effect on manners. Every master of slaves is born a petty tyrant. They bring the judgement of heaven on a Country. As nations can not be rewarded or punished in the next world, they must be in this. By an inevitable chain of causes and effects providence punishes national sins by national calamities...

In this connection, you may wish to comment on this excerpt from a letter by Robert E. Lee, written to his wife in 1856:

> In this enlightened age, there are few I believe, but what will acknowledge, that Slavery as an institution, is a moral, political evil in any Country. It is useless to expatiate on its disadvantages. I think it however a greater evil to the White than to the black race, and while my feelings are strongly enlisted on behalf of the latter, my Sympathies are more strong for the former.

Epilogue: The Failure of the Founders' Policy

> This [anti-slavery] agitation has produced one happy effect at least; it has compelled us to the South to look into the nature and character of this great institution, and to correct many false impressions that even we had entertained in relation to it. Many in the South once believed that it was a moral and political evil; that folly and delusion are gone; we see it now in its true light, and regard it as the most

safe and stable basis for free institutions in the world.
—John C. Calhoun, Senator from South Carolina, 1838[2]

...he who would be no slave, must consent to have no slave. Those who deny freedom to others, deserve it not for themselves; and, under a just God, cannot long retain it. All honor to Jefferson—to the man who, in the concrete pressure of a struggle for national independence by a single people, had the coolness, forecast, and capacity to introduce into a merely revolutionary document, an abstract truth, applicable to all men and all times, and so to embalm it there, that today, and in all coming days, it shall be a rebuke and a stumbling-block to the very harbingers of reappearing tyranny and oppression.
—Abraham Lincoln, 1859[3]

Slavery did not wither and die in the generation after the founders. It was not enough to ban the importation of slaves; the American slave population, both African and mulatto, grew naturally, and sons and daughters were cruelly torn from their families and sold to owners who set out to clear the lands of Alabama, Mississippi, and the other western territories where slavery was allowed. Breeding human beings made slavery economically efficient, and the

The cotton gin, by eliminating the slow process of hand picking the seeds from the bolls, made cotton plantations immensely more profitable.

cotton gin and other mechanical inventions made the plantation system profitable on lands that Madison and Jefferson thought would never be hospitable to slavery. Slaves even began to be employed in the infant manufacturing facilities of the South. The great Lincoln scholar, Harry Jaffa, cites the example of "a famous iron company in Richmond, Virginia, which introduced slaves into its labor force in the 1840s, with the result that the free laborers struck in protest." The manager broke the strike as managers sometimes do: he would not rehire any of the strikers, and "Thereafter, the company employed only slaves."

---

[2]Senate Speech, January 10
[3]Letter to Henry Pierce and others, April 6

In the North, parties and groups sprang up to resist slavery's expansion or to press for its abolition. In 1819 and 1820, the proposal to admit Missouri to the Union was resisted by Northern congressmen, who demanded as a condition of their approval a plan for the gradual abolition of slavery in the newly admitted state. Madison wrote a friend that the debate gave him "no slight anxiety," and added that he saw nothing "to controul those great repulsive Masses [sectional factions, based on the approval of slavery or its condemnation] from awful shocks against each other. . ." A famous letter of Jefferson's on the same subject declared, ". . . this momentous question, like a fire-bell in the night, awakened and filled me with terror. I considered it at once as the knell of the Union."

Alexander Stephens (1812–1883) was Vice President of the Confederate States of America during the American Civil War. He also served as a U.S. Representative from Georgia (both before the Civil War and after Reconstruction) and as the 50th Governor of Georgia from 1882 until his death in 1883.

The failure of the policy of disapproval and patience, of voluntary manumission and non-importation, had made the issue a sectional question of the first magnitude. And worse, it began to produce sentiments like that of Calhoun quoted at the start of this section. Slavery apologist George Fitzhugh also explicitly rejected the moral sentiments of the previous generation of Southerners. Writing in 1857, he said that Southern writings of the previous generation "are like to be as absurd and as dangerous as the Declaration of Independence, or the Virginia Bill of Rights." Fitzhugh would have found nothing "absurd or dangerous" in what Alexander Stephens of Georgia would say in his famous "Cornerstone" speech at the March, 1861 Georgia convention called to ratify the Confederate Constitution:

> Our new government is founded upon exactly the opposite idea [namely, opposite to Jefferson's idea that slavery was wrong in principle]; its foundations are laid, its cornerstone rests upon the great

truth, that the negro is not equal to the white man; that slavery—subordination to the superior race—is the normal condition... This stone which was rejected by the first builders "is become the chief of the corner"—the real "cornerstone"—in our new edifice.

William Lloyd Garrison (1805–1879) was a fiery opponent of slavery.

The quote within his quote is from Psalms 118. Stephens did not go on to add the next verse, "This is the Lord's doing, and it is marvelous in our eyes," but surely the text echoed in his hearers' minds as he spoke.

The Northern abolitionists were no less immoderate than these Southerners. The most prominent, William Lloyd Garrison, who began as a proponent of the resettlement of free blacks in Africa, turned against it when he saw that it was being used to reduce the number of free blacks and preserve slavery. He espoused secession of the North from the Union, and carried out public burnings of the Constitution, which Garrison called a "covenant with death."

In this crisis of moral, political, and sectional strife, arose Abraham Lincoln.

Questions for Reflection

9. Our inquiry will now turn to Lincoln, who will dominate the next chapter. An important area for further reading would be the rise of the abolitionist movement, whose leading figure was William Lloyd Garrison. Garrison, too, cited the Declaration, and his failure to be moderate was no oversight. Consider these words from his journal, *The Liberator*:

   I will be as harsh as truth, and as uncompromising as justice. On this subject, I do not wish to think, to speak, or write, with moderation... I am in earnest—I will not equivocate—I will not excuse—I will not retreat a single inch—AND I WILL

BE HEARD.

The sparkling long essay by John Jay Chapman, a descendant of founder John Jay, is the best written, and perhaps the most informative source on Garrison. It may be found in *The Selected Writings of John Jay Chapman*. Chapman credits Garrison even more than Lincoln for the ending of slavery. Other leaders from this period, 1820 to 1860, are competently treated in John Hope Franklin's *From Slavery to Freedom*, pages 242–270. Many, including the North Carolina freedman, David Walker, make explicit and passionate reference to the Declaration in stating the case for abolition. The most famous of the black abolitionists was doubtlessly Frederick Douglass, whom we have already mentioned.

Chapter 6 Review Questions

1. What were the original Constitutional provisions with respect to slavery?
2. How did Jefferson refer to the slaves in the first draft of the Declaration? How does the Constitution refer to them?
3. What did Levi Hart refer to as a 'self-contradiction?'
4. What did Jefferson tell James Heaton that the ending of slavery required?
5. What percentage of the population of South Carolina were slaves at the time of the Constitution?
6. What did South Carolina and the other slave states gain in the Constitution? What did they fail to get? What did the anti-slavery men gain?
7. What factors led anti-slavery men to expect the eventual end of slavery?
8. What did Alexander Stephens call 'the cornerstone' of the Confederacy?

The Politics of Abraham Lincoln　　　　　7

7.1　The Need for Statesmanship

> Four score and five years after the signing of the Declaration of Independence, the daring republican experiment consciously undertaken by the American Founding Fathers very nearly failed ignominiously, and it had to be revived by a man of even greater stature than Washington, Jefferson, Adams, Hamilton, and Madison—and at a cost in suffering and lives that seems staggering even in an epoch distinguished by mass murder and genocide. Abraham Lincoln's accomplishment was made even more wondrous by the fact that he anticipated the renewed need for grand statesmanship a quarter-century before he delivered the Gettysburg Address.[1]

Those who know principles are philosophers; those who know particulars are experts; those who bring them together are statesmen. The wisdom of the philosopher is made potent and the knowledge of the expert is made beneficial through the sagacity of the statesman.

Statesmanship recollects the past, acts with wisdom in the present, and so fosters better things in the days to come. It requires experience, but it is more than experience. It knows the loves and the character of the political community that it shepherds, and it keeps that community faithful to what is good in its founding. In a few cases, statesmanship even elevates that founding. Statesmanship is rare.

American statesmanship, in its noblest moments, we will call "Declaration Statesmanship." We call it that because of what we have argued in earlier chapters, namely, that the Declaration is the American covenant, the public and written source of the principles that make the country what it is. Because

---

[1] Paul Rahe's *Republics Ancient and Modern*

we have such a founding document, together with a written constitution and similar "secular scripture" ('scripture' being Latin for 'writing'), American statesmanship has a striking similarity to our religious heritage, Jewish and Christian. When we need national revival, we go back to the "book."

Abraham Lincoln spoke in quintessentially American fashion when he said:

> I have never had a feeling politically that did not spring from the sentiments embodied in the Declaration of Independence...I have often inquired of myself, what great principle or idea it was that kept this Confederacy so long together. It was not the mere matter of separation of the colonies from the mother land; but something in that Declaration giving liberty, not alone to the people of this country, but hope to the world for all future time. It was that which gave promise that in due time the weights would be lifted from the shoulders of all men, and that all should have an equal chance. This is the sentiment embodied in that Declaration of Independence.
>
> Now, my friends, can this country be saved upon that basis? If it can, I will consider myself one of the happiest men in the world if I can help to save it. If it can't be saved upon that principle, it will be truly awful. But if this country can't be saved without giving up that principle—I was about to say I would rather be assassinated on this spot than to surrender it.[2]

Lincoln, who spoke these words on his way to assume the duties of the presidency, to which he had been elected that fall, showed another virtue of the statesman besides wisdom. Courage. He gave this speech, in public, having been warned of a plot to kill him.

But all this was in 1861. What does Paul Rahe mean in the text we cited at the beginning of this section, that Lincoln anticipated the need for "grand statesmanship" more than twenty years before this speech, when he was still a young man? Professor Rahe's reference is to a speech Lincoln gave in his home state of Illinois, in his hometown, Springfield, on January 27, 1838.

---

[2] *Speech*, Independence Hall, February 22, 1861

126

The Address to the Young Men's Lyceum of Springfield, Illinois

The Perpetuation of Our Political Institutions:
Address to the Young Men's Lyceum
Springfield, Illinois
Abraham Lincoln
January 27, 1838

As a subject for the remarks of the evening, the perpetuation of our political institutions, is selected.

In the great journal of things happening under the sun, we, the American People, find our account running, under date of the nineteenth century of the Christian era. We find ourselves in the peaceful possession, of the fairest portion of the earth, as regards extent of territory, fertility of soil, and salubrity of climate.

This daguerreotype is the earliest-known photograph of Abraham Lincoln, taken in 1846 when he was a frontier lawyer in Springfield and Congressman-elect from Illinois.

We find ourselves under the government of a system of political institutions, conducing more essentially to the ends of civil and religious liberty, than any of which the history of former times tells us. We, when mounting the stage of existence, found ourselves the legal inheritors of these fundamental blessings. We toiled not in the acquirement or establishment of them—they are a legacy bequeathed us, by a once hardy, brave, and patriotic, but now lamented and departed race of ancestors. Theirs was the task (and nobly they performed it) to possess themselves, and through themselves, us, of this goodly land; and to uprear upon its hills and its valleys, a political edifice of liberty and equal rights; 'tis ours only, to transmit these, the former, unprofaned by the foot of an invader; the latter, undecayed by the lapse of time, and untorn by usurpation—to the latest generation that fate shall permit the world to know. This task of gratitude to our fathers, justice to ourselves, duty to posterity, and love for our species in general, all imperatively require us faithfully to perform.

How, then, shall we perform it? At what point shall we expect the approach of danger? By what means shall we fortify against it? Shall we expect some transatlantic military giant, to step the Ocean, and crush us at a blow? Never! All the armies of Europe, Asia and Africa combined, with all the treasure of the earth (our own excepted) in their military chest; with a Buonaparte for a commander, could not by force, take a drink from the Ohio, or make a track on the Blue Ridge, in a Trial of a thousand years.

At what point then is the approach of danger to be expected? I answer, if it ever reach us, it must spring up amongst us. It cannot come from abroad. If destruction be our lot, we must ourselves be its author and finisher. As a nation of freemen, we must live through all time, or die by suicide.

I hope I am over wary; but if I am not, there is, even now, something of ill omen amongst us. I mean the increasing disregard for law which pervades the country; the growing disposition to substitute the wild and furious passions, in lieu of the sober judgement of Courts; and the worse than savage mobs, for the executive ministers of justice. This disposition is awfully fearful in any community; and that it now exists in ours, though grating to our feelings to admit, it would be a violation of truth, and an insult to our intelligence, to deny. Accounts of outrages committed by mobs, form the every day news of the times. They have pervaded the country, from New England to Louisiana;—they are neither peculiar to the eternal snows of the former, nor the burning suns of the latter;—they are not the creature of climate—neither are they confined to the slaveholding, or the non slaveholding States. Alike, they spring up among the pleasure hunting masters of Southern slaves, and the order loving citizens of the land of steady habits. Whatever, then, their cause may be, it is common to the whole country.

It would be tedious, as well as useless, to recount the horrors of all of them. Those happening in the State of Mississippi, and at St. Louis, are, perhaps, the most dangerous in example, and revolting to humanity. In the Mississippi case, they first commenced by hanging the regular gamblers: a set of men, certainly not following for a livelihood, a very useful, or very honest occupation; but one which, so far from being forbidden by the laws, was actually licensed by an act of the Legislature, passed but a single year before. Next, negroes, suspected of conspiring to raise an insurrection, were caught up and hanged in all parts of the State: then, white men, supposed to be leagued with the negroes; and finally, strangers, from neighboring States, going thither on business, were, in many instances, subjected to the same fate. Thus went on this process of hanging, from gamblers to negroes, from negroes to white citizens, and from these to strangers; till, dead men were seen literally dangling from the boughs of trees upon every road side; and in numbers almost sufficient, to rival the native Spanish moss of the country, as a drapery of the forest.

Turn, then, to that horror striking scene at St. Louis. A single victim was only sacrificed there. His story is very short; and is, perhaps, the most highly tragic, of any thing of its length, that has ever been witnessed in real life. A mulatto man, by the name of McIntosh, was seized in the street, dragged to the suburbs of the city, chained to a tree, and actually burned to death; and all within a single hour from the time he had been a freeman, attending to his own business, and at peace with the world.

Such are the effects of mob law; and such are the scenes, becoming more and more frequent in this land so lately famed for love of law and order; and the stories of which, have even now grown too familiar, to attract any thing more, than an idle remark.

But you are, perhaps, ready to ask, "What has this to do with the perpetuation of our political institutions?" I answer, it has much to do with it. Its direct consequences are, comparatively speaking, but a small evil; and much of its danger consists, in the proneness of our minds, to regard its direct, as its only consequences. Abstractly considered, the hanging of the gamblers at Vicksburg, was of but little consequence. They constitute a portion of population, that is worse than useless in any community; and their death, if no pernicious example be set by it, is never matter of reasonable regret with any one. If they were annually swept, from the stage of existence, by the plague or small pox, honest men would, perhaps, be much profited, by the operation. Similar too, is the correct reasoning, in regard to the burning of the negro at St. Louis.

He had forfeited his life, by the perpetration of an outrageous murder, upon one of the most worthy and respectable citizens of the city; and had he not died as he did, he must have died by the sentence of the law, in a very short time afterwards. As to him alone, it was as well the way it was, as it could otherwise have been. But the example in either case, was fearful. When men take it in their heads to day, to hang gamblers, or burn murderers, they should recollect, that, in the confusion usually attending such transactions, they will be as likely to hang or burn some one, who is neither a gambler nor a murderer as one who is; and that, acting upon the example they set, the mob of tomorrow, may, and probably will, hang or burn some of them, by the very same mistake. And not only so; the innocent, those who have ever set their faces against violations of law in every shape, alike with the guilty, fall victims to the ravages of mob law; and thus it goes on, step by step, till all the walls erected for the defence of the persons and property of individuals, are trodden down, and disregarded. But all this even, is not the full extent of the evil. By such examples, by instances of the perpetrators of such acts going unpunished, the lawless in spirit, are encouraged to become lawless in practice; and having been used to no restraint, but dread of punishment, they thus become, absolutely unrestrained. Having ever regarded Government as their deadliest bane, they make a jubilee of the suspension of its operations; and pray for nothing so much, as its total annihilation. While, on the other hand, good men, men who love tranquility, who desire to abide by the laws, and enjoy their benefits, who would gladly spill their blood in the defence of their country; seeing their property destroyed; their families insulted, and their lives endangered; their persons injured; and seeing nothing in prospect that forebodes a change for the better; become tired of, and disgusted with, a Government that offers them no protection; and are not much averse to a change in which they imagine they have nothing to lose. Thus, then, by the operation of this mobocratic spirit, which all must admit, is now abroad in the land, the strongest bulwark of any Government, and particularly of those constituted like ours, may effectually be broken down and destroyed—I mean the attachment of the People. Whenever this effect shall be produced among us; whenever the vicious portion of population shall be permitted to gather in bands of hundreds and thousands, and burn churches, ravage and rob provision stores, throw printing presses into rivers, shoot editors, and hang and burn obnoxious persons at pleasure, and with impunity; depend on it, this Government cannot last. By such things, the feelings of the best citizens will become more or less alienated from it; and thus it will be left without friends, or with too few, and those few too weak, to make their friendship effectual. At such a time and under such circumstances, men of sufficient talent and ambition will not be wanting to seize the opportunity, strike the blow, and overturn that fair fabric, which for the last half century, has been the fondest hope, of the lovers of freedom, throughout the world.

I know the American People are much attached to their Government;—I know they would suffer much for its sake;—I know they would endure evils long and patiently, before they would ever think of exchanging it for another. Yet, notwithstanding all this, if the laws be continually despised and disregarded, if their rights to be secure in their persons and property, are held by no better tenure than the caprice of a mob, the alienation of their affections from the Government is the natural consequence; and to that, sooner or later, it must come.

Here then, is one point at which danger may be expected.

The question recurs "how shall we fortify against it?" The answer is simple. Let every American, every lover of liberty, every well wisher to his posterity, swear by the blood of the Revolution, never to violate in the least particular, the laws of the country; and never to tolerate their violation by others. As the patriots of seventy six did to the support of the Declaration of Independence, so to the support of the Constitution and Laws, let every American pledge his life, his property, and his sacred honor;—let every man remember that to violate the law, is to trample on the blood of his father, and to tear the character of his own, and his children's liberty. Let reverence for the laws, be breathed by every American mother, to the lisping babe, that prattles on her lap—let it be taught in schools, in seminaries, and in colleges;—let it be written in Primers, spelling books, and in Almanacs;—let it be preached from the pulpit, proclaimed in legislative halls, and enforced in courts of justice. And, in short, let it become the political religion of the nation; and let the old and the young, the rich and the poor, the grave and the gay, of all sexes and tongues, and colors and conditions, sacrifice unceasingly upon its altars.

While ever a state of feeling, such as this, shall universally, or even, very generally prevail throughout the nation, vain will be every effort, and fruitless every attempt, to subvert our national freedom.

When I so pressingly urge a strict observance of all the laws, let me not be understood as saying there are no bad laws, nor that grievances may not arise, for the redress of which, no legal provisions have been made. I mean to say no such thing. But I do mean to say, that, although bad laws, if they exist, should be repealed as soon as possible, still while they continue in force, for the sake of example, they should be religiously observed. So also in unprovided cases. If such arise, let proper legal provisions be made for them with the least possible delay; but, till then, let them if not too intolerable, be borne with.

There is no grievance that is a fit object of redress by mob law. In any case that arises, as for instance, the promulgation of abolitionism, one of two positions is necessarily true; that is, the thing is right within itself, and therefore deserves the protection of all law and all good citizens; or, it is wrong, and therefore proper to be prohibited by legal enactments; and in neither case, is the interposition of mob law, either necessary, justifiable, or excusable.

But, it may be asked, why suppose danger to our political institutions? Have we not preserved them for more than fifty years? And why may we not for fifty times as long?

We hope there is no sufficient reason. We hope all dangers may be overcome; but to conclude that no danger may ever arise, would itself be extremely dangerous. There are now, and will hereafter be, many causes, dangerous in their tendency, which have not existed heretofore; and which are not too insignificant to merit attention. That our government should have been maintained in its original form from its establishment until now, is not much to be wondered at. It had many props to support it through that period, which now are decayed, and crumbled away. Through that period, it was felt by all, to be an undecided experiment; now, it is understood to be a successful one.

Then, all that sought celebrity and fame, and distinction, expected to find them in the success of that experiment. Their all was staked upon it:—their destiny was inseparably linked with it. Their ambition aspired to display before an admiring world, a practical demonstration of the truth of a proposition, which had hitherto been considered, at best no better, than problematical; namely, the capability of a people to govern themselves. If they succeeded, they were to be immortalized; their names were to be transferred to counties and cities, and rivers and mountains; and to be revered and sung, and toasted through all time. If they failed, they were to be called knaves and fools, and fanatics for a fleeting hour; then to sink and be forgotten. They succeeded. The experiment is successful; and thousands have won their deathless names in making it so.

But the game is caught; and I believe it is true, that with the catching, end the pleasures of the chase. This field of glory is harvested, and the crop is already appropriated. But new reapers will arise, and they, too, will seek a field. It is to deny, what the history of the world tells us is true, to suppose that men of ambition and talents will not continue to spring up amongst us. And, when they do, they will as naturally seek the gratification of their ruling passion, as others have so done before them. The question then, is, can that gratification be found in supporting and maintaining an edifice that has been erected by others? Most certainly it cannot. Many great and good men sufficiently qualified for any task they should undertake, may ever be found, whose ambition would aspire to nothing beyond a seat in Congress, a gubernatorial or a presidential chair; but such belong not to the family of the lion, or the tribe of the eagle.

What! think you these places would satisfy an Alexander, a Caesar, or a Napoleon? Never! Towering genius disdains a beaten path. It seeks regions hitherto unexplored. It sees no distinction in adding story to story, upon the monuments of fame, erected to the memory of others. It denies that it is glory enough to serve under any chief. It scorns to tread in the footsteps of any predecessor, however illustrious. It thirsts and burns for distinction; and, if possible, it will have it, whether at the expense of emancipating slaves, or enslaving freemen. Is it unreasonable then to expect, that some man possessed of the loftiest genius, coupled with ambition sufficient to push it to its utmost stretch, will at some time, spring up among us? And when such a one does, it will require the people to be united with each other, attached to the government and laws, and generally intelligent, to successfully frustrate his designs.

Distinction will be his paramount object; and although he would as willingly, perhaps more so, acquire it by doing good as harm; yet, that opportunity being past, and nothing left to be done in the way of building up, he would set boldly to the task of pulling down.

Here then, is a probable case, highly dangerous, and such a one as could not have well existed heretofore.

Another reason which once was; but which, to the same extent, is now no more, has done much in maintaining our institutions thus far. I mean the powerful influence which the interesting scenes of the revolution had upon the passions of the people as distinguished from their judgment. By this influence, the jealousy, envy, and avarice, incident to our nature, and so common to a state of peace, prosperity, and conscious strength, were, for the time, in a great measure smothered and rendered inactive; while the deep rooted principles of hate, and the powerful motive of revenge, instead of being turned against each other, were directed exclusively against the British nation. And thus, from the force of circumstances, the basest principles of our nature, were either made to lie dormant, or to become the active agents in the advancement of the noblest of cause—that of establishing and maintaining civil and religious liberty.

But this state of feeling must fade, is fading, has faded, with the circumstances that produced it.

I do not mean to say, that the scenes of the revolution are now or ever will be entirely forgotten; but that like every thing else, they must fade upon the memory of the world, and grow more and more dim by the lapse of time. In history, we hope, they will be read of, and recounted, so long as the bible shall be read;—but even granting that they will, their influence cannot be what it heretofore has been. Even then, they cannot be so universally known, nor so vividly felt, as they were by the generation just gone to rest. At the close of that struggle, nearly every adult male had been a participator in some of its scenes. The consequence was, that of those scenes, in the form of a husband, a father, a son or a brother, a living history was to be found in every family—a history bearing the indubitable testimonies of its own authenticity, in the limbs mangled, in the scars of wounds received, in the midst of the very scenes related—a history, too, that could be read and understood alike by all, the wise and the ignorant, the learned and the unlearned. But those histories are gone. They can be read no more forever.

They were a fortress of strength; but, what invading foemen could never do, the silent artillery of time has done; the levelling of its walls. They are gone. They were a forest of giant oaks; but the all resistless hurricane has swept over them, and left only, here and there, a lonely trunk, despoiled of its verdure, shorn of its foliage; unshading and unshaded, to murmur in a few more gentle breezes, and to combat with its mutilated limbs, a few more ruder storms, then to sink, and be no more.

They were the pillars of the temple of liberty; and now, that they have crumbled away, that temple must fall, unless we, their descendants, supply their places with other pillars, hewn from the solid quarry of sober reason. Passion has helped us; but can do so no more. It will in future be our enemy. Reason, cold, calculating, unimpassioned reason, must furnish all the materials for our future support and defence. Let those materials be moulded into general intelligence, sound morality and, in particular, a reverence for the constitution and laws; and, that we improved to the last; that we remained free to the last; that we revered his name to the last; that, during his long sleep, we permitted no hostile foot to pass over or desecrate his resting place; shall be that which to learn the last trump shall awaken our WASHINGTON.

Upon these let the proud fabric of freedom rest, as the rock of its basis; and as truly as has been said of the only greater institution, "the gates of hell shall not prevail against it."

Remarks

We will make a few remarks in the way of analysis of this speech, but first we will give a word of praise to our forefathers, who cared enough for reason and civic life that they could and did spend their precious leisure hours meeting to listen to speeches like this. The Young Men's Lyceum was a kind of civic and educational society that sponsored events like the one featuring the gangly young hometown lawyer's speech on "the perpetuation of our political institutions." One of the ways to perpetuate our liberties, to perform what Lincoln called "this task of gratitude" is to use our minds in understanding and hence cherishing our "legacy," our republican inheritance.

Life was rough in Springfield in 1838, but even on the frontier, tired men found time and energy to devote to the art of being free.

One bit of fact that underlies the speech is noteworthy. About ten weeks before Lincoln spoke in Springfield, not sixty miles away, in Alton, Illinois, an armed mob had shot and killed a newspaper editor, Elijah P. Lovejoy. Mr. Lovejoy, an abolitionist and also anti-Catholic agitator, had castigated the people and authorities in Missouri for the

Lovejoy's murder: the grim result of mob violence.

lynching so vividly described in the earlier part of the speech. Three times his presses had been thrown into the Mississippi; he died, gun in hand, defending a newly purchased fourth press. Lincoln acknowledges these events in passing, in the words, "throw printing-presses into rivers, shoot editors." The connection between the Lovejoy episode and the Negro murdered in St. Louis means that race, slavery, and abolitionism lurked in the background, though, it should be stressed, the background only, of Lincoln's account of the dangers that violence and passion posed to American institutions.

We now give a somewhat oversimplified sketch of the plan of the speech:

1. Introduction and theme: the task of perpetuation
2. Three dangers and their remedies
   a) Mob rule, either from passion or from idealist extremism, and its remedy, reverence for the laws
   b) Great ambition in great men, provoked by the once-for-all character of the founding, and a partial remedy, resistance by a united people
   c) Weak attachment to the founding, due to the passing away of the revolutionary generation, and to dimming memory, and the consequent increase in the danger posed by the passions of the people, and its remedy, sober reason
3. Conclusion, comparison of the American republic to the church, and the implied marriage of reason and reverence

What may be seen about Lincoln's purpose, his statesmanship, in this speech?

In a way, everything is implied in its theme: *on the perpetuation of our political institutions*. Lincoln saw that the revolutionary generation was

136

dying, and with it the living memory of the fight for the principles of the Declaration. He saw too that the experiment had been so far a success, with the exception of the continuation and spread of slavery. In particular, he saw that the blessings of liberty implied prosperity and comfort, and a consequent decline in the noble ambitions and spirit of sacrifice that made the founding possible. In the vigilante justice of his day, he saw a tendency for the "old Adam," the man of selfish and violent passions, to resurface. In our own day, we note in passing, coldness of soul, sloth, and indifference, might undermine the laws more than the heat that leads to riots.

The Declaration had asserted self-evident truths. That meant, as we have said in earlier chapters, truths accessible to and sometimes held only by reason. These truths are mightily bolstered by religious faith, but not all men are believers, and not all believers are equally fervent and faithful throughout their lives. Declaration principles, the creed of the founders, had been upheld by *feelings* not to be counted on long beyond the lives of the original patriots. As the text runs: "But this state of feeling *must fade, is fading, has faded,* with the circumstances that produced it."

Lincoln gives as the remedy for this fading, in his account of the third danger, "sober reason." But his words there can be misleading. For he had urged earlier that "as the patriots of seventy-six did to the support of the Declaration," so now Americans of later generations should to the laws and Constitution, pledge, life, property, and "sacred honor." He urges mothers, teachers, preachers, politicians—all Americans—to have and inculcate "reverence for the laws," and he concludes this section, which deals with the first danger, mob violence, whether of vigilantes, or of bigots, or of abolitionists, by prescribing as remedy reverence for the laws. But he calls this reverence, not "reason," but "a state of feeling."

We may say, then, that Lincoln's prescription for the health of the American body politic is to fight the eternal dangers posed by the passions with reason fortified with an almost religious reverence for the spirit and letter of the laws. Like St. Paul, he places the spirit over the letter, since, as he freely acknowledges, the letter can be in error: "Let me not be understood as saying there are no bad laws, or that grievances may not arise for the redress of which, no legal provisions have been made. I mean to say no such thing." Bad laws are not to be idolized, they are to be changed, and in the meantime, unless they are intolerable, to be obeyed, "for the sake of example."

Lincoln's forceful admonition that Americans be habituated to "reverence for the laws" has been characterized as "civic religion," and criticized by some believers as verging on idolatry. Perhaps there are dangers in that direction, but the language of devotion is traditional in American political discourse. Here is a nice instance from Calvin Coolidge. Note the use of the word, "faithfully."

> These principles of independence, of the integrity of the Union, and of local self-government have not diminished in their importance since they were so clearly recognized and faithfully declared in the Virginia convention of 150 years ago. We may wonder at their need of constant restatement, reiteration, and defense. But the fact is that the principles of government have the same need to be fortified, reinforced, and supported that characterize the principles of religion. After enumerating many of the spiritual ideals, the Scriptures enjoin us to "think on these things." If we are to maintain the ideals of government, it is likewise necessary that we "think on these things." It is for this purpose that educational institutions exist, and important anniversaries are observed.[3]

Lincoln had been reading *The Federalist* in the period before he gave this speech. Perhaps his thought was provoked by the passage below. Note the exact expression, used by Lincoln in 1838, "reverence for the laws."

> The reason of man, like man himself, is timid and cautious when left alone, and acquires firmness and confidence in proportion to the number with which it is associated. When the examples which fortify opinion are *ancient* as well as *numerous*, they are known to have a double effect. In a nation of philosophers, this consideration ought to be disregarded. A reverence for the laws would be sufficiently inculcated by the voice of enlightened reason. But a nation of philosophers is as little to be expected as the philosophical race of kings wished for by Plato. And in every other nation, the most rational government will not find it a superfluous advantage to have the prejudices of the community on its side.[4]

Lincoln's project, the work for which he finally gave the last, full measure of devotion, was to ennoble these "prejudices," filling them with reason, morality, and a feeling of reverence for the rule of law and for the principles

---

[3] Coolidge's speech *On the Inspiration of the Declaration,* given on its 150th anniversary, July 4, 1826
[4] *Federalist 49*

138

of eternal right enshrined in the founding. That is how he dedicated himself to perpetuate our political institutions.

Questions for Reflection

1. What do you think of the charge that "civic religion" is idolatry, that such reverence should be reserved for God alone?

2. Coolidge was a wonderful writer. Note, in the passage quoted above, the threefold repetitions, "restatement, reiteration, and defense," "fortified, reinforced, and supported." What effect do they have on you as a reader? What does the word "faithfully" mean in the first sentence? Does it suggest religion? Should it? Do you think it would follow from what he says that Americans should spend some time on the Fourth of July re-reading the Declaration? Do we? What do you think of his strong statement that educational institutions exist so that we may "think on these things"?

3. Do you think that Publius was right in saying that when examples that buttress opinions are "ancient" they are stronger? What do we think of the wisdom of our parents and other ancestors?

4. Lincoln said in his 1857 speech on the *Dred Scott* decision, "prosperity [has a tendency] to breed tyrants." In the Lyceum Address he states, "As a nation of freemen, we must live through all time, or die by suicide." Are these two ideas connected? The first seems to be about the bad leader, the second about a depraved people. Is he right in stating that prosperity breeds tyrants? Why, or why not, would one think so?

Postscript: The Second Danger and the Great Man

Lincoln says nothing about a *self-imposed* remedy for the danger posed by the great man, for him of the "family of the lion, or the tribe of the eagle." He almost seems to be warning *himself* about this danger, when he goes on to say of such a genius, "It thirsts and burns for distinction; and, if possible, it will have it, whether at the expense of emancipating slaves, or enslaving freemen." Perhaps he means to leave reflection on this danger to similar souls, and gives only a glimpse of it here, to the rest of us. Perhaps this great man will find his satisfaction in the work that history gives him, to revive and re-establish the founding, a work whose need will arise as long as men forget their high calling under the laws of nature and nature's God, and devote themselves to mere interest, comfort, and private gain.

Order of Events V: *The House Divided*

1775   first **abolition society** formed, by Benjamin Franklin and Benjamin Rush, in Philadephia

1786   7 of the 13 original states have either **abolished slavery**, or limited it with a view to its extinction

1787   **Northwest Ordinance**: Congress keeps slavery out of U.S. territory

1793   first **Fugitive Slave Act**

1803   **Louisiana Purchase** adds large tract of land to U.S. territory

1807   Great Britain **outlaws slave trade**

1808   U.S. Congress **ends African slave trade**, earliest date allowed by Constitution

1814   **Hartford Convention** meets in Conn. to discuss limiting federal power, and (possibly) **secession** of New England

1820   **Missouri Compromise**: Missouri will be admitted as a slave state; Maine as a free state; Arkansas (a territory) will retain slavery; slavery prohibited in territory north of 36°30′

1822   **Vesey Slave Plot** suppressed in S. Carolina; 37 participants executed

1826   Pennsylvania passes a "personal liberty" law in order to **nullify Fugitive Slave laws**; other northern states follow suit

1828   National Tariff Law passed, called the **Tariff of Abominations** by the South

1831   **William Lloyd Garrison** founds *The Liberator*, an abolitionist paper. Georgia's Senate offers a $5000 award for his capture and conviction. **Nat Turner** leads a slave revolt in Virginia. 55 whites, 100 blacks killed; 20 blacks executed

1832   S. Carolina passes **Ordinance of Nullification** to defy tariff law; revokes it in 1833

1833	**American Antislavery Society** formed to abolish slavery and slave markets in D.C. and all U.S. territories. Great Britain **outlaws slavery** at home and in its colonies
1834	**pro-slavery riots** in N.Y.C. and Philadelphia; the latter destroys 40 Negro homes
1835	**William Lloyd Garrison mobbed** by hostile crowd in Boston; forced to find refuge in the jail
1836	House of Representatives makes it a rule that all petitions on slavery must be **tabled without discussion**
1837	**Elijah P. Lovejoy** killed defending his presses from pro-slavery rioters in Illinois
1838	**Lincoln's speech to the Young Men's Lyceum** Joshua Giddings of Ohio elected—becomes the **first abolitionist in Congress**
1839	**Atherton Gag Rule** created to eliminate all discussions of slavery in the House
1841	**Amistad Incident**: Supreme Court rules that slaves who mutinied against their Spanish captors, and were later captured by U.S. Navy, are free
1844	**Atherton Gag Rule lifted** by the House
1846	**Lincon elected to Congress** as representative from Illinois, on the Whig ticket
1848	**Mexican War** results in acquisition of more territory below the 36°30′ line. **Lincoln returns to Illinois**, deciding not to run for re-election
1850	**Compromise of 1850** allows California admission as free state, Utah and New Mexico as either slave or free; abolishes slave trade in D.C.; and strengthens Fugitive Slave Law. **Southern Rights Association** formed to oppose abolitionists and other anti-slavery actions
1851	*Uncle Tom's Cabin* by Harriet Beecher Stowe published in serial form
1854	**Missouri Compromise repealed** by passage of the Kansas–Nebraska Bill, allowing slavery in territories above 36°30′

1855   **Bleeding Kansas**: violence follows replacement of anti-slavery governor with pro-slavery man; "Border Ruffians" from Missouri kill some anti-slavery settlers, and **John Brown** retaliates by executing pro-slavery settlers

1856   **first Republican Party presidential nominee**, John C. Fremont, loses to Franklin Pierce

1857   March: **Dred Scott decision**
       June: Lincoln speaks against the decision

1858   **Kansas** rejects pro-slavery constitution twice, and becomes a free territory. Lincoln's **"House Divided" speech** given to Republican Party state convention. **Lincoln–Douglas debates** held from Aug. to Oct. in their race for the U.S. Senate; Douglas is chosen (by the Illinois state legislature) in Nov.

1859   **John Brown's Raid on Harper's Ferry** in Virginia. **Fugitive Slave Act declared unconstitutional** by Supreme Court

1860   February: Lincoln's **Cooper Union Address**
       May: Lincoln nominated for President on Republican ticket
       November: **Lincoln elected President** with Hamlin as Vice-President
       December: **South Carolina secedes from the union**

1861   March: **Cornerstone Speech** given by Alexander Stephens, vice-president of the Confederacy
       April: **Fort Sumter attacked**; Lincoln arms militia to put down rebellion; four more states secede
       July: **First Battle of Bull Run**: the Civil War Begins in earnest

1862   **Congress bans slavery in all U.S. territories**, in defiance of the *Dred Scott* decision

1863   **Emancipation Proclamation** frees slaves in rebel-held areas of the Union

7.2 The House Divided

> ...In 1846 I was once elected to the lower House of Congress. Was
> not a candidate for re-election. From 1849 to 1854, both inclusive,
> practiced law more assiduously than ever before. Always a whig in
> politics, and generally on the whig electoral tickets, making active
> canvasses. I was losing interest in politics, when the repeal of the
> Missouri Compromise aroused me again. What I have done since then
> is pretty well known.
>
> —Abraham Lincoln, 1859[5]

The Missouri Compromise

The Missouri Compromise is the name commonly used for a number of
legislative and political acts taken in 1820, chief among which were the
admission of two states to the Union, Missouri and Maine, and the prohibition
of slavery in the portion of the Louisiana Purchase north of the line of latitude
36°30′, approximately the southern boundary of the state of Missouri, Missouri
itself being allowed to retain slavery. The debate on the question of Missouri's
admission as a slave state had been bitter and sectional. In the House, where
they had a numerical advantage of 105 to 81, the representatives of the North
voted almost unanimously for a phased-in prohibition of slavery. The Senate,
however, where the numbers were equal, consistently blocked this prohibition.
John Quincy Adams, Madison, and Jefferson were all aghast at the stark
sectionalism of the vote, and Jefferson's remark, quoted in chapter 6, that it
was "like a fire-bell in the night," has become famous. Adams, who was then
secretary of state, wrote in his diary that, "If the Union must be dissolved,
slavery is precisely the question upon which it ought to break."

The struggle over Missouri did not appear to all the men of the day
as altogether about the morality or justice of slavery. The new Western
lands, and the natural increase of the slave population, augmented by legal
importation before 1808, and by slave smuggling after then, had kept the
South a region of agriculture, and with the invention of the cotton gin,
an agriculture that included a significant portion of profitable, large scale,
slave labor operations. The 'advanced' farmers of the South, and certainly
the wealthiest of them, found in slaves the chief source of their labor force.
The agricultural and slave-owning interest also constituted a commercial

---

[5]Letter to Jesse W. Fell to be used for a campaign biography, December 20, 1859

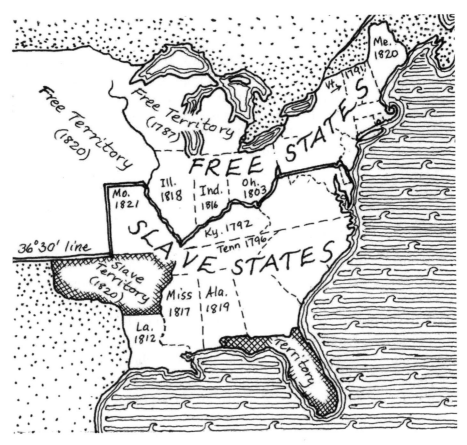

Slave vs. Free: 1821

	Free States		Slave States	
original 13 states: 6 slave 7 free	New Jersey New Hampshire Massachusetts Connecticut	Rhode Island New York Pennsylvania	Maryland Delaware Virginia	N. Carolina S. Carolina Georgia
by 1819: 11 slave 11 free	Vermont Ohio	Indiana Illinois	Kentucky Tennessee Louisiana	Mississippi Alabama
by 1821: 12 slave, 12 free	Maine		Missouri	

faction opposed to tariffs. Tariffs are import taxes on foreign goods, mostly manufactures. The infant Northern manufacturing interest sought tariffs to protect itself against European, and especially English, competition. A Missouri with slavery would presumably also be a state whose representatives would support Southern, agrarian, and anti-tariff policies in future congresses.

When the Missouri question arose, the Senate had exactly the same

144

number of free states and slave states, eleven. Maine's desire for admission as a separate state (it had hitherto been a portion of Massachusetts) gave both parties a way out of the standoff. The opponents of slavery obtained the prohibition north of the 36°30′ line, an extension of the policy of the founders in the Northwest Ordinance, which had contained a similar provision. Maine was admitted as a free state in 1820, and Missouri was to be admitted as a slave state in 1821, though it had to accept a second compromise, demanded by Henry Clay, to recognize the constitutional rights of Negro citizens of the United States.

Almost all of the remaining territory owned by the United States at that time (the sole exception was the portion of the Louisiana Purchase that was to become the state of Arkansas; Florida was not acquired until 1821) was thus under a federal ban against slavery. This put into the national law an obstacle to further growth of slavery, much as the Ordinance of 1787 had, and it reaffirmed the moral principle behind that ordinance. It is also reaffirmed the right of Congress to legislate about slavery, and everything else, in United States' territories. The three chief goods of the compromise, as they appeared to Lincoln, were these: the fact of territory freed of slavery north of the Line, the right of the national government so to act, and the moral disapprobation of slavery effected through its having so acted.

The Compromise Holds: 1821–1850

We now compress our story even further. In this period of Western expansion, the states formed out of the old Northwest Territory or above 36°30′ came in as free states: Michigan in 1837 through Wisconsin in 1848. Arkansas, below the line, entered with slavery in 1836, and Florida in 1845. Texas, after a period of independence, came in with slavery in 1845. The numerical equality of slave and free states was maintained, now 15 and 15. The boundary disputes between Texas, now an American state, and Mexico, culminating in the Mexican–American War (1846–1848), gave rise to new disputes over the prohibition of slavery in any territory to be acquired from Mexico. As in the Missouri controversy, Congress was split by section and between the two houses. Lincoln, who was in the House of Representatives, consistently voted with the majority for the prohibition, which was called the Wilmot Proviso (after its author, a Democrat from Pennsylvania). The South was outnumbered in the House, but in the Senate they had parity with the North, and so consistently blocked the Wilmot Proviso.

The Missouri Compromise had not granted those favoring the extension of slavery the right to have it in federal territory south of the 36°30′ line; it had only banned slavery north of it. Hence, Lincoln and the "Proviso men" resisted a motion by Senator Douglas to extend the line to the Pacific Ocean. It would have cut California, which was filling up with gold miners and other immigrants, and already seeking admission to the union in 1849, into two regions. They feared that one would produce a state with slavery and the other, one without it, and they wanted the whole of California free. California, like Texas, had been (very briefly) an independent republic. Its request for admission to the Union was blocked in the Senate because the inhabitants wished to come in with a prohibition of slavery.

Patching the Cracks: the Compromise of 1850

The California question headed a list of slavery related matters that were resolved in the Compromise of 1850. As with the Missouri Compromise, each side gave something. The North yielded on a fugitive slave law and certain payments to Texas. The South accepted California as a free state and let restrictions be placed on the slave market in the District of Columbia. Utah and New Mexico were allowed to choose to enter the Union, at some later date, as slave or free, but no concession was made limiting the federal power to govern them while they were territories. Most of the leading politicians declared themselves tolerably well satisfied with these arrangements, and both major parties, at that time the Whigs and the Democrats, endorsed it in their national conventions.

Among the people, the deeper questions simmered and sometimes flared. Direct denunciations of the equality taught by the Declaration began to be heard from apologists for slavery, while abolitionists like the doomed Lovejoy made equally fierce attacks on the Constitution. Small but frightening slave rebellions, few in number, but big with terror, prompted Southern states to patrol the roads at night for black men breaking curfew, and to prohibit teaching reading and writing to slaves, lest they should catch a contagion of liberty from Northern abolitionists. The great Protestant denominations— Methodists, Baptists, and Presbyterians—began to divide on sectional lines. Sentiment in the lower south, the "Cotton Kingdom," was clearly shifting from toleration of slavery as a perplexing and troublesome evil to defense of it as a positive good.

These underlying differences were not settled by the Compromise. In

146

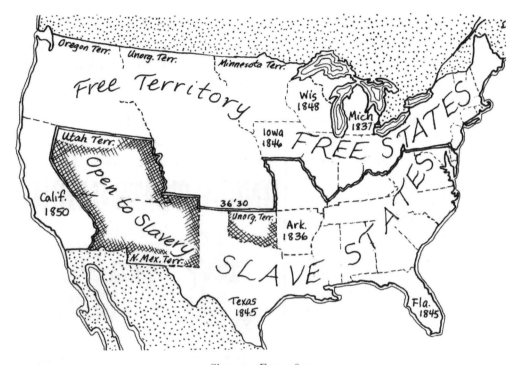

Slave vs. Free: 1850

The compromise of 1850 upset the balance of fifteen slave and fifteen free states by adding California as a free state. (The dates on the map are the dates of admission to the Union.)

some respects they may have worsened. Bitterness over the obligation to obey the hated fugitive slave law fueled defiance and sometimes non-compliance in New England. Indeed, as prominent a man as Ralph Waldo Emerson advised his fellow citizens to break it "on the earliest possible occasion." Confiding to his diary, he was yet more strident: "This filthy enactment was made in the nineteenth century, by people who could read and write. I will not obey it, by God!"

It was the fugitive slave law that set Harriet Beecher Stowe to writing *Uncle Tom's Cabin*, one of the most incendiary novels of all time. It was a Northern and an international sensation, translated into twenty languages and selling over a million copies in the first couple of years after its publication. The dramatic depiction of the cruel slave master and his suffering slaves infuriated the more humane slave owners who knew how it caricatured their own practice. Forgotten, perhaps, or overlooked, was how much of it was true. The passionate reaction of slavery apologists culminated in the defiant writings of George Fitzhugh, whose polemics included statements like, "The

147

negro slaves of the South are the happiest, and in some sense, the freest people in the world," and, "the whole literature of free society is but a voice proclaiming its absolute and total failure." Fitzhugh has in mind here the scandals of child labor, and the discarded and poor elderly, discussed and lamented in the liberal and Northern press. He goes on to conclude, "Hence the works of the socialists contain the true defence of slavery."[6]

It is hard to know what the leaders who had worked out the Compromise of 1850 would have thought of these deep fault lines. They were among the great names of American history: Webster, Clay, Calhoun, Stephen Douglas, Jefferson Davis, and William Seward. The first three were all dead within two years of the agreement, and the last two found themselves on opposite sides of the Civil War a dozen years later. Senator Douglas would soon act to end the ban on slavery north of the 36°30' line, a key element of the Compromise, taking an action that he knew, as he himself put it, would "raise a hell of a storm." But this

When President Lincoln met Stowe in 1862, he is said to have exclaimed, "So you are the little woman who wrote the book that started this great war!"

would not happen until 1854. In 1850, the nation's leaders had avoided open schism, and the lovers of the Union continued to live in hope.

Congressman Lincoln, whose popularity had declined in his House district because he had raised objections to the war of conquest in Mexico, did not run for re-election to the House. He returned to Illinois, and gave himself to the practice of law.

---

[6]George Fitzhugh's *Cannibals All*, 1857

"Popular Sovereignty" and Stephen A. Douglas

I regard the great principle of popular sovereignty, as having been vindicated and made triumphant in this land, as a permanent rule of public policy in the organization of Territories and the admission of new States...

I deny their [Congress's] right to force a good thing upon a people who are unwilling to receive it. The great principle is the right of every community to judge and decide of itself, whether a thing is right or wrong, whether it would be good or evil for them to adopt it; and the right of free action, the right of free thought, the right of free judgement upon the question is dearer to every true American than any other under a free government. —Stephen A. Douglas, 1858[7]

The North has only to will it [the saving of the Union] to accomplish it; to do justice by conceding to the South an equal right in the acquired territory, and to do her duty by causing the stipulations relative to the fugitive slaves to be faithfully fulfilled; to *cease the agitation of the slavery question...*
—John C. Calhoun, 1850, emphasis added[8]

As we saw above, Lincoln wrote in his sketch for his Presidential campaign biography that, "the repeal of the Missouri Compromise aroused me again." Draft language of that repeal was announced in a Washington newspaper in mid-January of 1854 as follows:

[An amendment will be added to the Nebraska bill stipulating that] the Constitution, and all laws of the United States which are not locally inapplicable, shall have the same force and effect within the said Territory of Nebraska as elsewhere within the United States, except the eighth section of the act preparatory to the Admission of Missouri into the Union, approved March 6, 1820, which was superseded by the principles of the legislation of 1850, commonly called the compromise measures, and is hereby declared inoperative.

Senator Stephen A. Douglas of Illinois was the chairman of the Senate Committee on Territories; Douglas consented to the amendment, and the bill passed. This meant that the federal ban on slavery in the Territory, which

[7]Speech in Chicago
[8]Speech to the Senate, March 4, 1850

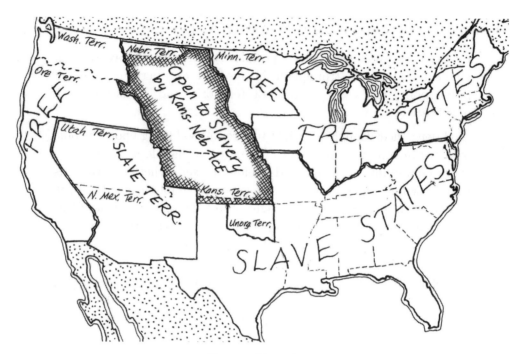

Slave vs. Free: 1854

The Kansas–Nebraska Bill of 1854, which repealed the Missouri Compromise, opened new areas to slavery. There were still sixteen free and fifteen slave states.

was divided into a southern portion, the Kansas Territory, and a northern, the Nebraska Territory, was void. As Douglas had predicted, "a hell of a storm" arose.

What did Douglas intend? There can be no doubt that he wanted the Union to survive and prosper. Moreover, he was not, like Calhoun, of the "slavery as a positive good" school. Indeed, Douglas had supported the admission of California as a free state, and the organization of the Oregon Territory, in which Congress adopted an amendment authored by Douglas recognizing the existing ban on slavery, enacted by the settlers themselves.

Douglas was an intelligent and bold politician, ambitious for the Presidency. He would be the candidate of the Northern Democrats in 1860, running against Lincoln. He saw the threat of disunion, and he had heard the resentment in his Southern Democratic colleagues like Calhoun. Calhoun had all but demanded that no one even talk about slavery as a political question. That is what he meant in saying that the North could bring an end to the threat of disunion by ceasing to "agitate" the issue of slavery. Douglas sought a bold answer to the Union's troubles. It would require practical

"Bleeding Kansas"—pro-slavery "border ruffians" are shown shooting down anti-slavery "free-soilers." The violence went both ways; prior to his 1859 raid on Harpers Ferry, Virginia abolitionist John Brown killed five slavery supporters in Kansas.

politics and principle. He called his answer "Popular Sovereignty."

As a policy, "Popular Sovereignty" meant that Congress would no longer prohibit slavery in any United States' territories. The question would be handed over to the people of the territories as they organized themselves. It would be addressed again in their conventions when they grew ripe for statehood. Since the fugitive slave law was now in effect, and since the overseas slave trade had been illegal for nearly 50 years, this meant that there should be no reason for any discussion, or "agitation," on the issue to arise in Congress again. He further promised not to "care" about what the people of any territory seeking admission had decided on the issue in preparing for admission as a state, so long as they had done it fairly.

This was meant to satisfy the demands of Calhoun's heirs in the South. The national argument, as a political argument, was to cease, because the issue, as some say now about abortion, "didn't belong in politics." But on the question of the spread of slavery, Douglas's solution had some appeal to the anti-slavery faction in the North, since many thought it unlikely that the northern climate would be hospitable to the plantation agriculture, chiefly cotton and rice, that had been home to slavery in the South. If this hunch about the economics of the spread of slavery were true, then the Union would become progressively more and more dominated by free states, without anyone having to raise the question of the morality of slavery, and thereby offend the slave interest in the South.

To make all this work, Douglas had to persuade his fellow Americans that "Popular Sovereignty" was the corner-stone of the republic. He had some reason to think that it was, and that he could make a majority think so. For one thing, the principle squared with the American fondness for local control. Douglas would point out in his 1858 debates with Lincoln that liquor laws, and agricultural laws, and a host of other ordinances differed from Maine to Louisiana, and that we liked it that way. Jefferson himself had been a strong proponent of states' rights and of local self-government. At the same time, within these local communities, the will of the people had been held sovereign. Jeffer-

Stephen A. Douglas

son had called the rule of the will of the majority a "sacred principle" in his first inaugural address.

But there were problems with Douglas's formulation. He might say, "I don't care," about local decisions on slavery, but people did care. In the case of Kansas, they would care enough to send armed bodies of settlers to inflate the votes of their side in the territorial disputes on the way to statehood. These men cared enough to shed blood over the question. Further, it was not perfectly evident that slavery could only prove profitable growing cash crops in warm climates; we noted above that in Richmond a successful factory enterprise employed slave labor exclusively. In our century, tyrants like the Communist Chinese have made effective, if inhumane, use of slaves, as did the old Soviet Union, in very cold climates. Poor workers, especially "guest workers" and illegal immigrants, not to mention innocent and poor young women and children, can find themselves in conditions similar to slavery even at present, in all kinds of climate and in various occupations. Slavery, *de jure*, and *de facto*, is an endemic disease among mankind, alas!

Moreover, it was not clear, when Douglas was setting forth "Popular Sovereignty" in the 1850s, what would happen if Southern settlers brought their slaves with them. Would the territorial government be obliged to pass laws to protect their 'property'? In that case, slavery would be established *de facto* before any vote on it. Most important of all, popular sovereignty, in its fundamental sense, majority rule, is not a complete statement of the American creed. Jefferson's exact words, from his first inaugural address, in which he called the popular will "sacred," deserve quotation in full:

> All, too, will bear in mind this sacred principle, that though the will of the majority is in all cases to prevail, that will to be rightful must be reasonable; that the minority possess their equal rights, which equal law must protect, and to violate would be oppression.

Douglas's policy and that of the founders were alike in key points, but different in others. Both thought that the preservation of the Union was paramount. Both agreed in refusing to interfere with slavery where it existed. Both looked to a change to be produced by time and patience. But the founders had used the power of Congress to block the expansion of slavery and to strengthen the conviction that it was wrong. Douglas looked to "Popular Sovereignty" to produce the first effect while he took affirmative action to see that the second, the conviction that it was wrong, would not be expressed in the public arena. This meant that he differed from the founders in principle, and not only in policy. Douglas had made *self-rule*, and not *self-evident truths*, the deepest principle of free government. Lincoln thought the policy harmful; he was convinced that the principle, as Douglas's understanding would have it, was false. That is what "aroused" him in 1854.

7.3 Declaration Statesmanship in Action

> The doctrine of self-government is right—absolutely and eternally right—but it has no just application as here attempted. Or perhaps I should rather say that whether it has such application depends on whether a negro is *not* or *is* a man. If he is *not* a man, why in that case, he who *is* a man may, as a matter of self-government, do just as he pleases with him. But if the negro *is* a man, is it not to just that extent a total destruction of self-government, to say that he too shall not govern *himself*? When the white man governs himself that is self-government; but when he governs himself, and also governs *another* man, that is *more* than self-government—that is despotism. If the negro is a *man*, why then my ancient faith teaches me that

153

"all men are created equal;" and that there can be no moral right in connection with one man's making a slave of another.

Judge Douglas frequently, with bitter irony and sarcasm, paraphrases our argument by saying: "the white people of Nebraska are good enough to govern themselves, *but they are not good enough to govern a few miserable negros!!*"

Well I doubt not that the people of Nebraska are, and will continue to be as good as the average of people elsewhere. I do not say the contrary. What I do say is, that no man is good enough to govern another man *without that other's consent.* I say that this is the leading principle—the sheet anchor of American republicanism.

—Abraham Lincoln, Peoria, Illinois, 1854

Lincoln Aroused: the Peoria Speech

Lincoln's Peoria speech merits our attention for several powerful reasons. It was an immediate success in its day. It is carefully researched. And it gives the heart of his disagreement with Douglas on facts, policy, and principles.

Lincoln gave essentially the same speech at least four times, writing out the second, the one given in Peoria, for publication in the *Illinois State Journal.* Lincoln had asked Douglas to have the Peoria event be a debate; Douglas told a friend that he didn't want to debate Lincoln, saying "... [he is] the most difficult and dangerous opponent that I have ever met." Instead of holding a debate, they spoke one after another to the same crowd, Douglas going first. Lincoln's shrewd political sense manifested itself in the timing; he told the tired crowd to go have dinner and come back before hearing him. Douglas had worn them out with a three hour address on a warm afternoon! To make sure they returned, he also offered Douglas an hour's rebuttal to "skin me."

The opening sentence gives the subject of the speech in plain, homespun simplicity: "The repeal of the Missouri compromise, and the propriety of its restoration, constitute the subject of what I am about to say." The first quarter or so is a thorough review of the policy of Congress regarding slavery from the time of the Articles of Confederation down to the present day. We have summarized that history above. It establishes conclusively that Congresses from before the Constitution up to the 1850s held that they had the power to restrict slavery in national territories, and had often used it.

Statesmanship: Fidelity to Principles

The heart of the speech is Lincoln's treatment of the contradiction between popular sovereignty as applied to slavery, and natural right as enshrined in the Declaration. If anyone, black, white, yellow, or brown, is a man, and if I arrogate to myself, and to men of my race only, the right to choose whether that man and his kind shall be slaves or not, I cannot have grounded that decision in the universal proposition that "all men are created equal" and hence "endowed by their creator with certain unalienable rights." Since I am no

Francis Marion, the gallant and daring
'Swamp Fox' of the Revolution

longer measured, that is, held to a moral measure, in my choice, how shall I make it? Douglas's understanding of popular sovereignty comes to saying that the "sacred right of self-government" allows a moral right in one man's enslaving another. Lincoln says that the real meaning of Douglas's doctrine would lead men "into an open war with the very principles of civil liberty—criticizing the Declaration of Independence, and insisting that there is no right principle of action but *self-interest*."

Indeed, not only *would* the popular sovereignty basis of the Nebraska Bill lead men to disparage the Declaration, it had already done so, and not only the chieftains of the slave power, like Calhoun. The eloquence of the following passage from the Peoria speech demands that it be quoted:

> ... Little by little, but steadily as man's march to the grave, we have been giving up the OLD for the NEW faith. Near eighty years ago we began by declaring that all men are created equal; but now from that beginning we have run down to the other declaration, that for SOME men to enslave OTHERS is a "sacred right of self-government." These principles cannot stand together. They are as opposite as God and mammon; and whoever holds to the one, must despise the other.

> When Pettit [Senator from Indiana], in connection with his support of the Nebraska bill, called the Declaration of Independence "a self-evident lie," he only did what consistency and candor require all

other Nebraska[9] men to do. Of the forty odd Nebraska Senators who sat present and heard him, no one rebuked him. Nor am I apprized that any Nebraska newspaper, or any Nebraska orator, in the whole nation, has ever yet rebuked him. If this had been said among [Francis] Marion's men, Southerners though they were, what would have become of the man who said it? If this had been said to the men who captured [Major] Andre, the man who said it, would probably have been hung sooner than Andre was. If it had been said in old Independence Hall, seventy-eight years ago, the very door-keeper would have throttled the man, and thrust him into the street.

Statesmanship: Our Place in History

Americans had, and have, a special duty because we have natural right spelled out in our founding "scripture." Our British brethren, against whom we had written the Declaration, abolished slavery in 1832 because they felt themselves measured by the standard of human equality and Christian morality. So had the newly liberated South American republics. (Brazil, as a self-styled "Empire," was a special case. It kept slavery until 1888; the next year it became a republic and abolished it.)

It may have been fairly easy for the British to end slavery, given that there was none of it in the home island, and Spanish Latin America did not have as extensive or as regional a slave establishment as did the United States. Still, they had cleansed themselves of the evil, and we had not. Our reputation, our prestige, was at issue. Lincoln was not alone in feeling ashamed at our loss of moral leadership, and he said so in the speech: "I hate it [Douglas's declared 'indifference' to slavery] because of the monstrous injustice of slavery itself. I hate it because it deprives our republican example of its

THE UNITED STATES—A BLACK BUSINESS

A southern planter and a northern businessman stand by and watch the destruction of the union. A cartoon from the British paper Punch in 1856.

---

[9]Here and in what follows "Nebraska" is not the territory itself, but is used a shorthand for "supporters of the Nebraska Bill."

156

just influence in the world—enables the enemies of free institutions, with plausibility, to taunt us as hypocrites—causes the real friends of freedom to doubt our sincerity..."

The thought that America has a special duty to mankind to vindicate republican government was, of course, not original with Lincoln. We have already seen that it was prominent in *Federalist 1*. If the young republic failed, it would be, according to Publius, "the general misfortune of mankind." Washington told his fellow citizens, in his first inaugural address, "...the preservation of the sacred fire of liberty and the destiny of the republican model of government are justly considered, perhaps, as deeply, as finally, staked on the experiment intrusted to the hands of the American people." In the twentieth century, Presidents Eisenhower and Kennedy, among others, have spoken along the same lines regarding the scandal of race discrimination. Here is Eisenhower, addressing a national television audience in response to the defiance of Arkansas state authority to the desegregation of Central High School in Little Rock: "At a time when we face grave situations abroad because of the hatred that Communism bears towards a system of government based on human rights, it would be difficult to exaggerate the harm that is being done to [our] prestige and influence..." Or Kennedy in 1963: "[Racial discrimination] hampers our world leadership by contradicting at home the message we preach abroad." It is interesting that both of these recent presidents cited the Declaration in their inaugural addresses. In making the charge that he did, that Douglas's "Popular Sovereignty" doctrine and his 'don't care' posture "deprive...our ... example of its just influence..." Lincoln showed the breadth of vision and the goodwill, as well as the attitude of a wise servant, that characterizes high statesmanship.

Opinion, the Matter of the Statesman, and Words, his Instrument

As we read the Peoria speech today, one element jars our sensibilities: Lincoln does not take a stand for full political and social equality of the races. Some of the abolitionists of his day, especially the Quakers and other religious abolitionists, did. The 1854 laws of Maine set up in almost all respects what we would recognize today as equal civil rights, including jury duty and voting rights. But Maine was almost alone. Illinois' laws did not allow blacks to vote or serve on juries, and Illinois was typical of the free states.

In Peoria, Lincoln said this: "Let it not be said that I am contending for the establishment of political and social equality between the whites and blacks. I have already said the contrary." Was this statesmanlike too, or was it either weak or unwise, or even unjust?

We think Lincoln's position in the Peoria speech can be vindicated, and that it can be reconciled with his support for expanded civil rights towards the end of the Civil War, if two things are kept in mind. First, as Lincoln himself said in 1859, "In this country, public opinion is everything." Second, the knowledge of the statesman is prudence, or practical wisdom, which consists in knowing how to move toward moral goals by practicable steps, not in "the immoderate pursuit of moral perfection" which, in political life, "will more often lead to misery and terror than to justice and happiness," as Thomas G. West puts it in his book, *Vindicating the Founders*.

To begin with the first point, is it not self-evident that in a republic, where the citizens are governed by their consent, their opinion will be the court of last resort, the final arbiter of all disputes? That does not mean that those opinions will never change, or that it will not be the duty of a good man and especially of a statesman to mold them for the better. But a public man will ignore them at his peril. Lincoln turns this weapon back on Douglas in the Peoria speech, when he tells him that he will never be able to suppress the voice of the people crying out that slavery is unjust:

> . . . the great mass of mankind . . . consider slavery a great moral wrong; and their feeling against it, is not evanescent, but eternal. It lies at the very foundation of their sense of justice; and it cannot be trifled with—It is a great and durable element of popular action, and I think, no statesman can safely disregard it.

Sir Francis Bacon wrote long ago that, "Nature, to be mastered, must be obeyed." The saying is equally true of the nature of the physical body and of the body politic. Public opinion, the soul of the political body, was ailing in the days after the Nebraska Bill, and Douglas was prescribing as medicine what Lincoln thought poison. That the patient should also take up a regimen of vigorous exercise after his recovery was not and should not have been the first thing on the doctor's list.

Lincoln never said that political equality between the races was *wrong*; the expression of his early views on equality are clothed entirely in the language of feeling. In 1854 (in the Peoria speech) he said, "my own *feelings* would not admit a social and political equality between the black and white races, and...even if my own *feelings* would admit of it, I still knew that

AN HEIR TO THE THRONE,
OR THE NEXT REPUBLICAN CANDIDATE

A Democratic Party cartoon from the presidential campaign of 1860, mocking Lincoln for his defense of human equality. He is standing in front of a circus sign with Horace Greeley, editor of the *New York Tribune*, suggesting that bringing blacks into politics would be like a circus sideshow.

the public *sentiment* of the country would not, and that such a thing was an utter impossibility, or substantially that. Whether this *feeling* accords with justice and sound judgement, is not the sole question, if indeed, it is any part of it. A universal *feeling*, whether well or ill-founded, can not be safely disregarded. We can not, then, make them equals [emphases added]." Four years later, in the 1858 debates, he quoted his own earlier statement about feelings in regard to equality, and also said this about justice: "I agree with Judge Douglas that he [the Negro] is not my equal in many respects, certainly not in color—*perhaps* not in intellectual and moral endowments;

159

but in the right to eat the bread without the leave of any body else which his own hand earns, he is my equal and the equal of Judge Douglas, and the equal of every other man [emphases added]."

Prudence in Shaping Public Opinion

It must be remembered that the young Lincoln had said in 1838 that our passions, our feelings, were to be the enemy of our freedom in the future, and that reason, "cold sober reason," would be the friend of the principles of the Declaration, Only one feeling, an almost religious reverence for the founding ideals, would buttress that reason. It should also be pointed out that Lincoln said that he knew only that the feelings of his fellow citizens would not admit of equality. He was certain that there was an inequality of "color." He did *not* say that he was certain of the infinitely more important inequality of "intellectual and moral endowments." These he said, *might* be unequal. . . "*perhaps.*"

Many causes, including prominently the religious conviction that all men are brothers, conspired to change public opinion in the United States towards the end of the Civil War. The Emancipation Proclamation, by altering the legal status of slaves and by encouraging them to flee their masters and seek refuge in the Union armies, had some effect. But the greatest source of the change was probably the testimony given in blood by the black soldiers who had served the Union. The number enlisted was reported by the President to Congress in January of 1864 to be over 100,000,[10] and Lincoln and many others thought that without their services, the war could not have been won. To a complaining Northern politician, James C. Conkling, who objected to fighting "to free negroes," Lincoln penned these memorable words:

> [When peace comes] it will then have been proved that, among free men, there can be no successful appeal from the ballot to the bullet; and that they who take such appeal are sure to lose their case, and pay the cost. And then, there will be some black men who can remember that, with silent tongue, and clenched teeth, and steady eye, and well poised bayonet, they have helped mankind on to this great consummation; while, I fear, there will be some white ones, unable to forget that, with malignant heart, and deceitful speech, they have strove to hinder it.

---

[10]By the end of the war, over 200,000 blacks had served in the Union armed forces, and 37,000 had died serving their country.

When a man will not fight to preserve his people and his principles, we call him a slave; when a slave does fight, we see in him a man. In antiquity, slaves who risked their lives to save their masters were often manumitted. They had proved their manhood. Lincoln wrote Conkling in the same letter, "If they stake their lives for us, they must be prompted by the strongest motive—even the promise of freedom. And the promise being made, must be kept."

It cannot, alas, be said that the promise was perfectly kept. It would take a century more after the abolition of slavery for a new exercise of Declaration Statesmanship to establish political equality without regard to race in this country. But the start was made in the time of Lincoln's stewardship.

Men fit to be free. Men of Company E, 4th USCT, circa 1864.

Let us be blunt; if Lincoln had taken the full position of equal social and political rights, he would not have been electable to any statewide office in Illinois, neither in 1854, when he first sought election to the U.S. Senate and nearly won, nor again in 1858, when he and Douglas had their memorable debates. He would not have become president in 1860, nor would any member of his party who might take up the banner of full social and political equality. He accomplished the good that he could, always insisting on the fundamental principles that, in the fullness of time, would yield yet

161

more perfect results. To achieve both these goods, he had to rekindle a reverence for the Declaration. Let us look briefly at how he did that in the Peoria speech.

The Power of the Word

Words, words, words. "Mere words" men say, and yet it is by the power of words that we take common counsel and learn to govern ourselves. We are free because we are made in the image of the all-wise God, and we have a bit of His light in our minds, and by that bit we strive to live according to His laws, the "laws of Nature, and of Nature's God." Of divine things, St. Paul writes, "But how are men to call upon him in whom they have not believed? And how are they to believe in him of whom they have never heard? And how are they to hear of him without a preacher?"

Lincoln preached in Peoria. He preached the political religion he had declared must be preached years ago in Springfield. Douglas and the doctrine of "Popular Sovereignty" were "giving up the OLD faith." Human equality and "Popular Sovereignty" were "as opposite as God and mammon." Three times he calls the proposition that all men are created equal, the "ancient faith." Of the Nebraska Bill he says, "It hath no relish of salvation in it." He calls the founders, "our revolutionary fathers," and "the fathers of the republic," stirring memories of Abraham, Isaac, and Jacob. He says that slavery is founded on the consequence of Adam's sin, "the selfishness of human nature." He says, "Our republican robe is soiled, and trailed in the dust. Let us re-purify it. Let us turn and wash it white, in the spirit, if not the blood, of the Revolution."

Lincoln was like a great preacher in more than his scriptural language and his vision that America was founded on the Declaration as a kind of covenant or original creed, the "ancient faith." He endeavored to emulate the charity of great preaching, too, as when he admitted that "the Southern people" were "just what we would be in their situation," and when he said that "I surely will not blame them." He stressed that Thomas Jefferson, the 'father Abraham' of the American covenant was "a Virginian by birth...a slaveholder." He opened his speech by announcing that he did not "propose to question the patriotism, or to assail the motives of any man, or class of men." He added that he wished "to be no less than national in all the positions" he would take. When he had suggested that "a gradual emancipation might be adopted," he immediately added, "but for their tardiness in this I will

162

not undertake to judge our brethren of the south." Thus, to political faith, he added political charity.

The climax of the speech begins with "Our republican robe is soiled..." and ends with these words of salvation and hope:

> Let us re-adopt the Declaration of Independence, and with it, the practices, and policy, which harmonize with it. Let north and south— let all Americans—let all lovers of liberty everywhere—join in the great and good work. If we do this, we shall not only have saved the Union; but we shall have so saved it, as to make and keep it, forever worthy of the saving. We shall have so saved it, that the succeeding millions of free happy people, the world over, shall rise up, and call us blessed, to the latest generations.

In the Lyceum speech, Lincoln had concluded by urging the statesmen of his day to take the materials supplied by reason and mold them into intelligence, morality, and reverence for the law. At Peoria, he took his own advice, and became such a statesman.

7.4   The Supreme Court Betrays the Declaration

> ...Congress is neither "to legislate slavery into any Territory or State nor to exclude it therefrom, but to leave the people thereof perfectly free to form and regulate their domestic institutions in their own way, subject only to the Constitution of the United States."
>
> A difference of opinion has arisen in regard to the point of time when the people of a Territory shall decide this question for themselves.
>
> This is, happily, a matter of but little practical importance. Besides, it is a judicial question, which legitimately belongs to the Supreme Court of the United States, before whom it is now pending, and will, it is understood, be speedily and finally settled. To their decision, in common with all good citizens, I shall cheerfully submit, whatever this may be...
>
> The whole Territorial question being thus settled upon the principle of popular sovereignty—a principle as ancient as free government itself—everything of a practical nature has been decided...Most happy will it be for the country when the public mind shall be diverted from this question to others of more pressing and practical

importance.

—President James Buchanan, *Inaugural Address*, 1857

I know that Mr. Calhoun and all the politicians of his school denied the truth of the Declaration...But I say...that three years ago there had never lived a man who had ventured to assail it in the sneaking way of pretending to believe it, and then asserting it did not include the negro. I believe the first man who ever said it was Chief Justice Taney in the *Dred Scott* case, and the next to him was our friend Stephen A. Douglas. And now it has become the catchword of the entire [Democratic] party.

—Abraham Lincoln, *Seventh Debate with Douglas*, 1858

Dred Scott v. Sandford

Dred Scott was a black slave, born in Virginia. His owner, an army officer, had taken him into the free state of Illinois and the then territory of Minnesota, also free soil under the Missouri Compromise of 1820. When Scott's owner died, having willed Scott, Scott's wife, whom he had married in the North, and their children to his wife, Scott sued for his freedom in the state court of Missouri, where the family had been taken and the owner had died. The case reached

Dred Scott

the United States Supreme Court, which decided against Scott on March 6, 1857, just two days after President Buchanan's inauguration.

Chief Justice Taney's opinion was long and convoluted in its reasoning. The key elements for anti-slavery men were these: it declared that Congress had never had the power to prohibit slavery in the territories, and hence that the Ordinance of 1787 and the Missouri Compromise were never valid; and that blacks were not and could not be citizens of the United States. These were intended by the high court's majority to be legally binding precedents.

Buchanan, who had been in private correspondence with at least two members of the court prior to their handing down the decision, desired this outcome. It meant that no legal power could prevent the introduction of slaves into federally controlled territory, not only before a territorial government had been set up, but also under the territorial government itself. Neither Congress nor its delegated substitute, the territorial legislature, could do anything whatever to block slavery.

Consequences of the Decision

Supreme Court decisions do more than settle the case before them (here, they reduced Scott and his family to the status of slaves again) and establish precedents for closely related future cases. They also include the spirit and reasoning by which future decisions may be made on less closely connected matters. These additional elements of the justices' opinions are called "*obiter dicta*." In Taney's written opinion, the *obiter dicta* included the claim that the founders did not intend to include blacks in the Constitution or in the Declaration of Independence. Assuming that the humanity of the black man was not a constitutional principle, Taney went on to reason that the opera-

The infamous Roger B. Taney

tive parts of the Constitution would be those governing him as a species of property. Accordingly he wrote, "And no word can be found in the Constitution which gives Congress a greater power over slave property, or which entitles property of that kind to less protection than property of any other description. The only power conferred is the power coupled with the duty of guarding and protecting the owner in his rights."

165

The *Dred Scott* decision provoked a storm of controversy in the North. The nationally known editor of the *New York Tribune*, Horace Greeley, wrote that the decision was about as respectable as an opinion reached by "a majority of those congregated in any Washington bar-room." It also caused both Lincoln and Douglas serious political problems, though for opposite reasons, as we shall see. Let's start with Douglas.

Buchanan had said in his inaugural that the territorial question was being settled on the basis of Douglas's principle of "Popular Sovereignty." In 1854, "Popular Sovereignty" as taught by Douglas meant that the people of a territory would be free to keep slavery out by making a law. Congress had chosen not to make such a law, by the repeal of the Missouri Compromise in the Nebraska Bill, but the people of Kansas still could, before they applied to become a state. Now the Court had decided that not only Congress, but also the people of the territory, had no such power. How could Douglas now say that "Popular Sovereignty" meant anything? And if, as Lincoln was to hammer home in the great debates of 1858, slavery was hard to abolish once even a sizeable minority of the inhabitants held slaves, did *Dred Scott* mean anything other than the total victory of Calhoun and the more extreme pro-slavery men in the South? After the Court's decision, the only part of the governmental structure in the country that could ban slavery was the state government.

James Buchanan, president from 1857 to 1861

Lincoln's statesmanship faced a problem of its own. After all, the highest court in the land had declared that the central reason for the existence of his party, the use of the national power to block the expansion of slavery in the territories, was unconstitutional. And Lincoln himself had said in the Lyceum speech that American statesmanship required an almost religious "reverence for the constitution and laws." Was *Dred Scott* not, as a precedent, "the constitution and laws"? Had he not said, just a year ago, that "We [Republicans] will submit to its [the Court's] decisions; and if you [Democrats] do also, there will be an end of the matter"?

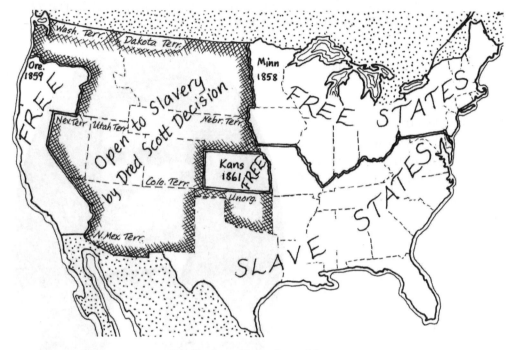

Slave vs. Free: 1857–1861

The *Dred Scott* decision of 1857 opened up more territory to slavery, but by 1860, with the admission of Oregon and Minnesota, the free states outnumber the slave states 18 to 15. In 1861 Kansas will make it 19 to 15.

Rarely has there been a Supreme Court decision as partisan in its effects as *Dred Scott*...perhaps never. Douglas was forced by the probing questions of Lincoln in the second of the Lincoln-Douglas debates of 1858, to advocate resistance to passage or enforcement of laws to protect legally held property, i.e., slaves, as a last resort for territories opposed to slavery. Southern Democrats pointed out that he was advocating local action, or inaction, that undermined the Constitution as interpreted by *Dred Scott*. This issue was to cause a split in the Democratic Party in 1860: the platform of the Northern Democrats will include Douglas's doctrine, and that of the Southern Democrats will explicitly call for a *federal* slave code, to be applied to the territories by the national government. Douglas will lose every Southern state in the Presidential election of 1860.

On the other hand, Lincoln had said while campaigning for Fremont, the Republican candidate in the 1856 election, that there was only one question, the answer to which defined his party: "Shall the government of the United

States prohibit slavery in the [territory of] the United States?" Now his party was to be defined by advocating a position solemnly held in the *Dred Scott* decision to be unconstitutional! What was he to do?

For three months he thought, and held his peace. Then, in June of 1857, after Douglas had joined Taney in holding that the Declaration did not include blacks, who were, according to the Senator, "an inferior race," and "incapable of self-government," Lincoln struck.

Reverence for the Law, Fidelity to Principle

In a forceful speech given in Springfield on June 26, 1857, Lincoln withdrew his unqualified promise of acquiescence in the dictates of the Court. He granted that Scott and his family must stay in slavery, granted too that any future decisions made in accordance with that decision as a precedent would bind him as to action, but he emphatically denied that it had any moral force

Abraham Lincoln in 1858

that would keep him or anyone else from direct, peaceful, and legal political measures aimed at its overthrow. Legal precedents have great force if they are unanimous, impartial, consistent with our legal expectations and traditions, and if they are based on what is true. The *Dred Scott* decision, Lincoln held, met none of these standards. He said, "...we think the...decision is erroneous. We know the court that made it, has often overruled its own decisions, and we shall do what we can to have it overrule this. We offer no *resistance* to it."

Quoting President Andrew Jackson, Lincoln implied that the executive and legislative branches could act in ways contrary to the decision of the court, taken as precedent and authority. Jackson had said, "The Congress, the Executive and the Court must each for itself be guided by its own opinion of the Constitution. Each public officer, who takes an oath to support the Constitution, swears that he will support it *as he understands it*, and not as it is understood by others." Lincoln drops his argument here, but he has raised a difficult and powerful point. Was he saying that when an egregiously wrong decision has been reached by the Court, the other branches may legislate and act contrary to it as authority and precedent, and must only go along with the Court's understanding when particular cases are decided? Such a teaching would greatly impair the power of the Court to decide fundamental questions, where public opinion is divided or hostile. It would surely be prudent to resort to it only in matters of great import. But was not slavery such a matter? And without such an understanding of constitutional law, how could judicial tyranny be effectively resisted?

The rest of the speech, and the part where it soars, is devoted to showing that it is historically false to say that the black man had no part in the Declaration, and to expounding the Declaration as a standard of human action and a beacon for human hopes. We give two excerpts from the speech, which can be read in its entirety in the *Book of Readings*:

> ...In those days [the period of the founding], our Declaration of Independence was held sacred by all; but now, to aid in making the bondage of the negro universal and eternal, it is assailed, and sneered at, and construed, and hawked at, and torn, till, if its framers could rise from their graves, they could not at all recognize it.

> ...They [the founders] defined with tolerable distinctness, in what respects they did consider all men created equal—equal in "certain inalienable rights, among which are life, liberty, and the pursuit of happiness." This they said, and this they meant. They did not mean to assert the obvious untruth, that all were then enjoying that equality, nor yet, that they were about to confer it immediately upon them. In fact they had no power to confer such a boon. They meant simply to declare the *right*, so that the *enforcement* of it might follow as fast as circumstances should permit. They meant to set up a standard maxim for free society, which could be familiar to all, and revered by all; constantly looked to, constantly labored for, and even though never perfectly attained, constantly approximated, and thereby constantly spreading and deepening its influence, and augmenting the happiness

169

and value of life to all people of all colors everywhere. The assertion that "all men are created equal" was of no practical use in effecting our separation from Great Britain; and it was placed in the Declaration, not for that, but for future use. Its authors meant it to be, thank God, it is now proving itself, a stumbling block to those who in after times might seek to turn a free people into the hateful paths of despotism. They knew the proneness of prosperity to breed tyrants, and they meant when such should re-appear in this fair land and commence their vocation they should find left for them at least one hard nut to crack.

I have now briefly expressed my view of the meaning and objects of that part of the Declaration of Independence which declares that "all men are created equal."[11]

Lincoln perhaps goes beyond what was in Jefferson's mind in his account of the meaning of the Declaration. In this speech equality is still the basis of resistance and possibly revolution, but Lincoln also finds in it a deeper meaning for the perpetuation of the nation, the standard to be aspired to, looked to, approached, approximated, although perhaps never perfectly attained. Slavery remains a violation of rights, but now it is also, and more importantly, *not right*. As Lincoln will say in the next to last debate, when confronted by Douglas's presentation of the rights of the people to choose slavery, to have slaves, "...he is perfectly logical if there is nothing wrong in the institution; but if you admit that it is wrong, he cannot logically say that anybody has a right to do wrong."

You might almost say that the attack of the Taney Court and Stephen Douglas upon the Declaration gave Lincoln a golden opportunity to advance the fortunes of his party and preserve the principles of his country. The argument about slavery had been mired in discussions of legal technicalities when conducted by the political moderates, and had been intemperate, uncharitable, and divisive when pressed by abolitionists and Southern "fire-eaters." Lincoln took the argument and connected it to the fundamental principles that give the Union stability and purpose. We also learned something about the fallibility of the Supreme Court,.

Reflections

---

[11] *Speech*, Springfield, Illinois, June 26, 1857

We leave our consideration of Lincoln's Declaration Statesmanship here, aware that his story and that of the nation's final struggle with slavery was only to be consummated in the fiery trial of civil war. As we have said before, our subject is not American history, but American *principles*. We have argued that the exercise of statesmanship we have studied was guided by a deep reflection on the principles of the Declaration, and brought about a new and deeper understanding of and love for those principles. A sign that this greater understanding was

Col. Robert E. Lee in a U.S. Army uniform before the war.

achieved is that every congressional act admitting a new state, starting in 1864 with Nevada and continuing through Hawaii in 1959, has contained a provision specifying that the state government would be faithful to the principles contained in the Declaration of Independence.

Perhaps a word of respect for the courage and honor of the men of the South would be in order here. Most of them fought for hearth and home, whatever the reasons of the political men who brought on the war may have been. Estimates vary, but probably no more than one in three came from a slave-owning household. The spirit and valor of the Confederate armies has impressed everyone who has read the record of their lost cause. The capacity and personal dignity of many Southern generals, particularly Robert E. Lee, have been admired by Americans of all regions and parties from the days of their doomed but gallant campaigns to the present. Lee's agonizing choice to join the Southern cause, which historian Samuel Eliot Morison wrote, "[showed] the distress of a noble mind," is best seen in his own words:

> Secession is nothing but revolution...In 1808,...and [when] the Hartford Convention assembled, secession was termed treason by Virginia statesmen; what can it be now? Still, a Union that can only be maintained by swords and bayonets, and in which strife and civil war are to take the place of brotherly love and kindness, has no charm

171

for me. If the Union is dissolved, the government disrupted, I shall return to my native state and share the miseries of my people. Save in her defense, I will draw my sword no more.[12]

Questions for Reflection

Perhaps no other period in American history has been so extensively described by historians as the Civil War and the events leading up to it. Any reading the student does in this area will be beneficial; we make no attempt to cover the wealth of materials that exist, except for the following brief remarks.

Harry V. Jaffa's *Crisis of the House Divided*, University of Chicago Press, 1982, is the best, fullest, and most useful book for the purpose of studying Lincoln's statesmanship in the period leading up to the Civil War, and we heartily recommend it to all our readers. We are deeply indebted to Professor Jaffa. All of the book is outstanding; we particularly recommend chapter XIV, "The Universal Meaning of the Declaration of Independence." The third volume of Paul Rahe's *Republics, Ancient and Modern*, has also proved invaluable.

For Southern efforts to suppress speech about slavery, besides Calhoun's 1850 speech (in the *Book of Readings*), we recommend William Lee Miller's *Arguing About Slavery*, which treats in lively and memorable prose the story of John Quincy Adams and the "gag rule". Miller's recent books, *President Lincoln* and *Lincoln's Virtues*, are also excellent. Miller calls them "ethical biography," since they consider not the policy or the history of Lincoln's actions, but their basis in his thought and character.

A reader can get a fine introduction to the abolitionist movement from Henry Mayer's *All on Fire, William Lloyd Garrison and the Abolition of Slavery*.

The best single volume treatment of the Civil War era, political, social, and military, is James M. McPherson's *Battle Cry of Freedom*. We strongly recommend the coverage of the events leading up to the war, chapters 3–8.

We *do not* recommend another recent book of some notoriety, Thomas J. DiLorenzo's *The Real Lincoln*, except as a specimen of

---

[12]Col. Robert E. Lee, to his son, January, 1861, quoted in Morison's *The Oxford History of the American People*

careless reasoning and special pleading. If, however, the student is well read on the subject of Lincoln's policies and thinking, this book can be useful as a model of how not to think, and as a preparation for meeting the hatred of Lincoln that persists in some corners of national life to the present day.

Jaffa's latest book, *A New Birth of Freedom*, should be read by anyone wanting to think through the issue of secession, and the nature of the American Union.

5. Read chapter XIV in Jaffe's *Crisis of the House Divided* and summarize or comment on his argument.

6. Original sources are irreplaceable in thoughtful study. Again, a full list would be excessively long, but we cannot forbear urging more reading of Lincoln, and of the Lincoln–Douglas debates, both of which are available in many editions and forms. Every American should read the Gettysburg Address and Lincoln's Second Inaugural (included in the *Book of Readings.*) Supreme Court decisions, too, are easily obtained from libraries and elsewhere. *Dred Scott* is long, but repays the efforts of a serious student. An abridged version of this decision can be found in the *Book of Radings.* Can you summarize the arguments for and against?

7. A reader whose interest is piqued by the quotation from President Jackson on coordinate responsibility for Constitutional interpretation might wish to consider how that teaching would play out as applied to *Roe v. Wade*, the abortion case. Suppose you were President, what would you do?

8. A recent book on Lee and Grant ends with the following paragraph, which is both touching and merits some reflection:

> "In the mid-1970s a government clerk was riffling through old files in a Washington bureau and discovered a yellowed piece of paper dated October 2, 1865.
>
> 'I, Robert E. Lee of Lexington, Virginia do solemnly swear, in the presence of Almighty God, that I will henceforth support, protect and defend the Constitution of the United States, and the Union of the States thereunder, and that I will, in like manner, abide by and faithfully support all laws and proclamations which have been made during the existing

rebellion with reference to the emancipation of slaves, so help me God.'

No one knew how Lee's oath came to be forgotten in an old file drawer, but it was commonly believed that the notarized document had been hidden in 1865 to suppress evidence that former Confederates were willing to restore the United States. More than a hundred years after his death, Robert E. Lee's oath was finally acted upon and his citizenship restored by the United States House of Representatives. The vote was not unanimous." (from Nancy Scott Anderson and Dwight Anderson *The Generals*, page 470)

Discuss why the document might have been suppressed. What arguments, if any, could be made for refusing to restore his citizenship? Who do you suppose voted against it? Can you find out?

9. We gave an outline of Lincoln's Lyceum speech at the start of this section. Find another of the great speeches of this period, by Calhoun, Clay, Webster, Douglas, Lincoln, or another, and give such an outline yourself. You might want to make an oral or written report, in which you read or recite parts of the speech, and explain or paraphrase the rest from your outline.

Chapter 7 Review Questions

1. What did Abraham Lincoln say about the role of the Declaration in his life?
2. Answer the following with quotations from Lincoln's speech to the Young Men's Lyceum:
   a) "The alienation of their affections from the government is the natural consequence" of what?
   b) "While ever a state of feeling, such as this, shall... very generally prevail throughout the nation, vain will be every effort... to subvert our national freedom." To what "state of feeling" does Lincoln refer?
   c) "It thirsts and burns for distinction, and, if possible, it will have it, whether at the expense of emancipating slaves, or enslaving freemen." What is it?

    d) "It will in future be an enemy." What is it?

3. Chapters 6 through 8 refer to historical events crucial for understanding the Declaration Statesmanship of the founders, Abraham Lincoln, Martin Luther King, Jr., and others. To help see the relationship between these events, construct a timeline incorporating the following events. You will find some answers in chapter 6 and 7, some in Order of Events V in this chapter, or in Orders of Events VI and VII in chapter 8. You may use other references to find dates.

The Founding

    a) First Congressional ban on the importation of slaves

    b) Northwest Ordinance outlaws slavery in Federal territories

    c) Pennsylvania passes a gradual emancipation law

    d) Jefferson proposes abolition of slavery in Virginia

    e) Jefferson and Madison die

    f) slave trade ended by U.S. Congress

Abraham Lincoln

    g) Lincoln's speech to the Young Men's Lyceum

    h) Dred Scott decision

    i) Lincoln's Peoria Speech

    j) Missouri Compromise

    k) *Uncle Tom's Cabin*

    l) Gettysburg Address

    m) Compromise which allowed admission of Calif. as a free state

    n) Lincoln's First Inaugural

    o) Repeal of the Missouri Compromise

    p) Lincoln Assassinated

    q) Lincoln–Douglas debates

    r) Lincoln's Second Inaugural

Civil Rights

    s) 'Black codes' enacted

    t) *Regents of Univ. of Ca. v. Bakke*

    u) *Brown v. Board of Education*

    v) Fourteenth Amendment passed

    w) *Plessy v. Ferguson*

    x) Martin Luther King, Jr.'s *I Have a Dream* speech

    y) Jim Crow Laws enacted (a span of about two decades)

    z) Segregation of federal workplaces in Washington, D.C.

4. What did Lincoln see as the three chief goods of the Missouri Compromise?

5. Of what did Emerson write: "I will not obey it, by God!"

6. What is the 'great principle' of the American republic proclaimed by Stephen Douglas? How did he think this principle would help save the Union? How did it differ from the principle of the founders?

7. What did Lincoln say is the leading principle of American Republicanism?

8. What does Thomas West say "will more often lead to misery and terror than to justice and happiness"?

9. What did Lincoln think prevented the social and political equality of the white and black races?

10. What were the key elements of the *Dred Scott* decision? How did the decision threaten Douglas's great principle? How did Lincoln react to the decision?

Jim Crow and the Civil Rights Movement   8

This section will be somewhat shorter than our treatment of the struggle over slavery, and it will culminate in events much closer to our own time. We will look at the failure to realize the equality promised in the fourteenth and fifteenth amendments to the Constitution and see once again the living force of appeals to the Declaration of Independence, and to its religious roots, in American politics. A look at events following the Civil War is necessary to set the stage.

8.1   Reconstruction and Its Aftermath

The Emancipation Proclamation had been an executive act, and applied only to slaves in the Confederacy. After Lincoln's re-election in November of 1864, with the war still dragging on, the President recommended the adoption of an amendment to the Constitution abolishing slavery. Congress passed the amendment on January 31, 1865; it would be ratified by the states on December 6th of that same year. Shortly after, with the surrender of the Confederate armies in the spring of 1865, the war came to an end. Lincoln had been pondering how to reconcile the states that had been in rebellion; his famous second inaugural address in March, while stating no policy, proposed the spirit in which Americans should act: "With malice toward none; with charity for all; with firmness in the right, as God gives us to see the right, let us strive on to finish the work we are in; to bind up the nation's wounds..." What that would have meant no one can know. Lincoln was taken from this life by the assassin's bullet, dying on the morning of April 15th. His Vice-President, Democrat Andrew Johnson of Tennessee, and thc Congress, dominated by the Republican Party, would have to undertake the task of restoring the Union and dealing with the emancipated slaves.

Re-Constructing the Union

President Lincoln with son 'Tad' in 1865

The *Oxford History* states that the economic conditions in the South were worse than those in Central Europe after either of the World Wars. Deaths in both armies had been at levels similar to those experienced by the European powers—much higher, in proportion to the population, than those America suffered in the Second World War. Nonetheless, there was remarkably little bitterness or resistance to the verdict of the battlefield. Lee and the other Southern chieftains counseled acquiescence and reunion, and civilian governments were quickly set up in all the states of the former Confederacy. Since there was some doubt about the relation of the Southern states to the Union, and since the state governments were in need of some reconstitution—at the very least, their ordinances of secession would have to be repealed—a period of 'reconstruction' was called for.

What would happen, what *should* happen, to the former slaves, the 'freedmen,' as they were called? Sentiment in the North was still not altogether friendly to full "social and political equality," as Lincoln had termed it. Few blacks voted or served on juries in the North, and racial bigotry was strong there. Those who had looked ahead to the day when slavery was no more were not necessarily thinking of an integrated society. Many had talked of, and sometimes acted on, schemes to colonize free blacks in Africa or in some other distant and largely open land. Whether such a thing was just or practicable is not especially relevant; no one mustered the political and financial power needed to effect it, and surely the freedmen themselves had little desire for resettlement.

Those freedmen, and their black brethren who had served in the Union armies, had the manliness and independence of mind that military veterans often have, and were not about to be treated as servile or inferior creatures. At the same time, the federal executive power, now wielded by a Democrat, Andrew Johnson, would not be deployed to force anything harsh on the overwhelmingly Democratic South. (Lincoln, a Republican, had run with a Democratic vice-presidential candidate on a 'unity' ticket.) Moreover, the war had been fought by the Lincoln administration on the legal premise that the Southern states were in the Union, and only violently and temporarily controlled by rebels. Accordingly, as soon as state governments loyal to the Union were reconstituted, they were acknowledged by President Johnson. The first move would be up to the reconstructed state governments themselves.

Without giving the details, let it be said that, in brief, these governments did too little good, and too much that was positively harmful. Perhaps they need not have granted full citizenship to all freedmen, without a probationary period of education and economic help, as even some abolitionists had recommended. But they should not have enacted the "black codes," which limited freedom of contract, travel, and employment, and which were felt to amount almost to a re-imposition of slavery. Perhaps they should have enacted universal suffrage (voting rights), but failing in that, they should have allowed at least returning black sol-

Democratic Vice President Andrew Johnson

diers and the educated freedmen to vote. They most certainly should not have tolerated mobs' burning schools set up by the federally run Freedmen's Bureau.

The good they did do, including such fundamental things as recognizing the legitimacy of blacks' marriages and their rights to sue (and be sued), were not enough to overcome the indignation kindled by the 'black codes' and other burdens they placed on the freedmen. It seemed to many who had sacrificed for the Union cause that the victory won in the war was slipping away, and that the old order of slavery, or rather, a *de facto* equivalent, was on the rise. A reaction was soon to come from the North.

Radical Reconstruction: The False Spring of Political and Social Equality

Historians call the second phase of Reconstruction, "Radical Reconstruction." It began in the spring and summer of 1866, with the passage, over the President's veto, of the first federal Civil Rights Act and the Fourteenth Amendment, which would be ratified in 1868; both laws, if enforced, would overturn the 'black codes' and establish equal citizenship for all freedmen

Freed family, Richmond, Va., April 1865. War-damaged buildings are visible behind the group.

and their descendants. The Freedmen's Bureau was re-authorized with increased powers, and was bitterly resented in the South. These issues dominated the mid-term election of 1866, which gave the Republican Party, now bereft of its prudent head, Lincoln, a huge and veto-proof majority in the Congress. President Johnson now became irrelevant, and Congress took the initiative.

The new Congress acted swiftly. Civilian state governments were swept aside, replaced by military governors in five districts covering what had been ten states. These states then adopted new constitutions and laws enfranchising the blacks and disqualifying former Confederate officers; in five states this meant black majorities in registered voters. To the Republican politicians who engineered it, it presumably meant Republican electoral power all across the South. These states were not allowed congressional representation until they had ratified the Fourteenth Amendment (which understandably would enjoy less than potent authority in the South when white politicians recovered their power a decade later). To ensure that the local governments would respect the civil rights of the Fourteenth Amendment,

180

A gubernatorial campaign poster of 1866. On the left "The white man must work to keep his children and pay his taxes." Over the recumbent freedman, "Whar is de use for me to work as long as dey make dese appropriations?" "The Negro estimate of freedom," written as a motto on the Capitol dome, is "Freedom and no work," while its pillars are "Indolence," "Apathy," and "Idleness," with "white women" and "white sugar."

another amendment was added, the Fifteenth, prohibiting the United States or any state government from denying or abridging the right of citizens to vote "on account of race, color, or previous condition of servitude." This was meant to insure the black voters in the South against local intimidation, but its universal language would reasonably apply to naturalized or native-born American citizens of Mexican or Chinese ancestry wishing to vote in California, for example.

Despite these strong measures and the black majorities in the electorate, Southern state governments in the next few years were never in fact dominated by freedmen; there was only one black governor, P.B.S. Pinchback of Louisiana, and he served exactly 35 days, from December 9, 1872 to January 13, 1873. There was never a majority of freedmen in both houses of any state legislature, and only one black man on any state supreme court. Contrary to the bitter complaints of many ex-confederates, the south was never ruled by blacks, and never was likely to be so ruled. Instead, a three-part coalition formed in the reconstructing states. It was composed of Republican newcomers from the North, derisively termed 'carpetbaggers,' Southerners who thought it best to cooperate with the new regimes, like Lee's right hand man, General James T. Longstreet, and the freedmen themselves. The politicians of this coalition, overwhelmingly the white politicians,

The First Vote

held the reins of power for only a few years—no more than ten in any state—and though there were men, white and black, of talent and integrity among them, the performance of these governments was mixed. On the plus side, voting rights and civil rights were equalized throughout the region, a striking fact when contrasted with the North, where blacks had voted in only a few states. Public education was greatly extended; the public school systems of the South generally date from the years of radical reconstruction. Public works and what we would now call "social services" were initiated or extended.

Southern Backlash

However, largely in consequence of these new governmental functions, taxes and public debts skyrocketed. Moreover corruption was open and extensive, though it must be added, political corruption is always with us, and was equally gross in parts of the North, especially in the urban centers like New York City. The mood of the white and formerly pro-confederate majority, who felt left out of these political arrangements, turned ugly, their actions often violent. Lynchings and intimidation became the order of the day; the period saw the birth of the Ku Klux Klan and other vigilante groups.

One of the purposes of this intimidation—terrorism really—was reduction of the black vote. Another was the destruction of the most talented or assertive of the Republican political leadership, especially the black Republicans. Vandalism, beatings, and even murder were employed against officeholders. At one point, Sept. 14, 1874, an armed mob attacked the statehouse in New Orleans to overturn contested Republican electoral victories in Louisiana. Gen. Longstreet led a force of police and black state militia against the insurrectionists, but he was defeated and there were serious casualties—over one hundred dead and wounded on both sides. President Grant had to send 5000 United States Army regulars and three gunboats to restore order and to re-instate the legally elected representatives. In December, the President sent for his toughest and most trusted commander, Gen. Phil Sheridan. Sheridan arrived at the end of the year, and found the Democrats using force to seat five of their party members in the Louisiana House. Sheridan's soldiers ejected the five Democrats on January 4th, and the remaining Democrats walked out in protest. Grant backed up "little Phil," and the White League beat a retreat in New Orleans for a time. Although a Congressional investigation found Grant's and Sheridan's actions proper, press reaction, even in the North, was critical of the administration.

Although the federal government made efforts to suppress the Klan and to put down the worst of the violent and illegal political actions, these crimes continued to resurface. Under the pressure of the white resistance, and weakened by the corruption the radical reconstruction governments had spawned, or at the least, tolerated, the coalition shrank and fractured, while its Northern patron, the Republican Party,

The original text below this 1868 cartoon read: "The above cut represents the fate in store for those great pests of Southern society—the carpet-bagger and the scallawag—if found in Dixie's land after the break of day on the 4th of March next."

alarmed at the reports of corruption and debt, and still undermined by anti-black prejudice, grew weary of protecting it. It may seem hard to understand a century and a quarter later, but Grant's firm and just action in Louisiana in 1874 and 1875 actually hurt him and his party. An American consul, a Republican, wrote to a friend in January of 1875, "The truth is, our people

U.S. Grant sits atop "The Solid South" on a bag labeled "Carpet Bag and Bayonet Rule" in a cartoon representing southerners' political feelings during Radical Reconstruction.

are tired out with this worn out cry of 'Southern outrages' ... hard times and heavy taxes make them wish the 'nigger' 'everlasting nigger' were in Hell or in Africa."

Weakness in the national political will to support the Radical Republicans' power in the formerly confederate states, and the increasing strength of the white opposition there, led to an end of this phase of reconstruction by 1877. In the next 20 years, the Republican Party virtually ceased to exist in the former confederate states, but the newly empowered Democrat governments, the so-called "Redeemers," moderated and controlled the worst of the race-hatred from the days of Radical Reconstruction. The situation was unstable and uneven, a mixture of paternalism, considerable social mixing of the races, subtle and not so subtle oppression, and much black self-help and progress. But it was emphatically the White Man's rule, and marked the end of the most hopeful era for equality in the South for almost a century. This story has been told with great conviction and much exaggeration by all sides; our purpose has been not so much to settle old controversies as to understand the background for the next Declaration struggle, the defiance of the Fourteenth and Fifteenth Amendments and the victory of equal rights in the 1960s.

8.2   Populism, Mob Rule, and Jim Crow

It is a common misconception, indicative of prejudice against the South, that systematic oppression of the black man in the form of legally enforced segregation commenced immediately after the withdrawal of the protective umbrella of the federal power in the 1870s. This is substantially false. For two more decades, many blacks continued to exercise their constitutional right to vote, and much of the public transporta-

Lynchings: 1930

tion system was not racially segregated, to name only two facts contradicting this view. Moreover, state governments included elected and appointed black officers, and there was black representation from the Southern states in Congress up to 1901. In Louisiana, where the cosmopolitan influence of the great city of New Orleans was strong, there were 130,334 "colored people" registered to vote in 1896, according to the *Oxford History*. Eight years later, however, the number was 1,342. Similar drops occurred all over the South in the 1890s.

What happened? The story is convoluted and ironic. After 1873, a lawless and resentful faction in the South, which had continued the abominable practices of lynching and terror on and off through this period, turned against the "Redeemer" state governments, controlled by the conservative Democrats, many of them former officers in the Confederate armies, like Governor Wade Hampton of South Carolina. This was largely a reaction from below, a populist movement of the small farmer and working man, envious of the wealth and privilege enjoyed by the men of business who ran the government and bought their crops and labor at low prices and sold them for what seemed to these working men unjust profits. Initially, they welcomed support from the freedmen, who, of course, shared economic grievances with these poor white farmers. But the conservatives were able to use their power to steal black votes and intimidate black voters, as they attempted to stem the rising populist tide. At this point the populists turned on their former allies (the freedmen) and, strangely and tragically, joined with the conservatives they had been opposing to form a coalition united by hostility to social and political equality for the blacks. Segregation and disenfranchisement were now the *explicit* goals of the new white majority. These objectives became central to the Democratic party's political order in the South for the next 60 years.

An unflattering depiction of "Jim Crow" on sheet music c. 1832

Similar racist sentiments and economic fears in the West led to the formation of a virulently anti-Chinese "Workingman's Party" which was involved in vigilantism and riots in San Francisco and elsewhere in California. Nor were these excesses confined to the recovering South and the unruly West.

In 1908, within a half mile of Lincoln's Springfield, Illinois home, there was a vile case of lynching of two blacks by a white mob. The violence was set off when a white woman's accused of a black man, George Richardson, of rape. After his arrest, she testified to a grand jury that Richardson had nothing to do with the rape, and the authorities tried to remove him and another black man to a safe location. A mob, furious at their departure, went wild, destroying property and killing two other blacks with no connection to the case. The governor had to call out the militia, to the number of 5,000 men, to restore order. This was the very lawlessness proceeding from democracy and the passions that Lincoln had warned against in the Lyceum speech.

In short, it was a time of populism everywhere in the country; and in places like California, the lower Midwest, and the South, where populism easily blended with racism, the results were ugly. The astonishing drop in voter registration in Louisiana is a sign of the re-imposition of race-conscious law in many parts of the country but especially and systematically in the South. It was during these years, between 1890 and 1910, when white labor thought it would find a protection against black competition in laws restricting blacks or segregating them in the workplace, that laws began to be passed requiring employers to construct separate entrances or separate toilet facilities for blacks, for example. And it was at this time that public schools and transportation were entirely segregated, and black participation in the basic civic duties, not only voting, but also jury duty and public employment, were also sharply reduced, all by the power of state laws. The legislative acts that produced this effect were termed the "Jim Crow" laws, named after a colloquial Southern expression for the black man, and they persisted well beyond the period we are speaking of here, right through both World Wars and into the 1960's.

The Progressive Heresy

Jim Crow was a shameless attempt, at the state level, to nullify the Fourteenth and Fifteenth Amendments, amendments that sprang from Declaration principles. Why was this scofflaw attitude not resisted by the nation as a whole? A partial answer may be found in the intellectual and academic currents moving through the nation from the 1870s well into the 20th Century. Pseudo-scientific racism, drawing its origins from Darwin's work, or as it is sometimes called, "Social Darwinism," and Germanic Historicism, springing from Hegel, both undermined the Declaration principles of human equality and the eternal natural law and natural rights. Perhaps the most influential American historian in the first part of the 20th century was Charles Beard. In 1908, Beard said this of the intellectual movements of the period:

> ... in comparing the political writings of the last twenty-five years

with earlier treatises one is struck with decreasing reference to the doctrine of natural rights as a basis for political practice. The theory has been rejected . . . because we have come to recognize since Darwin's day that the nature of things, once supposed to be eternal, is itself a stream of tendency. . .

Locke mistakenly depended upon an understanding of nature, using abstract reason, rather than history, and the method of science, to understand politics. . . The influence of the historical school on correct thinking in politics has been splendidly supplemented by that of the Darwinians.[1]

Beard was active in the Progressive movement, whose most famous academic politician, Woodrow Wilson, became President in 1912. Wilson's stance on Declaration Principles is summarized in a recent essay by Professor Ronald J. Pestritto:

Perhaps the greatest obstacle to a progressive constitutionalism, according to Wilson, was that the founders' constitutional order rested upon the notion that the ends of government are permanent: namely, the protection of individual rights that are derived from the transhistorical 'laws of nature and of nature's God' . . . As long as the preeminence of individual natural rights was maintained, Wilson knew that it would be difficult to change the institutional arrangements of the Constitution, which were designed primarily to protect individuals from majority faction.[2]

At the beginning of the twentieth century Social Darwinism, the rise of the social sciences, and the decline of traditional philosophy, added to naked human self-love and the imperialism of the Spanish–American War, all contributed to a "respectable" racism. C. Vann Woodward writes in *The Strange Career of Jim Crow*: "At home and abroad, biologists, sociologists, anthropologists, and historians, as well as journalists and novelists, gave support to the doctrine that races were discrete entities and that the 'Anglo-Saxon' or 'Caucasian' was the superior of them all."

An example of the novelists Woodward had in mind was surely Thomas Dixon, author of *The Clansman*, the novel that was turned into the classic, and utterly white supremacist film, *Birth of a Nation*. The film had a

---

[1] From *Politics*, a lecture delivered at Columbia University
[2] Pestritto and West, eds., *Challenges to the American Founding*, ch. 10

screening in the East room of the White House, with President Wilson, a college classmate of Dixon's, in attendance. There is a story that Wilson called the film, "true," though in response to protest from the Boston chapter of the NAACP Wilson's press Secretary denied the story. However that may be, we know that Wilson supported the new race-conscious measures we have been covering in this chapter. With President Wilson in office, the District of Columbia, which was under Congressional rule, became as segregated by law as was Georgia. Starting in 1913 a number of federal agencies were officially segregated, including the Post Office Department and the Bureau of the Census. Workers who complained were fired. President Wilson himself wrote the editor of a religious journal, the *Congregationalist*, in September of 1913, defending his actions: "I would say that I do approve of the segregation that is being attempted in several of the departments."[3]

The Birth of a Nation glamorized the K.K.K. as knights defending the South.

McKinley and a Policy of Denial

A large faction of the Democratic Party was active in its resistance to realizing the promises of the Fourteenth and Fifteenth Amendments. What about the role of the Republican Party, the "Grand Old Party," or GOP, as it was beginning to be called, a generation after Lincoln? In the 1890's a newspaper from the Republican (and formerly abolitionist) stronghold of Massachusetts contained this brief description of the new state of affairs[4]: "[Southern race policy was] now the policy of the Administration of the very party which carried the country into and through a civil war to free the slave." The reference was to the Republican Administration of William McKinley. Consider the following:

---

[3]Woodrow Wilson to Rev. H.A. Bridgman, Sept. 8, 1913, cited in *Woodrow Wilson and the Progressive Era*, by Arthur S. Link.

[4]*Boston Evening Transcript*, Jan. 14th, 1899, cited in Woodward, page 73

Thirty years after the war, Republican President McKinley staked his political fortune on the claim that the Union's preservation was complete. It is a human failing to become entrenched in old battles long after the event and long after it matters who won and why. It is no doubt often the part of wisdom to point out that it is time to move on, to draw the curtain of history over disputes heavy with years and murky in their causes. This is particularly the case when the artificial perpetuation of such disputes prevents fruitful and edifying new friendships and common endeavor. Thus, in his 1897 inaugural, he says, "The North and the South no longer divide on the old lines... It will be my constant aim to do nothing, and permit nothing to be done, that will arrest or disturb this growing sentiment of unity and co-operation."

A McKinley campaign poster from 1900.

It sounds impressive. But it does raise a question—what exactly were the issues and divisions that were being left behind? Were they the kind that the national soul was wise to turn away from? What might it have been that McKinley suspected would require his "constant" attention, lest it "arrest or disturb this growing sentiment of unity and co-operation"?

In 1890, as head of the Ways and Means Committee in Congress, McKinley pushed a major tariff bill through the House of Representatives. Some senators blocked this bill and the Sherman Silver Purchase Act, demanding as their price that GOP senators give up on a voting rights bill which had passed in the House. This bill had been designed to protect the deteriorating access of southern blacks to the ballot box, and was awaiting passage by the Senate.

This voting rights bill, to which McKinley gave lip service, was called for by the Republican platform, urged by President Harrison, and passed in the House by a partisan 155 to 149 vote. The choice was between the human rights of black men, and silver and the tariff. The GOP leadership, including, prominently, McKinley, chose Mammon.

The repression of blacks, including Jim Crow laws and lynchings, intensified. The tariff bill is often cited as one of the chief instances of McKinley's "superb" political skills.

Between 1889 and 1893, the GOP was back in power, and made some efforts to enforce voting rights in accordance with the Fifteenth Amendment. And yet, 1892 saw the apex of lynchings—226 dead that year, 155 of them blacks. Lynching totals for 1889–1918 are 2,522 blacks and 702 others.

In 1896, the year of McKinley's first election, the Supreme Court handed down its decision in *Plessy v. Ferguson*, establishing the famous "separate but equal" doctrine for meeting the due process and equal protection clauses of the Fourteenth Amendment. The decision, in effect, constitutionally authorized Jim Crow laws, which proliferated as a result.

The McKinley administration directed its attention from the beginning to economic and foreign affairs, as the deterioration of the condition of American blacks intensified. In 1901, George White, of North Carolina, the last elected black congressman from the old Confederacy, left the House. There would be no more until 1965.

McKinley in his second inaugural address stated that, "sectionalism has disappeared. Division on public questions can no longer be traced by the war maps of 1861. These old differences less and less disturb the judgment."

The Persistence of Declaration Principles

In 1899, a group of "Massachusetts Negroes" wrote an eloquent, heart-breaking, and principled open letter to President McKinley, which read in part as follows:[5]

> We, colored people of Massachusetts in mass meeting assembled to consider our oppressions and the state of the country relative to the same, have resolved to address ourselves to you in an open letter, notwithstanding your extraordinary, your incomprehensible silence on the subject of our wrongs in your annual and other messages to Congress, as in your public utterances to the country at large. We

---

[5]You can find the whole letter in the *Book of Readings* or in Mortimer J. Adler's *Annals of America*.

address ourselves to you, sir, not as suppliants, but as of right, as American citizens, whose servant you are, and to whom you are bound to listen, and for whom you are equally bound to speak, and upon occasion to act, as for any other body of your fellow countrymen in like circumstances.

We ask nothing for ourselves at your hands, as Chief Magistrate of the republic, to which all American citizens are not entitled. We ask for the enjoyment of life, liberty, and the pursuit of happiness equally with other men. We ask for the free and full exercise of all the rights of American freemen guaranteed to us by the Constitution and laws of the Union, which you were solemnly sworn to obey and execute. We ask you for what belongs to us by the high sanction of Constitution and law, and the democratic genius of our institutions and civilization.

These rights are everywhere throughout the South denied to us, violently wrested from us by mobs, by lawless legislatures, and nullifying conventions, combinations, and conspiracies, openly, defiantly, under your eyes, in your constructive and actual presence. And we demand, which is a part of our rights, protection, security in our life, our liberty, and in the pursuit of our individual and social happiness under a government, which we are bound to defend in war, and which is equally bound to furnish us in peace protection, at home and abroad.

We have suffered, sir, God knows how much we have suffered! since your accession to office, at the hands of a country professing to be Christian, but which is not Christian; from the hate and violence of a people claiming to be civilized, but who are not civilized; and you have seen our sufferings, witnessed from your high place our awful wrongs and miseries, and yet you have at no time and on no occasion opened your lips on our behalf.

Note the explicitly Declarationist language employed in this appeal: "We ask for the enjoyment of life, liberty, and the pursuit of happiness equally with other men." One wonders why it had no effect on McKinley, who had served in the Union armies thirty-five years earlier, and had his nickname, "the Major," from that service.

The more than fifty years from the triumph of Jim Crow to the successful modern Civil Rights movement offer a rich field for historical inquiry, but the details are too manifold for coverage in this book. We mentioned above the little-known fact that Southern Democrat Woodrow Wilson oversaw, and approved, the *de jure* segregation of much of the federal government. Another Southern Democrat, Harry S. Truman, made a dramatic move in the opposite direction, opening all the Armed Services of the United States to men of all races in 1948–9. Truman himself was moved by the sacrifice of black soldiers in the Second World War, and indignant at the treatment some of those men had received upon returning to their native land. Something of the same sentiment had moved the leaders of the Republican Party in the post bellum period. One wonders why there was not a similar sentiment after the First World War. The subject is discussed in, among other places, John Hope Franklin's *From Slavery to Freedom*.

In this account we have paid little attention to the actions of the freedmen themselves. We were looking instead at the application, and in this case, the tragic absence, of Declaration Statesmanship on the part of the leaders of the day, and these were nearly all whites. But, it cannot be said often enough, political self-government requires personal self-government, and there is a long and impressive story of success in the lives of the freedmen and their families which we will only notice. Justice is done to that story by other authors, notably Alan Keyes in his book, *Masters of the Dream*. Suffice it to say here that under the persecution of the Klan, unequal application of the law, strict segregation in nearly all aspects of public social life after 1900, and with the weight of prejudice and sometimes hatred weighing them down, the free blacks of the South advanced in education and financial independence, lived a vibrant church and community life, and sustained and strengthened their families. This last point may surprise contemporary readers who are aware of, and lament, the breakdown of the American family, and especially the plague of family problems that beset blacks today. But it is a fact. The vast majority of black children born under Jim Crow grew up in marriage-based, two-parent households, in spite of poverty and prejudice.

Order of Events VI: *Reconstruction and Jim Crow*

1865 Feb: **Freedman's Bureau** created by Congress to provide basic needs and schools to former slaves
March: **Lincoln's Second Inaugural Address** "With malice toward none, with charity toward all..."
April: **Lincoln assassinated**
Dec: **13th Amendment ratified**, slavery abolished

First phase of **Reconstruction**–the southern states' governments re-form on their own
Black Codes restrict freedom of former slaves

1866   April: **Civil Rights Act** passes over Pres. Johnson's veto
Spring: **Fourteenth Amendment** sent to the states to be ratified

1866   Fall: Congressional elections result in veto-proof ($2/3$) majority for the (mostly northern) Republicans. **Radical Reconstruction** begins

1867   **First, Second and Third Reconstruction Acts.** Martial Law imposed in former rebel states

1868   **Fourteenth Amendment** grants citizenship to former slaves
Ku Klux Klan sets new goals of repressing Negro vote and driving out "carpetbaggers"

1870   **Fifteenth Amendment** grants voting rights to former slaves
First black congressman elected

1875   **Civil Rights Act**, equal rights in public places and right to serve on juries

1877   **Radical Reconstruction dissolves** with withdrawal of northern and federal support

1878   Equal accommodation on railroads denied by Supreme Court

1881   **Booker T. Washington** founds Tuskegee Institute

1883   Equal access in public places denied by Supreme Court

1890   Negro Suffrage restricted by Mississippi, beginning of **Jim Crow laws**

1896   *Plessy v. Ferguson* legalizes segregation, "separate but equal"

1901   Last black congressman from Reconstruction period retires

1906   **Anti-Negro riots in Atlanta:**18 blacks and 3 whites killed

1908   **Springfield, Illinois riots:** 7 deaths and much destruction of property

1913   Federal government buildings segregated by Woodrow Wilson

1921   **Ku Klux Klan** unleashes a wave of violence and intimidation

1923   Oklahoma placed under martial law due to **KKK terrorism**
Literacy test for voters upheld by NY State Court of Appeals

1948   **"States' Rights" Democrats** walk out of the national convention over civil rights plank

194

Questions for Reflection

1. Reflect on Truman's efforts to desegregate the armed forces, and if possible, read chapters 24–25 in Franklin's book *From Slavery to Freedom*. Is the fact of military service, with the attendant risk of life for country, grounds for or proof of aptness for citizenship?

2. A residue of the old civil rights heritage did continue in the GOP through the period from McKinley through the passage of the Civil Rights Act of 1964. You can find a moving and eloquent letter on the subject of equality of rights, from President Coolidge to a Mr. Charles F. Gardner of Fort Hamilton N.Y., August 9, 1924 (in the *Book of Readings*).

3. We recommend Alan L. Keyes's *Masters of the Dream: The Strength and Betrayal of Black America*. Also, C. Vann Woodward's *The Strange Career of Jim Crow*, Eric Foner's *Reconstruction: America's Unfinished Revolution*, and Jean Edward Smith's fine biography, *Grant*. There are many more books on the progress and setbacks of the rights of American Blacks; these four are outstanding. Read one of these books and give an oral or written report on it.

8.3 The Declaration Politics of the Civil Rights Movement

I say to you today, my friends, that in spite of the difficulties and frustrations of the moment, I still have a dream. It is a dream deeply rooted in the American Dream.

I have a dream that one day this nation will rise up and live out the true meaning of its creed: "We hold these truths to be self-evident: that all men are created equal."   —Martin Luther King, Jr.[6]

Our Constitution is color-blind, and neither knows nor tolerates classes among citizens...It is to be regretted that this high tribunal, the final expositor of the fundamental law of the land, has reached the conclusion that it is competent for a state to regulate the enjoyment by citizens of their civil rights solely upon the basis of race. In my opinion, the judgement this day rendered will, in time, prove to be

---

[6] *Speech at the Lincoln Memorial*, August 28, 1963

quite as pernicious as the decision made by this tribunal in the Dred
Scott Case.   —Justice John Marshall Harlan[7]

"All Men Created Equal" in the Courts

Jim Crow reigned unchecked
for nearly six decades, until
the passage of the 1964 Civil
Rights Act and the 1965 Voting Rights Act. Justice de-
layed for six decades (or even
a century, if one goes back to
the end of the Civil War) must
be regarded as a national failure. Part of the reason for
this failure was the Unites
States Supreme Court's un-
willingness to defend the Fourteenth and Fifteenth Amendments. But a deeper failure
took place in the citizenry. We
all failed, North, South, East,
and West, to live up to our
principles.

Justice John Marshall Harlan served from 1877 to 1911.

But principles are powerful things, and though they may sleep in the
hearts of Americans, they have never yet died. The second half of the
20th century saw a revival of Declaration thought in the legal arena, the
religious and moral life, and the political world. Jim Crow was beaten by
preaching, teaching, and lawsuits. Perhaps we should not say the victory was
final or total, especially in the legal and political world, where Declaration
principles are still striving to be realized in the fight against preferential
treatment based on race and sex. Still, this part of our story is chiefly a tale
of victory, a victory won largely on the basis of explicit and powerful use
of the Declaration in our common life as Americans. It, too, is a case of
Declaration Statesmanship.

---

[7]Dissent, *Plessy v. Ferguson,* 1896

A Color-Blind Constitution

The words of Justice Harlan quoted above come from his prophetic dissent in a Louisiana case in which the majority of the court upheld the right of that state to require a railway company to separate the races in its passenger coaches. Since the law takes rail service to be a public matter, and properly regulated by the state, the issue came down to whether the laws of a state could make a racial distinction between American citizens. That the black passengers who were to be segregated were American citizens was due to the Fourteenth Amendment, which overturned the part of the *Dred Scott* decision that held that blacks could not be U.S. citizens. Ever since the ratification of the Fourteenth Amendment, all persons born in the Unites States are, as the Amendment says, "citizens of the United States and of the state wherein they reside." The Constitution is color-blind with regard to citizenship.

The liberty that the founders declared to be an inalienable right is principally the freedom to live one's own life, tend to one's own business, travel freely, and, as Lincoln said to Douglas, "to eat the bread, without the leave of anybody else, which his own hand earns." Citizenship confers additional rights—and duties. And it is not automatic. Aliens do not become citizens by residence only; they must even now be "naturalized." A nation could live by Declaration principles, respecting liberty, and yet embrace a number, perhaps a large number, of free persons who are essentially resident aliens, like the guest workers in Germany and elsewhere. These free persons, who are not members of the civic community, have rights that must be respected, but they need not, and unless they become citizens, must not, vote, serve on juries, and the like. But they miss an important part of their full human potential if they are not eligible for the duties and advantages of citizenship. That was implied by Aristotle long ago, when he said that man was by nature a political animal.

You ought to have a good reason to deny citizenship to any group of inhabitants of your country, especially those who themselves were born there, or even whose parents and grandparents were born there. Your country will be their "native land," and they will be its "native sons." Though the founders, and almost all white Americans, once doubted whether black and white could ever be friends and brothers enough to justify universal black citizenship, the decision was made when the Fourteenth and Fifteenth Amendments were passed. There were even stronger doubts about whether Orientals and whites could be in single political community. Chinese culture seemed more removed from the American way than did the life of the freedmen, and restrictions on Far Eastern immigration reflected these doubts throughout the late 19th and early 20th century. Indeed, at the time of our Revolution, many Americans were concerned that the French would not make good citizens!

Pacific Chivalry

We have said above that black soldiers' valor in the Civil War was partly responsible for of the change of heart. So, doubtless, were the bonds of religion and a common language. Fear that the freedmen could not defend themselves without citizens' rights was also a factor, as was Republican electoral self-interest.

Once you have decided to include anyone as a citizen, he immediately has civil rights. The chief of these is equal treatment under the law. Since there had been a track record of unequal treatment right after the Civil War, during the first phase of Reconstruction, the Radical Reconstruction which replaced it went on to insist that the *states* must guarantee to all citizens *equal treatment*, regardless of race, and that the federal government would have the power to ensure that they would get it. The decision in *Plessy v. Fergusen* allowed the state to make laws enforcing segregation, effectively distinguishing between two 'classes' of citizens.

Harlan's reasoning in dissenting from the railway segregation case was clear and simple; citizenship was color-blind, civil rights were equal without regard to color, public access to public railways was part of civil freedom, therefore it was unconstitutional for Louisiana to, as he said, "...[separate] citizens, on the basis of race, while they are on a public highway."

Here is the conclusion of his dissent. As you read it, you may want to recall that his home state was Kentucky, and that he had been, before the War, a slaveholder:

> I am of opinion that the statute of Louisiana is inconsistent with the personal liberty of citizens, white and black, in that state, and hostile to both the spirit and letter of the Constitution of the United States. If laws of like character should be enacted in the several states of the Union, the effect would be in the highest degree mischievous. Slavery, as an institution tolerated by law, would, it is true, have disappeared from our country; but there would remain a power in the states, by sinister legislation, to interfere with the full enjoyment of the blessings of freedom, to regulate civil rights, common to all citizens, upon the basis of race, and to place in a condition of legal inferiority a large body of American citizens, now constituting a part of the political community, called the "People of the United States," for whom, and by whom through representatives, our government is administered. Such a system is inconsistent with the guaranty given by the Constitution to each state of a republican form of government, and may be stricken down by congressional action, or by the courts in the discharge of their solemn duty to maintain the supreme law of the land, anything in the constitution or laws of any state to the contrary notwithstanding.
>
> For the reason stated, I am constrained to withhold my assent from the opinion and judgement of the majority.

"Affirmative Action"

Perhaps the most famous act of the United States Supreme Court between the notorious cases of *Dred Scott* and *Roe v. Wade* is the 1954 *Brown v. Board of Education* decision. By its ruling, the Court made racially segregated public schools illegal. Most Americans will tell you that this decision meant that the Court had finally read the letter of the Fourteenth Amendment in the spirit of the Declaration; all men are created equal, and the Constitution is color-blind. Lawyers for the National Association for the Advancement of Colored People (NAACP) had made just such a point in arguing to the Court that school segregation ought to be struck down. Their briefs included passages like these: "...the Fourteenth Amendment prevents states from according differential treatment to American children on the basis of their color or race... The broad general purpose of the Fourteenth Amendment [is the] obliteration of race and color distinctions... that the Constitution is color-blind is our dedicated belief." And they won their case. The Court did strike down the segregated schools of Topeka, Kansas.

But arguments before the Court are not the law; the Court gives its own reasons for its decisions, and these are the binding interpretations for other judges, and the precedents for future Supreme Court decisions. Unhappily, most Americans have the wrong idea about *Brown v. Board of Education*. The Court did indeed outlaw segregation, but not because it accepted Harlan's 1896 dissent, that the "Constitution is color-blind." Instead, it ruled that the psychological harm it believed segregation inflicted on black school children was an unlawful injury. This may be true; it may be provable, psychologically, that segregation produces unjust "feelings of inferiority" in the minority child. But even if it is, by deciding the case on this basis, the Court missed the chance to re-establish the fundamental principle of equal justice without regard to color in the law.

This failure would show up in the question of race-conscious policy adopted to ensure equality of results by group twenty years later, when the Court began to consider the legality of 'affirmative action'. The most famous of these cases was to be *Regents of the University of California v. Bakke* (1978), in which Justice Brennan was to put the following in his opinion: "The position... summed up by the shorthand phrase 'our Constitution is color-blind'... has never been adopted by this court as the proper meaning of the Equal Protection Clause [of the Fourteenth Amendment.] Indeed, we have expressly rejected this proposition on a number of occasions."

More recent Court rulings have moved, slowly, towards Harlan's color-blind doctrine, but it has yet to be adopted. At present, the government may treat Americans differently on the basis of race, but it must have strong reasons to do so. In the words of Justice O'Connor in *Adarand v. Peña* (1995), "All racial classifications, imposed by whatever federal, state, or local governmental actor, must be analyzed by a reviewing court under strict scrutiny." Strict scrutiny is hard to survive, but not impossible. As of

200

this writing, there are hundreds of federal and state programs and judicial dictates that still treat Americans differently on the basis of race.

From Reconstruction to the present day, then, the courts have not concluded that the principle of equality found in the Declaration and the Fourteenth Amendment, and the promise of a republican form of government consistent with the principles of the Declaration of Independence, require that American law be color-blind. Perhaps it will do so in our lifetimes, but that remains to be seen.

Maybe we expect too much from our courts. The Constitutional structure makes them the most cautious and least creative branch of government, and rightly so. And all of government, even the two more political branches, is finally only the servant of a free and sovereign people. To assess the real progress America has made towards color-blind law, we should turn to our political life, and the hearts and minds of our fellow citizens.

The Sovereign People Decides

> America has strayed to the far country of racism. The home that all too many Americans left was solidly structured idealistically. Its pillars were solidly grounded in the insights of our Judeo-Christian heritage: all men are made in the image of God; all men are brothers, all men are created equal; every man is the heir to a legacy of dignity and worth; every man has rights that are neither conferred by nor derived from the state, they are God-given. What a marvelous foundation for any home! What a glorious place to inhabit!
>
> —Martin Luther King, Jr.[8]

There is no way one can separate faith from politics in the change of heart that led to the end of Jim Crow and the resolve to live according to the letter and spirit of the Fourteenth and Fifteenth Amendments, culminating in the Civil Rights and Voting Rights legislation of 1964 and 1965. A look at the words of Martin Luther King Jr., who was prominent in securing the passage of both acts, will confirm what we have said. King moves effortlessly from quoting Scripture "... in the image of God... " to citing the Declaration "... all men are created equal... " And he calls this house of Scriptural stones and Declaration rafters, the American "home." That is what he meant in the great "I Have a Dream" speech when he told the multitude gathered before

---

[8] *Where Do We Go from Here?: Chaos or Community*, 1967

201

the Lincoln Memorial that his dream was "deeply rooted in the American dream."

None of this should surprise the readers of this book by now. The conjunction of Biblical faith and natural reason that led to the Declaration gave it a religious significance so great that Samuel Adams was moved to say of the people's response to it: "[They] seem to recognize this resolution as though it were a decree promulgated from heaven." President Coolidge, in his Sesquicentennial address on the Declaration, had pointed out that "the principles of human relationship which went into the Declaration... are found in the... sermons and the

The Rev. Martin Luther King, Jr. giving his address, 'Where Do We Go From Here?' in Atlanta, 1967.

writings of the early colonial clergy... They preached equality because they believed in the fatherhood of God and the brotherhood of man. They justified freedom by the text that we are all created in the divine image, all partakers of the divine spirit." How strikingly similar this is to Martin Luther King's lament in *Where Do We Go from Here*, "We fail to think of them [men not of our own race or creed] as fellow human beings made from the same divine stuff as we are, molded in the same divine image."

Knights and Martyrs: Two Sides of the Religious Response to Jim Crow

Jews, Catholics, and Protestants were all prominent in the debates and demonstrations that led up to the Civil Rights Act of 1964. Perhaps a bit of reflection on the principal stances that the Judeo-Christian tradition has taken towards injustice will prove helpful here. We will characterize the religious citizen as martyr or knight, admittedly an simplification, but one that may prove helpful.

The basic question is whether to "take up the sword." Recognizing as he does that injustice is not put right until the judgment or the coming of

202

the Messiah, and that the wicked sometimes prosper while the just suffer, what is the man of faith to do? One response is to seek personal perfection, suffer meekly, even unto death if necessary, and make one's own the love with which God loves even the sinner. Be ready to be a martyr. If you are not asked to give your life, you may have to sacrifice your career or your ambition. Do so patiently. Pray for the king, even in Babylon, and put away your sword. Make no alliance with Egypt, as Jeremiah taught, and become the faithful remnant. "He who lives by the sword shall die by the sword."

The other stance is, while praying to avoid the temptation to hate one's enemies, to stand up and fight for one's rights and people, trusting to Divine Judgment, but entering the fight. Of course, we are using the word "sword" chiefly metaphorically. We are not especially concerned with fighting to the death, but with political warfare, with the confrontation of demonstration and argument. Even without bloodshed, this kind of fighting can reduce friendship and civil concord and bring about personal and family strife that is most serious. Many American families saw that in the arguments here in our country about the Vietnam War, or about abortion, just as in the past town and clan were divided over slavery.

Booker T. Washington (1856–1915)

BOOKER T. WASHINGTON

What made the martyr's course attractive in the decades after the Civil War was the end to be achieved. It was not only recognition in law and policy of the legal equality of the races that friends of the freedmen sought, but the civic and personal friendships, the genuine good will, that underlies a civil community. This required respect and affection, and respect and affection are sometimes better won by silence and deeds than by protests and demands. The name of Booker T. Washington is associated with this Christian choice of submissive and charitable patience and amity. The following is typical of his writings:

The bedrock upon which every individual rests his chances of success

203

in life is securing the friendship, the confidence, the respect, of his next door neighbor of the little community in which he lives...There is at present no other safe course to pursue. If the Negro in the South has a friend in his white neighbor and a still larger number of friends in his community, he has a protection and a guarantee of his rights more potent and more lasting than any our Federal Congress or any outside power can confer.[9]

Or the following:

If any white man would be mean, let us be good;
if any white man would be little, let us be great;
if any white man would push us down, let us push him up.
If others can excel us in hating, let us excel them in loving.
If others can excel us in cruelty, let us excel them in acts of mercy.
You may call this cowardice; if so, it is the kind of cowardice that
Christ taught and practiced, and it is the kind of cowardice that in
the long run will win our cause.[10]

If these sentiments are not inconsistent with the dignity of man as taught in the Declaration, that they omit or minimize the notion of 'rights', makes them significantly different. Booker T. Washington thought that the strategy of raising up the black man by political defense of his rights in the Reconstruction had failed, and he also thought that he should order his life and the aspirations of his race to higher things, things that transcended politics. He would, and did, enter into political life quietly, backstage, as it were, to ameliorate the legal and social status of the black man, but he would lead no political crusade.

W.E.B. DU BOIS   The way of the knight, defense of one's own rights and those of others, was signaled by a "Declaration of Principles" adopted in 1905 by a group called the "Niagara Movement." Many of the leaders and principles of the Niagara Movement were later incorporated in the National Association for the Advancement of Colored People (NAACP). Its most famous leader was W.E.B. Du Bois, whose career shows the power, and the temptations, of the knight's way. The following is taken from the "Declaration of Principles":

---

[9]From "The Case of the Negro," published in *The Atlantic Monthly* of Nov. 1889
[10]From an address given May, 1900

We note with alarm the evident retrogression in this land of sound public opinion on the subject of manhood rights, republican government and human brotherhood, and we pray God that this nation will not degenerate into a mob of boasters and oppressors, but rather will return to the faith of the fathers, that all men were created free and equal, with certain inalienable rights...

We refuse to allow the impression to remain that the Negro-American assents to inferiority, is submissive under oppression and apologetic before insults...

We urge upon Congress the enactment of appropriate legislation for securing the proper enforcement of those articles of freedom, the thirteenth, fourteenth, and fifteenth amendments of the Constitution of the United States...

The Negro race...needs justice, and is given charity, needs leadership, and is given cowardice and apology...

Of the above grievances, we do not hesitate to complain, and to complain loudly and insistently. To ignore, overlook, or apologize for these wrongs is to prove ourselves unworthy of our freedom. Persistent manly agitation is the way to liberty...

This statement, complaint, and prayer we submit to the American people and Almighty God.

There are three things that merit our attention in this "Declaration of Principles." It looks to action, "persistent manly agitation" in the political arena. It explicitly cites Declaration principles. And it looks to "Almighty God," so much so that it terms itself both a complaint and a prayer.

Here is Du Bois himself, addressing the second annual meeting of the Niagara Movement.

W.E.B. Du Bois
Address to the Nation
Delivered at the second annual meeting of the Niagara Movement
Harper's Ferry, West Virginia, 16 August 1906

The men of the Niagara Movement coming from the toil of the year's hard work and pausing a moment from the earning of their daily bread turn toward the nation and again ask in the name of ten million the

---

privilege of a hearing. In the past year the work of the Negro-hater has flourished in the land. Step by step the defenders of the rights of American citizens have retreated. The work of stealing the black man's ballot has progressed and the fifty and more representatives of stolen votes still sit in the nation's capital. Discrimination in travel and public accommodation has so spread that some of our weaker brethren are actually afraid to thunder against color discrimination as such and are simply whispering for ordinary decencies.

Against this the Niagara Movement eternally protests. We will not be satisfied to take one jot or tittle less than our full manhood rights. We claim for ourselves every single right that belongs to a freeborn American, political, civil and social; and until we get these rights we will never cease to protest and assail the ears of America. The battle we wage is not for ourselves alone but for all true Americans. It is a fight for ideals, lest this, our common fatherland, false to its founding, become in truth the land of the thief and the home of the slave—a byword and a hissing among the nations for its sounding pretensions and pitiful accomplishment.

Never before in the modern age has a great and civilized folk threatened to adopt so cowardly a creed in the treatment of its fellow citizens born and bred on its soil. Stripped of verbiage and subterfuge and in its naked nastiness, the new American creed says: Fear to let the black men even try to rise lest they become the equals of the white. And this is the land that professes to follow Jesus Christ. The blasphemy of such a course is only matched by its cowardice. In detail, our demands are clear and unequivocal. First, we would vote; with the right to vote goes everything: freedom, manhood, the honor of your wives, the chastity of your daughters, the right to work, and the chance to rise, and let no man listen to those who deny this.

We want full manhood suffrage, and we want it now, henceforth and forever.

Second. We want discrimination in public accommodation to cease. Separation in railway and street cars, based simply on race and color, is un-American, undemocratic, and silly. We protest against all such discrimination.

Third. We claim the right of freemen to walk, talk, and be with them that wish to be with us. No man has a right to choose another man's friends, and to attempt to do so is an impudent interference with the most fundamental human privilege.

Fourth. We want the law enforced against rich as well as poor; against capitalist as well as laborer; against white as well as black. We are not more lawless than the white race: we are more often arrested, convicted and mobbed. We want justice even for criminals and outlaws. We want the Constitution of the country enforced. We want Congress to take charge of Congressional elections. We want the Fourteenth Amendment carried out to the letter and every state disfranchised in Congress which attempts to disfranchise its rightful voters. We want the Fifteenth Amendment enforced and no state allowed to base its franchise simply on color.

The failure of the Republican Party in Congress at the session just closed to redeem its pledge of 1904 with reference to suffrage conditions in the South seems a plain, deliberate, and premeditated breach of promise, and stamps that party as guilty of obtaining votes under false pretense.

Fifth. We want our children educated. The school system in the country districts of the South is a disgrace, and in few towns and cities are the Negro schools what they ought to be. We want the national government to step in and wipe out illiteracy in the South. Either the United States will destroy ignorance or ignorance will destroy the United States.

And when we call for education we mean real education. We believe in work. We ourselves are workers, but work is not necessarily education. Education is the development of power and ideal. We want our children trained as intelligent human beings should be, and we will fight for all time against any proposal to educate black boys and girls simply as servants and underlings, or simply for the use of other people. They have a right to know, to think, to aspire.

These are some of the chief things we want. How shall we get them? By voting where we may vote, by persistent, unceasing agitation, by hammering at the truth, by sacrifice and work.

We do not believe in violence, neither in the despised violence of the raid nor the lauded violence of the soldier, nor the barbarous violence of the mob, but we do believe in John Brown, in that incarnate spirit of justice, that hatred of a lie, that willingness to sacrifice money, reputation, and life itself on the altar of right. And here on the scene of John Brown's martyrdom we reconsecrate ourselves, our honor, our property to the final emancipation of the race which John Brown died to make free.

Our enemies, triumphant for the present, are fighting the stars in their courses. Justice and humanity must prevail. We live to tell these dark brothers of ours—scattered in counsel, wavering and weak—that no bribe of money or notoriety, no promise of wealth or fame, is worth the surrender of a people's manhood or the loss of a man's self-respect. We refuse to surrender the leadership of this race to cowards and trucklers. On this rock we have planted our banners. We will never give up, though the trump of doom find us still fighting.

And we shall win. The past promised it, the present foretells it. Thank God for John Brown! Thank God for Garrison and Douglass! Sumner and Phillips, Nat Turner and Robert Gould Shaw, and all the hallowed dead who died for freedom! Thank God for all those today, few though their voice be, who have not forgotten the divine brotherhood of all men, white and black, rich and poor, fortunate and unfortunate.

We appeal to the young men and women of this nation, to those whose nostrils are not yet befouled by greed and snobbery and racial narrowness: stand up for the right, prove yourselves worthy of your heritage and whether born North or South dare to treat men as men. Cannot the nation that has absorbed ten million foreigners into its political life without catastrophe absorb ten million Negro Americans into that same political life at less cost than their unjust and illegal exclusion will involve?

Courage, brothers! The battle for humanity is not lost or losing. All across the skies sit signs of promise. The Slav is rising in his might, the yellow millions are tasting liberty, the black Africans are writhing toward the light, and everywhere the laborer, with ballot in his hand, is voting open the gates of opportunity and peace. The morning breaks over blood-stained hills. We must not falter, we may not shrink. Above are the everlasting stars.

This is the creed of a knight. It intends to make a fight. If the drawback in the martyr's way is that it may change nothing, that of the knight's is that he may lose his soul in the wasteland of pride and finally hate. Manly agitation may lead to manly pride, and then to sentiments like these from Du Bois's later writings: "No race ever gave Passive resistance and Submission to Evil longer, more piteous trial. Today we raise the terrible weapon of self-defense... No human group has ever achieved freedom without being compelled to murder thousands of members of other groups who were determined that they should be slaves..." Du Bois's personal vision of justice did not, in the end, include the principles of the Declaration, which he explicitly repudiated as "individualistic," nor did he rest in faith; he actually praised Josef Stalin and held that a chief glory of Soviet socialism was the repression of religion, which he thought bred the passivity and submission he so despised. It was part of

W.E.B. Du Bois in 1918

his political agenda to nurture the "memory of slavery" and the "experience of caste." John Hope Franklin, a writer not unfriendly to Du Bois, reports that, "After seventy years of crusading for civil rights, W.E.B. Du Bois had joined the Communist Party, renounced his United States citizenship, and moved to Ghana in 1961." Du Bois died, two years later, self-exiled from his native land.

The Statesmanship of Martin Luther King, Jr.

Declaration Statesmanship has been the theme of this chapter. The greatest instances of Declaration Statesmanship, the founding and the response to slavery, may be epitomized by the names of Jefferson and Lincoln. Of course they were aided (and opposed) by many men of talent and goodwill, and we would not be taken as saying that they alone stood like gods astride the concourse of history, determining events by their sovereign wills. Nor would we say that their every decision was wise or just. At the same time, their prudence and resolution changed the course of affairs, and we have tried to learn from them. We will conclude this chapter by making a similar effort with Martin Luther King, Jr.

Statesmen act in the real world, and their deeds are conditioned by what is actually possible. The founders faced the momentous task of establishing the first human government devoted to the propositions of natural right. They had a people on their side, and so it was proper for them, they argued, to revolutionize. They became the generals, congressmen, secretaries, and officers of that revolution and its government.

Lincoln faced the task of breathing new life into the founding principles when they were in danger of expiring. He foresaw that they would even be denied and trampled in the defense of slavery. His country chose him president because of his stance, founded in the Declaration, against slavery. After that time, he taught and reformed his country as its head of state. His triumph, which he paid for with his life, was the re-establishment and deepening of those principles.

For almost a century after Lincoln's death, those principles, though widely honored and accepted, had not been applied to all Americans. Some in the academic world, indeed, denied them, but most Americans still cherished them while failing to apply them in the matter of race. Though this failure spread all over the country, and meant injustice for Asian-Americans, Mexican-Americans, American Indians, and others, everyone knew that the case was worst for blacks in the South. The blacks themselves had tried Christian submission and political agitation, without making a fundamental change.

CITIZEN-STATESMAN   King was a preacher and a citizen, not an elected official. His cause was not, in the first instance, the cause of a nation, but of a racially distinct segment of that nation, only about 12% of the population. He and his movement had on their side the great moral prestige that Lincoln had won for the Declaration, the legal provisions of the Fourteenth and Fifteenth Amendments, still largely paper guarantees, and the religious sensibilities of many of his fellow citizens. The black churches of the South, centers of education and community for more than a century, were a strong base of support. He also had a large number of whites of both parties who thought that Jim Crow was wrong, but who had not shown much strength or success in resisting it.

King could not operate from the seat of government, but he could take the higher ground of religion and moral principle. As a citizen, he could lead protest and discussion, and his allies could bring lawsuits. Since his cause was immediately in the interest of only one American in eight, he needed

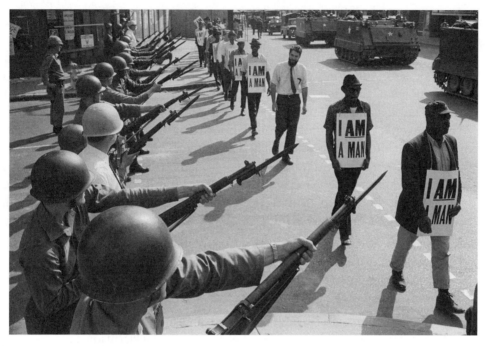

Protest march in Memphis TN, 1968, shortly before Martin Luther King, Jr.'s assasination.

the goodwill of his fellow citizens; he needed to win their hearts and minds. Beyond this practical need, he wanted that goodwill, wanted it more than he wanted anything else. His dream was of human brotherhood, both as a Christian minister and as an American. In this, he was closer to Booker T. Washington than to the NAACP and Du Bois. His own organization was called the Southern Christian Leadership Conference, and its motto was "To save the soul of America." He was a man of faith, and his horizon included more than politics. But even in politics, he knew that legal rights are grounded on human respect and friendship.

LIFTING HEARTS AND ENLIGHTENING MINDS King's creative solution to the practical political problem was to force the evil in Jim Crow to show itself in the face of peaceful protest, engendering a non-hateful courage in his people and moderating the fears of those who fought with them. It was, when it worked, a wonderful blend of the knight and the martyr. It broke the spell of unmanliness in the Southern black, while it shielded protesters from the worst temptations to hatred and violence. National sympathy swung decisively to King's side when the dignified and brave protesters were arrested singing hymns and offering no physical resistance to the sheriff's men and their dogs.

At the same time, he interpreted these feelings in accordance with religious and Declaration thought, thereby ennobling them. He helped people to think about what they felt. The movement he led, and the moral success it obtained, enabled him to turn to politics and the law in a way that Booker T. Washington's earlier efforts could not. King said of the law, "[It] is a form of education. The words of the Supreme Court, of Congress, and of the Constitution are eloquent instructors." When President Kennedy was ready to ask Congress to pass what would become the Civil Rights Act of 1964, his words had been prepared by the labors of American statesmen from Jefferson to Lincoln to King:

> This nation was founded by men of many nations and backgrounds. It was founded on the principle that all men are created equal, and that the rights of every man are diminished when the rights of one man are threatened...
>
> We are confronted primarily with a moral issue. It is as old as the Scriptures and is as clear as the American Constitution...
>
> We have a right to expect that the Negro community will be responsible, will uphold the law, but they have a right to expect that law will be fair, that the Constitution will be color blind, as Justice Harlan said at the turn of the century.[11]

When the civil rights legislation that the president had called for passed, the people had every reason to believe that they had set an unalterable course to make their laws reflect the Declaration principle of equality, and the Judeo-Christian principle of brotherhood. No one could reasonably think that we had cured the ills of bigotry and pride in the human heart, but we had made a solemn commitment, as a people, to do what King had asked for in "I Have a Dream": to make a nation in which our children would be judged, "not by the color of their skin, but by the content of their character."

Order of Events VII: *Civil Rights Movement*

1905 **Niagara Movement** formed, adopts a "Declaration of Principles"

1909 National Association for the Advancement of Colored People (**NAACP**) forms in response to the Springfield riots

1948 Armed forces desegregated by Pres. Truman

---

[11] *Address to the Nation*, June 11, 1963

1954 *Brown v. Board of Education* decision strikes down school segregation, reverses *Plessy v. Ferguson*

1955 **Rosa Parks** inspires a bus strike in Montgomery, Alabama

1957 Integration of public schools enforced by federal troops in Little Rock, AR

1960 Civil Rights Bill is filibustered by 18 southern senators, and passes with weakened provisions

1961 **"Freedom Riders"** demonstrate the ineffectiveness of court orders integrating interstate buses

1962 Ku Klux Klan claims 'credit' for **bombings of four black churches**

1962 Segregation of both inter- and intra-state transportation outlawed by Supreme Court ruling

1962 Racial discrimination in housing built or purchased with federal funds prohibited by executive order of Pres. Kennedy

1963 Martin Luther King, Jr. leads the March on Washington; **"I Have a Dream" speech**

1964 **Twenty-fourth Amendment** abolishes poll taxes

1964 **Civil Rights Act of 1964** passes after a 75 day filibuster

1965 **Voting Rights Act** further removes barriers to registering and voting

1966 **KKK investigated** in public hearings. 7 leaders cited for contempt; the "Imperial Wizard" sentenced to a year in prison

1967 Interracial marriage protected from state prohibitions by the Supreme Court

1968 Assassination of Martin Luther King, Jr.

1968 Discrimination in housing outlawed by **Civil Rights Act of 1968**

1978 *University of Ca. v. Bakke* allows race preferences in university admissions

1995 *Aderand v. Peña* allows racial considerations in awarding federal contracts, under a "strict scrutiny" test

1996 **California Civil Rights Initiative** bans race preferences in state government and schools

1998 I-200, a similar voter initiative, passes in Washington State

Chapter 8 Review Questions

1. What were the 'black codes'?
2. What did the Fourteenth Amendment promise the freed blacks? Why was its authority questioned in the South?
3. What percentage of colored voters were there in Louisiana in 1904 compared to 1896? What caused the drop?
4. What philosophies contributed to a 'respectable' racism in the Progressive Movement?
5. What notable success did McKinley achieve in Congress? What did he give up for it?
6. Why did Justice Harlan dissent from the majority opinion in *Plessy v. Ferguson*?
7. Why did the Court in *Brown v. the Board of Education* overturn racial segregation in schools? Why did the NAACP argue that it should be overturned?
8. Why did Booker T. Washington encourage submissive patience in the face of discrimination?
9. What did the Niagara Movement declare to be the "way to liberty"?
10. What was the name of Martin Luther King's own organization? What was its motto?

A People Worthy of the Declaration 9

Throughout this book we have attended to the subject of Declaration Statesmanship. Most of our statesmen, like the founders or Lincoln, held high office. Others were non-official leaders like Du Bois or King. But it is to be kept in mind that ours is a government "of the people." So, though each and every citizen need not hold office, still, in some sense he rules the republic, together with his fellows. The Constitution opens, "We the People..." This is a popular government, a republic. We think it proper, accordingly, to consider what kind of people, with what loves and what virtues, can live out Declaration principles. To this subject, by way of conclusion, we now turn, and we will take as our guide Alexis de Tocqueville.

9.1   The Character of Our Forefathers

> The nations of our time cannot prevent the conditions of men from becoming equal, but it depends upon themselves whether the principle of equality is to lead them to servitude or freedom, to knowledge or barbarism, to prosperity or wretchedness.
> —Tocqueville, final sentence of *Democracy in America*

In 1831, 55 years after the Declaration of Independence and 42 years after the adoption of the Constitution, a young French nobleman came to visit America. His name was Alexis de Tocqueville. Although of noble birth, the young Tocqueville was a friend of democracy. Democracy, however, had not had a happy history in France. The French Revolution of 1789, although founded on some of the same principles as the American Revolution (notably not, however, acknowledgment of the Creator as the source of human rights) had never attained stability. Bloody struggles for power among its leaders culminated in the elevation to power of an emperor, Napoleon. After

Napoleon's fall, the French were governed by unstable monarchical regimes, the first under a restored House of Bourbon, and the next headed by the so-called "citizen king," Louis Philippe.

Democratic ideals did not die under the restored monarchy, and Tocqueville believed that the power of the idea of equality would make some form of democracy the government of the future for all Western countries. But he was troubled by the lack of political stability and the tendency toward tyranny that France's first democratic efforts had shown. Similar problems were experienced in Central and South America, where the former Spanish colonies had been unable to establish stable, peaceful, popular rule. Many others in Europe held a more pessimistic view than Tocqueville. They believed that ordinary people could never rule themselves, and would always be prey to enterprising, ruthless men promising them the stability of dictatorial rule. They argued that only a king or an aristocracy, a small group of men who were trained to rule from birth, could provide stable, peaceful government for a country.

Alexis de Tocqueville (1805–1859)

Amidst the turbulent sea of floundering democracies, the United States rose up like an island of refuge. For over half a century, the people of the United States, and the millions of immigrants who had joined them, had managed to rule themselves successfully. Democracy in America had prospered and expanded. Tocqueville came to America hoping to discover the secrets of its success, some of which might help to guide France and other European countries on their road to democratic rule.

216

Tocqueville concluded that neither the natural advantages of the land nor the written constitution were sufficient to explain America's peace, stability and prosperity. Instead, he thought that these goods came from what he called her customs, what we might call the character or the culture of the people.

> The customs of the Americans of the United States are, then, the peculiar cause which renders that people the only one of the American nations that is able to support a democratic government... I am convinced that the most advantageous situation and the best possible laws cannot maintain a constitution in spite of the customs of a country; while the latter may turn to some advantage the most unfavorable positions and the worst laws. —Tocqueville[1]

In this chapter, we investigate the character that has made our country the most successful democracy in history.

Self-Government: Self-Control

As we noted above, self-government prevailed in America long before the Revolution. For various reasons, no aristocracy had ever been established in the colonies. The colonists were permitted by their charters from the king (which authorized them to settle the land claimed by the Crown) to form their own governments. The popularly elected colonial assemblies did not have to share power with an aristocracy, as the House of Commons in Britain did. For 150 years, these assemblies, with the approval of governors, generally appointed by the king, enacted nearly all necessary legislation. As old Captain Preston said, "We had always ruled ourselves." And, as his taking up his musket proved, we loved the liberty we had experienced.

Because there was no aristocracy, the colonists gained valuable experience in freedom in a wider sense. Under aristocratic rule, the noblemen owned much of the land in England, while commoners were often tenants on the lord's property. In the colonies, ownership of property was more widely diffused. Workmen owned the tools they employed in their trade. Most farmers owned the land they farmed. Other colonists owned small workshops or merchant ships. Many colonists were used to the responsibility that comes with ownership. They knew the risks that come with property, and they also

---

[1] *Democracy in America*, Vol. I, book 2, ch. 9

knew the profit that comes with managing it diligently and intelligently. They learned how to associate with others with similar goals, to share resources to achieve more. All these exercises in freedom required self-control. Moreover, because of their experience in managing their own affairs, both privately and in associations, and their love of the liberty involved in such management, the colonists naturally wished to share in decisions about matters affecting the whole colony. And they had learned the skills of such decision making. They could have self-government because they had self-control.

Self-Government: Association

These early Americans were, in one sense, independent before Independence. But in another sense, they were quite *inter*dependent. Tocqueville notes that only by common efforts could Americans compensate for the lack of an aristocracy:

> Aristocratic communities always contain, among a multitude of persons who by themselves are powerless, a small number of powerful and wealthy citizens, each of whom can achieve great undertakings single-handed... Among democratic nations, on the contrary, all the citizens are independent and feeble; they can do hardly anything by themselves, and none of them can oblige his fellow men to lend him their assistance. They all, therefore, become powerless if they do not learn voluntarily to help one another.[2]

Americans became masters of voluntary association. They combined to found a school, to set up a volunteer fire company, or to pitch in and help other families in difficulty without the command of a magistrate or sheriff. According to Tocqueville, Americans offered such help not only from charity, but also because they thought it in their own interest. They knew that the time would likely come when they also would need help or they saw in a project such as a school an increase of learning that would be beneficial to all. All this continued after 1776, and into the first half-century of the new republic, when Tocqueville came to visit and observe America.

Our forefathers were thus self-governing in two distinct, but related senses. They were largely independent owners of property, which they governed according to their own good sense, and they were also experienced in forming and sustaining self-governing associations so as to overcome their

---

[2] *Democracy in America*, Vol. II, Book 2, ch. 5

isolation and individual weakness, and to receive aid from others when they might need it. Both kinds of self-government required and fostered prudence and submission of appetite to reason. Self-government in associations also developed habits of lawfulness and compromise, and experience of the rules of debate and decision-making. These habits and experiences were vital to the experiment in full political self-government that the Declaration would inaugurate. They were also crucial to the design of limited government set out in the Constitution, since it was only by the capacity of the people in voluntary associations to conduct affairs in business, the arts, religion,

Benjamin Franklin epitomized the American aptitude for voluntary associations. He organized the first volunteer fire department and a subscription library in his adopted city of Philadelphia.

and education, that these affairs could be managed apart from government, and in particular, centralized government. Tocqueville put the last point this way:

> Nothing, in my opinion, is more deserving of our attention than the intellectual and moral associations of America. The political and industrial associations of that country strike us forcibly; but the others elude our observation, or if we discover them, we understand them imperfectly because we have hardly ever seen anything of the kind. It must be acknowledged, however, that they are as necessary to the American people as the former, and perhaps more so. In democratic countries the science of association is the mother of science; the progress of all the rest depends upon the progress it has made.[3]

---

[3] *Democracy in America*, Vol. II, Book 2, ch. 5

Individualism

America has been called the country of individual rights and individualism. The reason for the first is that the inalienable rights of the Declaration belong to the individual, not to groups, such as ethnic or racial groups, or to clans, or societies. They are the rights of man. Naturally, then, we tend to be "individualists" and to prize individualism. Tocqueville, who is sometimes credited with having invented the term, gives a definition of it, together with a sharp criticism. He writes:

> Individualism is a mature and calm feeling, which disposes each member of the community to sever himself from the mass of his fellows, and to draw apart with his family and his friends, so that after he has thus formed a little circle of his own, he willingly leaves society at large to itself... [Individualism makes] every man forget his ancestors... it hides his descendents and separates his contemporaries from him; it throws him back forever upon himself alone and threatens in the end to confine him entirely within the solitude of his own heart.[4]

Tocqueville looks to civic and political associations, and what he calls "the principle of self-interest rightly understood" to combat these evils. We will return to the problem of individualism in the next section.

9.2   The Character of a Free People

> I should have loved freedom, I believe, at all times, but in the time in which we live I am ready to worship it.   —Tocqueville[5]

What does it mean to be free? On the surface, being free means being able to do whatever you want. No one to tell you what to do, no one to answer to, no responsibilities. Can a free society exist with this sort of attitude?

Freedom & Responsibility

Perhaps you think we will answer this question with a firm "no." Well, you might be surprised that we will say instead, "Yes, sort of." Let us explain.

---

[4]*Democracy in America*, Vol. II, Book 2, ch. 2
[5]*Democracy in America*, Vol. II, Book 4, ch. 7

Unlike Peter Pan, who can wants to be a boy forever, the real young are impatient to grow up, especially when they are being told, "No," by their parents. And that is because they imagine, rightly, that when they are adults, they will be free. As children grow towards adulthood, the impatience to get out on their own, to make their own decisions, grows with them. This often leads to tension between parents and children, children pushing for independence, parents resisting. Both efforts are natural. On the one hand, the purpose of being a child is to turn into an adult, just as the purpose of being a caterpillar is to develop the butterfly's beautiful wings and fly. The role of parents, on the other hand, is to help the children develop their powers and to make sure they don't harm themselves before they're ready for independence, just as nature protects and develops the butterfly's powers in the chrysalis before it releases it to fly. Parents do this, in part, by slowly increasing the realm in which their sons and daughters act on their own and take responsibility for their actions, including their mistakes.

Again, consider what happens when a mistake is made, and the consequences, for which the boy or girl takes responsibility, are painful. Did they really do what they wanted to? Did they want to be pained or unhappy? Of course not. So, did they act freely? In one way, yes. No one else did the actions. They carried them out themselves. But, they did not wish the outcome, so how did they produce what they did not, ultimately, will? The answer is that they were, in fact, slaves of ignorance or passion. That is, not really free. It is to prevent this that we try to give them good habits to control passion, and good information to ward off ignorance.

In one respect, then, to be an adult *is* to decide for yourself what you are going to do. And to be free *does* mean having no one tell you what to do... because you don't *need* anyone to tell you what to do, because *you* can make good decisions for yourself and those who depend on you. But then freedom turns out not to be the absence of responsibility, but the reward of responsibility in the form of the capacity to do what promotes human flourishing. Although a child becomes free by attaining a certain age, a person becomes worthy of freedom when he is able to take responsibility for his own actions.

Courage & Prudence

"Live Free or Die!" "Don't Tread on Me!" These cries rang in the ears of the colonial soldiers as they went into battle. The nation founded on the Declaration depends for its existence on a thirst for independence. This thirst must be so strong that it is worth dying for. It must be the grounds for courage. Is it

President Truman in the White House.

an accident that the refrain of the national anthem, the *Star Spangled Banner*, ends with the phrase, "the land of the free and the home of the brave"? Because freedom entails both risking yourself and taking care of yourself, it is not the easiest way to live. It is much easier never to put yourself on the firing line, and to have someone else take care of you and make all the important decisions.

So the man worthy of freedom must all desire it above other goods—more than pleasure, than ease, than excitement, than security. This makes him into a man of moral courage. He will have not fail to take responsibility for his actions because he knows that is the mark of a free man. President Harry Truman was widely known for his motto, "The Buck Stops Here." When decisions he made turned out for the worse, he didn't want to blame it on anyone else, because that would have meant he was not responsible for his own actions. Even his political opponents had to admire this feature of his character.

But desire isn't enough. To want to take care of yourself and to be willing to take responsibility for your actions will not help you if you always make bad decisions. A young man who falls in with a bad crowd and winds up in prison might admit that he was responsible for his fate, but he has wasted much of his life. So has a woman who find herself stuck with a man who abuses her, cheats on her, and then abandons her. Or the head of a family who entrusts his money to swindlers. Even if they all accept the consequences, they have still erred, and erred disastrously.

Independence requires the ability to make sound judgments, in addition to the willingness to stand behind one's judgments. Traditionally, the habit of making good decisions was known as prudence. It comes from good education, experience, and heeding the advice of the wise.

Civic Duty

So far we have talked about what makes a man capable of taking care of himself. In America, freedom has a more profound meaning, because adults not only take care of themselves and their families, they also have a role to play in caring for their community, state and country. The freedom

School board meeting, San Leandro, CA, 1942.

that our founders fought for was the right to participate in making laws for themselves, in deciding what their taxes should be used for, in choosing their chief executives and legislators, in appling the laws—in short, what we have called "self-government".

We still enjoy this freedom, which we usually exercise by voting for people to represent us and by serving on juries. This means that, in this country, we are the rulers. *We* are "Caesar." Just as everything done by an ambassador is done by authority of the president, so everything done in our city, state or country is done on our authority.

With this kind of liberty comes a new level of responsibility. Because we are the rulers, we have to be able to make good decisions for the whole community. We have to stay informed about important issues, and about how our representatives are performing in office. We also need to participate in the public discussions that will play an important role in determining what decisions are made. The demand such civic participation makes on our time and understanding should not be taken lightly, particularly in light of the temptations of "individualism". To do our civic duty well requires that we work at it, just as with any other duty. And that work involves getting and understanding a good deal of information. This is one reason that the founding generation limited the national government. The further away from us decisions are made, the harder it is for us to participate in them intelligently. Participation in local civic and political and religious groups is accessible to us all, as are local school board or city council meetings. And so, thanks to the internet, are many other modes of common action and deliberation. But if all the important decisions are usurped by judges and bureaucrats, or made in unresponsive state capitals, or in Washington, D.C., we will have little say in what laws govern the place where we live.

9.3 Forming Citizens

Religion

> Our Fathers' God to Thee
> Author of Liberty,
> To Thee we sing...
> —*My Country 'Tis of Thee*,
> final stanza

> When [friends of republican government] attack religious opinions, they obey the dictates of their passions and not of their interests. Despotism may govern without faith, but liberty cannot. Religion is much more necessary in the republic which they set forth in glowing colors than in the monarchy which they attack; it is more needed in democratic republics than in any others. How is it possible that society should escape destruction if the moral tie is not strengthened in proportion as the political tie is relaxed? And what can be done with a people who are their own masters if they are not submissive to the Diety?
>
> ...Religion in America takes no direct part in the government of society, but it must be regarded as the first of their political institutions...   —Tocqueville[6]

Men and women of our times will sometimes say that there is no public role for religion in American life. Belief in God, or lack of it, they say, is merely a private matter; it makes, or ought to make, no difference to our public institutions. Ideological lobbies pushing this view, such as People for the American Way, cite the First Amendment and its interpretation by the Supreme Court in such matters as public school prayer and holiday displays to show that religion has no legitimate place in public life.

This was not the view of Americans at the time of the Declaration, or at the time when the religious liberty provisions of the First Amendment were adopted. As Supreme Court Justice Joseph Story put it a generation after the founding, "...Piety, religion, and morality are intimately connected with the well-being of the state...The promulgation of the great doctrines of religion...can never be a matter of indifference in any well-ordered community." And the Americans of those days were, on the whole, pious men. Most of

---

[6]*Democracy in America*, Vol. I, Book 2, Ch. 9

them practiced a religion, generally some form of Protestant Christianity, and even those who did not recognized its crucial importance for the success of the democratic experiment.

The First Amendment & Religion

In fact, the First Amendment to the Constitution was proposed, in part, as a way to *encourage* the influence of religious belief on the people. In the House debates on its ratification, Daniel Carroll, a Roman Catholic from Maryland, said in passing, in his argument for adoption, that it was backed by "many sects." Madison, who held a stronger view in favor of the separation of church and state than did many of the other founders, took notice of the effects of the religious liberty established by the founding generation in 1819, by remarking with pleasure that "there has been an increase of religious instruction since the revolution."

By forbidding the "establishment" of religion, preventing the national government from becoming identified with one religious sect, the First Amendment served two functions. It prevented people of differing religious beliefs from being persecuted by governmental power directed by one religious body at the expense of the others. Thus, it kept the Union free from misuse by a religious sect. It also prevented religion from becoming a mere tool of political power, an abuse that Madison called, "an unhallowed perversion of the means of salvation." Within two generations, all the states had similar religious liberty provisions in their constitutions. Before that time, there had been more or less effective, and more or less oppressive, establishment of religion in eight of the original thirteen colonies: the Congregationalist Church was established by the Puritans in New England; Virginia, Maryland, and the Carolinas were officially Anglican. But in Europe, where most countries still had established state religions, faith had been undermined when the church served tyranny and oppression, or when it used the power of the state to persecute believers of other sects. This was especially scandalous for American Christians who saw the laws of the Old World used to persecute other Christians, and for men of good will, including unbelievers, who recoiled from the horror of the religious wars in Europe and England. Indeed, some leading writers of the European "Enlightenment," including, in his later career, our own Thomas Paine, considered religious faith to be an enemy to freedom and knowledge.

225

The Role of Religion in a Democracy

But the early Americans knew from experience that some religious faith was essential to free institutions. One reason for this view is obvious. Where men are free to do anything, they will always be tempted to use their power to commit injustice against others. In America, where the desire of the majority could always be made into law and enforced on others, the temptation to seize the property or trample the liberty of the minority was always present. No benevolent monarch, no kindly lord stood ready to protect the few from the many.

George Washington taking the Inaugural Oath at Federal Hall, New York, New York.

With such unlimited power, only the people could restrain themselves from injustice. Reverence for God and His laws taught Americans the limits within which they could use their unlimited power. American children were schooled in the Ten Commandments, and in the Gospel injunction, "Do unto others as you would have them do unto you." And so, without direct establishment, American public opinion, always the deepest and most powerful force in our republic, strongly supported religion. Whatever the secrets of their own hearts, American statesmen, even the free-thinking Jefferson, patronised religion. Statesmen and citizens alike felt that men whose consciences are formed according to religious precepts are more able to govern themselves wisely, and less likely to abuse their power.

The near universal acceptance of common religious moral teaching made it more possible for one man to trust the decency or justice of another. Washington made a similar point in his *Farewell Address* when he asked, "Where is the security for property, for reputation, for life, if the sense of religious obligation desert the oaths which are the instruments of investigation in courts of justice?" The solemnity of a religious oath, made with the hand on the Bible, makes a pious soul less likely to lie, to cheat, to break the Ten Commandments. Of course, Christianity did not keep men from treating one another unjustly, and gravely unjustly, too, as we have seen in the case of slavery. But the moral ideals implanted by faith in God were powerful helps in hindering, in preventing, and even in reversing grievous errors. That these ideals were more or less agreed upon, while the mysteries and transcendental aspects of faith were left outside the public sphere, meant that some of the most exalted things, the things that command the deepest loyalties in men, were not subjects of political division. This had a pacifying effect on our politics, insulating us against the sectarian savagery seen too often on this globe.

> ... if any hold that the religious spirit which I admire is the very thing most amiss in America, and that the only element wanting to the freedom and happiness of the human race on the other side of the ocean [is the replacement of God by nature or scientific materialism], I can only reply that those who hold this language have never been in America and that they have never seen a religious or a free nation. When they return from a visit to that country, we shall hear what they have to say.
> —Tocqueville[7]

Questions for Reflection

1. Tocqueville's discussion of the remedies for individualism is found in Volume II of *Democracy in America*, the first nine chapters of the Second Book (in some editions the "Second Part"), less than 40 pages altogether. You might wish to consider whether he gave religious sentiment and duty a fair treatment in these pages, and whether what he warns of is more or less threatening in our day.

2. What is the importance of owning property for learning the skills of freedom? Can you think of examples in which owning something makes a person more responsible? Or more inventive and imaginative? Consider, too, the moral dangers of wealth and of the desire to increase one's wealth, a favorite subject of philosophers and preachers.

3. Madison denounced the use of religion as a tool of political power, calling it a "perversion." Do you think drawing attention to its

---

[7] *Democracy in America*, Vol. I, Book 2, Ch. 9

usefulness in helping men to be good is such a use?

4. Discuss the view of human nature in the quotation above from *Democracy in America*.

Forming Citizens: Education

It is in republican government that the full power of education is needed. Fear in despotic governments arises of itself from threats and chastisements; honor in monarchies is favored by the passions and favors them in turn; but political virtue is a renunciation of oneself, which is always a very painful thing.

One can define this virtue as the love of the laws and the homeland. This love, requiring a continous preference of the public interest over one's own, produces all the individual virtues; they are only that preference.

This love is singularly connected with democracies. In them alone, government is entrusted to each citizen. Now government is like all things in the world; in order to preserve it, one must love it...

Therefore, in a republic, everything depends on establishing this love, and education should attend to inspiring it.   —Montesquieu[8]

...no sort of comparison can be drawn between the pioneer and the dwelling that shelters him. Everything about him is primitive and wild, but he is himself the result of the labor and experience of eighteen centuries. He wears the dress and speaks the language of cities; he is acquainted with the past, curious about the future, and ready for argument about the present; he is, in short, a highly civilized being, who consents for a time to inhabit the backwoods, and who penetrates into the wilds of the New World with the Bible, an axe, and some newspapers.   —Tocqueville[9]

"What I do with my own life" always affects other people. This is especially true in a democracy, where each one of us bears in a particular way the responsibility of making decisions that affect all. To do this well, we need to have the moral character to take that responsibility seriously. But we also need to have an education that allows us to discern what is truly best.

---

[8] *Spirit of the Laws* Part I, Bk. 4, ch. 5

[9] *Democracy in America*, Vol. I, Book 2, Ch. 9

In monarchies, great attention was given to the education of the heir, the prince, who eventually would rule the people, making decisions affecting the whole nation. In a democracy, the students in our public and private schools, and in their homes, are the princes. They will soon have a role in determining the direction our communities, our state, our nation will take. Students who prefer feeling to reflection, or prejudice to reason, cannot make good decisions. Some appreciation of this truth has consistently led Americans to endeavor to include some amount of character formation in our common schools. And some of that formation is often recollected with gratitude for the beloved teachers or coaches who have changed and shaped our lives.

The most famous example of the elite education of the heir to power may be that of Phillip of Macedon, who brought Aristotle himself to his court to tutor his son, whom the world came to know as Alexander the Great.

Beyond Character Formation

We certainly need schools where traits of good character are supported and even encouraged. But a good heart without a clear head is blind. To act well, to achieve good, a good-hearted American student needs to *understand* the principles that have made his country. Since these principles stem from the two primary lights of western civilization, Natural and Divine Law, it will be well for our students to come to know books of Plato and Moses, the researches of Aristotle, the orations of Cicero, the teachings of Socrates and St. Paul, in short the prime students of Nature, and the prime students of Nature's God. Something of what is called a liberal education is essential for the free man. American students in particular must also come to know the great figures of our own republic, men in whose lives our principles shine.

Tocqueville considered the Americans to be as a whole the most enlightened nation in the history of the world. With the exception of slaves, who were generally, though not universally, illiterate, almost no American was without a basic education. While most Americans didn't proceed to a study of philosophy or the fine arts, they did understand the history of their country, its forms of government and its laws. Through their formal education, their newspapers, their conversations, and, above all else, their participation in government, Americans understood the fundamental rights described in the Declaration of Independence, and how their laws, their customs and their forms of government were arranged to maintain those rights.

> The American learns to know the laws by participating in the act of legislation; and he takes a lesson in the forms of government from governing. —Tocqueville[10]

George Custer in his study, 1874, Fort Riley, Kansas

Tocqueville, however, was not an uncritical observer. He also points out that, up to the 1830s our literature was scanty, our theoretical science of little value, and our philosophers non-existent. With melancholy reluctance, Tocqueville concluded that there would never be in America such a soul as a Blaise Pascal, the greatest Christian inquirer he knew of. An observer of the state of learning in America, he says, "must consider the same object from two different points of view. If he singles out only the learned, he will be astonished to find out how few they are; but if he counts the ignorant, the American people will appear to be the most enlightened in the world."

On the other hand, Morison, author of the *Oxford History*, when describing the education of the founding generation speaks of the "sound education in the ancient classics and political theory that young men obtained at the College of William and Mary." He adds, "running a plantation, serving on the council or in the house of burgesses, and reading Cicero, Polybius, and Locke gave Virginians an excellent training in statesmanship."

---

[10] *Democracy in America*, Vol. I, Book 2, Ch. 9

230

Perhaps this difference between authors can be traced to the periods they have in mind. The liberal education of the 18th century Virginians and others that Morison refers to was an inheritance from English and European tradition, and in some measure aristocratic. The American of Tocqueville's time was much more the frontiersman and democrat of the days of Davy Crockett and Andrew Jackson. Democracy had, in some measure, pushed aside common liberal learning, and replaced it with self-instruction or with the useful. Moral instruction continued of course, in the elementary school. One only need look at the McGuffey Readers to see that. But the higher learning was then, and seems always to be, in some peril in America.

Tocqueville thought that we Americans compensated for our lack of "book-learning" by political and social practice:

> It cannot be doubted that in the United States the instruction of the people powerfully contributes to the support of the democratic republic; and such must always be the case, I believe, where the instruction which enlightens the understanding is not separated from the moral education which amends the heart. But I would not exaggerate this advantage, and I am still further from thinking, as so many people do think in Europe, that men can be instantaneously made citizens by teaching them how to read and write. True information is mainly derived from experience; and if the Americans had not been gradually accustomed to govern themselves, their book-learning would not help them much at the present day.[11]

Higher Education: Reflection & Correct Action

But Americans did connect primary education with self-government in Tocqueville's day, and they made the case for higher education as well. The University of Virginia was a beloved project of Jefferson, and his *Rockfish Gap Report* of 1818 sketched the public purposes of higher education as including, besides such practical concerns as agricultural and commercial progress:

> ...To form the statesmen, legislators, and judges, on whom public prosperity and individual happiness are so much to depend...
>
> To develop the reasoning faculties of our youth, enlarge their minds, cultivate their morals, and instill into them the precepts of virtue and order;

---

[11] *Democracy in America*, Vol. I, Book 2, Ch. 9

> ... And, generally, to form them to habits of reflection and correct
> action, rendering them examples of virtue to others, and of happiness
> to themselves.

The report on the plans for the University of Virginia, quoted above, makes for fascinating reading. He says nothing of theoretical philosophy, and his only mention of mathematics and physics quickly links those studies to advances in medicine and technological applications. Jefferson himself could, and did, read Homer in the original Greek, but he does not praise the classics, though Latin, Hebrew, and Greek (and Anglo-Saxon!) are among the studies listed by name later in the report, with the brief remark that these languages are the foundation common to all the sciences. Presumably this has something to do with their roles as the sources of many words in the modern languages, a reason commonly given today for the study of Latin. The notion of the useful dominates that of the contemplative throughout. The only philosophy with a prominent place is political philosophy, a central element in the ideal of liberal education from the time of Plato.

One thing that strikes us is Jefferson's omission of theological and scriptural studies. He explains this omission as proceeding in conformity with the principles of Virginia's Constitution, which places all sects of religion on an equal footing, with the jealousies of the different sects

University of Virginia, Charlottesville,
by Henry Howe, circa 1845

guarding that equality, and with the sentiments of the legislature in favor of freedom of religion. But he goes on to add that proofs of the being of a God will be presented in the ethics courses; and he speaks of this God in language that takes one back to the Declaration: He is the source of the moral law and hence of political justice and all moral obligations, and is our maker and ruler. Still there will be no professor of divinity in Jefferson's university, and no teaching of the contents of scripture as sacred. And he has bitter words for what he considers the backward-looking universities of Europe, with their close bonds to the churches.

Jefferson's university was unique in its hostility to revelation. Nearly all our institutions of higher learning began as seminaries, and continued to include a strong religious element for decades after the founding of the University of Virginia. And some of them were also explicit in their devotion to what we would call liberal education. A famous document in our educational history, the 1828 *Yale College Report*, argues thus:

> As in our primary schools, reading, writing, and arithmetic are taught to all, however different their prospects; so in a college, all should be instructed in those branches of knowledge, of which no one destined to the higher walks of life ought to be ignorant. What subject which is now studied here, could be set aside, without evidently marring the system? Not to speak particularly, in this place, of the ancient languages; who that aims at a well proportioned and superior education will remain ignorant of the elements of the various branches of mathematics, or of history and antiquities, or of rhetoric and oratory, or natural philosophy, or astronomy, or chemistry, or mineralogy, or geology, or political economy, or mental and moral philosophy?[12]

Morality, Sobriety & Enterprise

Returning briefly to primary education, the same *Rockfish Gap Report* summarizes the purposes of the common schools of Virginia as instructing all its youth in their rights, interests, and duties, as men and citizens. Jefferson lays stress on the students' knowing their rights and improving their morals. As one might expect, for Jefferson, this moral aim is not closely tied to sectarian belief. In much of the rest of America, that tie was stronger. Tocqueville remarks of the public schools in the America of the 1830s: "The greater part of education is entrusted to the clergy," and Morrison, writing of the colonial schools in New England writes, "The religious sentiment was basic."

As we have seen before, Lincoln has a way of getting at the kernel of his countrymen's ways. So it is with education. Here is an excerpt from a speech given in his home state in 1832:

> Upon the subject of education, not presuming to dictate any plan or system respecting it, I can only say that I view it as the most important subject which we as a people can be engaged in. That every man may receive at least, a moderate education, and thereby be enabled to read the histories of his own and other countries, by which he may duly appreciate the value of our free institutions, appears

---

[12] *Reports on the Course of Instruction in Yale College by a Committee of the Corporation and the Academical Faculty*, page 19

to be an object of vital importance, even on this account alone, to say nothing of the advantages and satisfaction to be derived from all being able to read the scriptures and other works, both of a religious and moral nature, for themselves. For my part, I desire to see the time when education, and by its means, morality, sobriety, enterprise and industry, shall become much more general than at present, and should be gratified to have it in my power to contribute something to the advancement of any measure which might have a tendency to accelerate the happy period.[13]

What did Tocqueville find that made America successful as a republic? A people experienced in the responsibilities of property ownership and self government. A people educated in the principles of law, government, and justice. A people who elevated God's laws above their own desires. In short, a people worthy of freedom.

Questions for Reflection

5. See if you can find out whether the general literacy that Tocqueville admired was produced by public schools, or by private schools, or by the churches or other means. You may want to consult the Northwest Ordinance, histories of education, or Tocqueville himself.

6. Consider the remark of Tocqueville above about the relation of literacy and citizenship ("It cannot be doubted. . ."). Do you agree or disagree? Why?

7. The place of theological and scriptural studies in publicly funded education has been a matter of controversy since the founding. What do you think of Jefferson's exclusion of these subjects from the university curriculum? If they are to be excluded, would it be wise for our statesmen to assist, with public money, private colleges and universities in which such studies are offered? Does such aid imperil the independence of private colleges? What has been our policy on aid to religious colleges in the last 50 years?

8. Consider the last quotation from Lincoln. What do you think of the order of the goods that Lincoln sets out as proper to public education? Do you agree with his placing enterprise and industry in the list? Should they come where he puts them, and why?

---

[13] *To the People of Sangamo County*, March 9, 1832

Epilogue:
Dangers to Freedom in Our Time

At what point then is the approach of danger to be expected? I answer, if it ever reach us, it must spring up amongst us. It cannot come from abroad. If destruction be our lot, we must ourselves be its author and finisher. As a nation of freemen, we must live through all time, or die by suicide. —*Address to the Young Men's Lyceum*

America, America, God mend thine every flaw.
Confirm thy Soul in Self-control,
Thy Liberty in Law. —*America the Beautiful*

A False Idea of Freedom

At no time in our country's history have we been a nation of saints or philosophers. Even the generation of people who founded our country failed to meet the demands of authentic freedom in many ways, most notably in the case of slavery. However, the idea of the free man was always present. Even when we didn't meet the demands of responsibility and self control, we knew that was how free men should behave. We honored the idea in our homilies and speeches. Our idea condemned corruptions of freedom; it rallied us in time of great national trial. Throughout our history, it has shown its great power to reform, to call our nation back to its founding principles.

Today, however, the very idea of freedom is under attack. We saw in the last section that freedom demands responsibility. But we are all aware that a very different understanding of what it means to be free permeates our society. According to this view, freedom means more than making our own decisions; it means not having anyone tell us that we should behave any differently. In this view, no legislator, no teacher, no parent, no governor, no preacher, not even God Himself has the right to tell a person what he should do.

This specious view, which takes freedom to be license to do anything at all, makes self-governing undesirable and finally impossible. The more we indulge our desires, the less interested we become in making the effort to live according to reason. The man of passion may look strong and free on the outside, but inside he is personally and politically weak. What will our political future be if we succumb to this false dream of freedom? Like a self-indulgent monarch who turns all the state's affairs over to a Grand Vizier only too eager for the power, and finds himself the slave of his former servant, we could continue to give more of our authority to our magistrates so that we might indulge ourselves. As long as our leaders continued to flatter and pamper us, we would continue to increase their power. If those in positions of power also believed freedom equaled license, they would have no reason not to use their power to fulfill their own desires, as long as they could get away with it. The more power they had, the more they would be able to get away with. They would become tyrants. And we would wake up one day to find that we had become slaves.

This is the pattern that republics all too often follow. In the last years of the Roman Republic, ordinary citizens were happy to give power to ambitious men who promised to feed and entertain them. The Roman authors even had a phrase for it: "*panem et circenses*," "bread and circuses." Julius Caesar, Pompey, Mark Anthony, and other glamorous and ambitious men then used their

One example of the extravagant public spectacles put on by Roman emperors to distract the people, a mock sea-battle with real water and scaled-down warships.

influence to satisfy their own desires and increase their power. Defenders of the Republic, like Cato and Cicero, were swept aside; civil disorders and political murders multiplied; the honest suffered and the unscrupulous prospered. The corruption in both citizens and officials became so great that most were thankful when Augustus finally subjected everyone to his own supreme authority, in what the historians call, "the Peace of Augustus." The relatively mild Augustus was then followed by his grim nephew, Tiberius, and by such horrors as Caligula and Nero. How terrible was the peace of Augustus, we may read in Tacitus' *Annals*. Virtue, in Tacitus' narrative, is so rare that upon meeting it "we are surprised before we are delighted."

The partisans of license betray authentic freedom in two other ways. First, they deny the natural law, and maintain that what is evil is either good or neutral. Finding this difficult to defend to others or even to be believed by themselves, and wishing to justify their uncontrolled behavior in some particular arena, they find themselves tempted to deny that human beings can control their actions more generally. Our behavior is determined, they are led to believe, by our genes and hormones, by our upbringing, by oppressive social structures. The poor are now *expected* to steal; those of a group abused by the policeman, to riot. Teenagers can't control their sexual drives, ambitious types can't help lying and stepping on others, angry people can't help killing. What are in fact moral problems are treated as physical illnesses or addictions or weaknesses no one can be expected to resist.

We can see this clearly in the recent history of homosexual propaganda. When homosexual "rights" first became an issue, proponents argued that all men are free to make their own choices. Since, they argued, homosexual acts giving sexual pleasure were morally neutral, or even good, then to discriminate against homosexuality was to punish an acceptable use of freedom. Then, in an almost complete contradiction of this argument, they made another, denying that it was a free choice at all. They said that some people are born homosexuals: their genetic make-up forces them into their homosexual "lifestyle." So to discriminate against such people is just like discriminating against people of different races. A white or yellow or black man can't help the color of his skin; a homosexual can't help his lifestyle.

But this sort of argument makes freedom both impossible and dangerous. If this argument is true, why should it not apply to other kinds of behavior? People born with bad tempers, with propensities to lie or steal, with a taste for sexual relations with children, can't be expected to control themselves. Of course, these last examples rather plainly involve the pubic good. Accordingly, we are now faced with a policy question. What shall we do? When someone can't control actions dangerous for society, then his ability to act in those ways must be either curtailed or tolerated. We end in either license or repression. Plato foresaw this centuries before our times. This is from *The*

237

Republic, Book VIII:

> [Socrates is speaking:] "...And they [the members of the democratic city] end up, as you well know, by paying no attention to the laws, written or unwritten, in order that they may avoid having any master at all."
>
> "Of course, I know it," he said.
>
> "Well, then, my friend," I said, "this is the beginning...from which tyranny in my opinion naturally grows."

Undermining Marriage and the Family

> There is certainly no country in the world where the tie of marriage is more respected than in America or where conjugal happiness is more highly or worthily appreciated. In Europe, almost all the disturbances of society arise from the irregularities of domestic life...But when the American retires from the turmoil of public life to the bosom of his family, he finds in it the image of order and of peace. There his pleasures are simple and natural, his joys are innocent and calm; and as he finds that an orderly life is the surest path to happiness, he accustoms himself easily to moderate his opinions as well as his tastes. While the European endeavors to forget his domestic troubles by agitating society, the American derives from his own home that love of order which he afterwards carries with him into public affairs.
>
> —Tocqueville[14]

Today, the marriage-based two-parent family is under stress as never before. Our tax laws and social legislation encourage mothers to hand over the care of children to governmental agencies, our divorce rates are much higher than in the past, the police have their hands full tracking down 'deadbeat dads,' illegitimate births are at shockingly high levels, and the very notion of a normal family, consisting of two adults, a man and a woman, united in marriage, and their children, is questioned.

When family life fails, so do the strong moral habits that make the exercise of freedom in public life possible. Within the family, parents learn how to care for others. They learn to think beyond the present moment, because they have to plan for the future of their children and grandchildren.

---

[14] *Democracy in America*, Vol. 1, Book 2, ch. 9

238

The effort to keep their marriage vows schools husband and wife in the habits of controlling passion and keeping promises. Children learn how to control their own actions from the example, instruction, and discipline of their parents. Even value-free social studies confirm that children raised *outside* of the marriage-based, two-parent family have worse chances in life, greater incidence of crime and drug addiction, lower grades in school, and higher rates of poverty and disease.

A Golden Wedding Anniversary in 1947

"For better or worse, for richer and poorer, in sickness and in health, till death do you part." When the kids are sick, during times of unemployment, through a difficult pregnancy, in the event of lasting disability, "even then will I love you and care for you." When one is grumpy, when times are tough, when someone else seems more attractive, "even then will I stick by you." This is what the marital commitment means. It is sealed by a vow made to God. Only if we believe in the possibility and nobility of self control can we even contemplate such a vow. Only if freedom exists, can marriage exist. Only if we can take responsibility for our own choices can marriage survive.

The political movement for homosexual 'marriage,' ironically, testifies to the truth of normal and traditional marriage, at least in one respect. Same-sex couples are blind to the deep roots of fertility, the complementarity in soul and body of the two sexes, and the necessity of giving oneself to the truly different, sexually different, other that give marriage its full meaning. But they rightly see the bond of committed married couples as somehow respectable and genuinely good. Their own erotic friendships may be contrary to nature, but what good they do have is even more defective without a pledge to resist promiscuity and total reduction to mere pleasure. So a kind of parasitic homage is paid to actual marriage by this movement. It cannot, however, be justified in a republic founded on "the laws of Nature and of Nature's God." And to call such a partnership marriage is to falsify the common language. One is reminded of one of Lincoln's jokes here. Question: "How many legs does a dog have, if you call a tail a leg?" Answer: "Four; calling a tail a leg does not make it one."

239

There is an evil spirit abroad today (it often comes to us through the airwaves, on television and radio) that whispers to us that the marital commitment doesn't mean much: "You don't have to wait for marriage to enjoy sex. . . if an inconvenient child is conceived, you may destroy it in the womb. . . if you are unhappy in your marriage, you should be free to abandon spouse and children to find your own personal fulfillment." We justify heeding this voice by telling ourselves that our right to be happy trumps every other concern. When we undermine marriage, we tell ourselves that the *children* would be unhappy if *we* are not personally fulfilled. But the fact is that when we do this, we have refused the duty to place our children's happiness over our own comfort. If we won't make the sacrifices necessary to take care of our own children, how will they be taught to make any sacrifices for strangers? Or fellow citizens?

Tocqueville thought that there would never be a people both free and irreligious. We may wonder whether there can long be a people politically free and at the same time indifferent to marriage and careless of innocent children.

Education as Workforce Training

The state of public education in our country has been a growing concern for decades. Education professionals have been echoing the public outcry for reform, but somehow things never seem to get any better. Part of the reason is a fundamental flaw in what reformers think the goal of education should be. Today, many universities and an increasing number of high school and elementary schools are focused on one goal for education: to get a job. Increasingly, schools are judged only on the extent to which they properly prepare students to take their place in the world of the multi-national corporations and government bureaucracies which will provide for them. There is something slavish in such a reduced view of education and life. There is more to life than a job.

Americans have always combined moral consensus and stability with economic innovation and flexibility. Now we teach moral uncertainty, or relativism, and are on the cusp of teaching a kind of timidity and narrow-mindedness in preparation for work. If we look only to immediate job placement, not long-term job creation via original thought, enterprise, and investment, we will have sacrificed growth for security, and we will have a future more like the mature, and slow-growth, economies of Western Europe. Like those nations, we will also have nothing by way of national confidence or moral resolve to set against the threat of radical Islamism, or whatever new enemy to human progress and dignity may arise.

Moreover, "workforce education" has formed an unholy alliance with multiculturalism. It has produced an emphasis on forming relativistic habits of mind and heart, because, in the opinion of educationists and corporate leaders, these workplaces must be free of the "divisive" arguments that might arise if someone says that some ways of life really are better than others. But such relativism implies a denial of the possibility that reason and reflection can reach a judgment in matters ethical and moral. It is a counsel of despair about the very end of education, namely, some degree of human wisdom about human goods. It also means removing authority and respect from professors, whose love is teaching and learning, and transfer-

Educating young people for work in a bureaucracy would not be likely to encourage a questioning or speculative attitude.

ring them to administrators, economists, and bureaucrats, who claim to know how to plan for the "needs of the 21st century." But these planners have never successfully foreseen human needs. Their follies have made an economic and environmental wasteland of the riches of Eurasia, as may be seen by reviewing the experiments and enterprises of Stalin and his successors. Nor have they created wealth. They have only robbed Peter to pay Paul, and slowed the progress of human dynamism deployed in the pursuit of happiness.

Reduction of the aim of education to workforce preparation began with the Progressive Movement. We have seen a gradual but steady change from the ways of our forefathers. As we have seen, at the beginning, students at all levels were educated chiefly to understand and to practice the principles that make a free society possible. They read history, literature, and moral treatises; some learned a foreign language and all a bit of mathematics. Having developed their capacity to think, many graduates were able to make important decisions about what is best, what is wise, and what is just, for themselves and society. By first being good humans, capable of reasoning for themselves, they were then able to exercise their minds in inventive ways to build up the vast, energetic, and wealthy economy the United States enjoys today.

None of this is meant to say that American education in our age of bountiful technology should have no room for development of suitable skills. On the contrary, it is essential that instruction of this sort be widely available, in and outside of educational institutions. But what earlier times called liberal or basic education, with a vigorous element of moral and civic study, must never be abandoned or crowded out by mere training.

We need to rethink the goals of education if our country is to survive. A democracy in which the public comes to think that one way of life is no better than any other, will soon judge everything by its price, including themselves, whom they will hardly value any more.

God in Exile

We have said that religious worship has always been the keystone of the arch of the American republic. Over the last forty years, however, God has been exiled from our public life. He can't be supplicated in public schools. He can't be honored in public displays. He is generally unwelcome in our movies and TV shows, except those that mock the simple or hypocritical people who worship Him. The mention of God in the Pledge of Allegiance has been challenged in court. It used to be a sign of character, or at least propriety, when a political official submitted his actions to the judgment of a higher being; now, in some circles, it is a cause of suspicion if a public man admits he prays.

Moral revolutions do not stand still. Thus we see that first comes the attack on moral restraint in the name of freedom, and then soon after comes, in the name of that same, now immoral, freedom, the denial that there can be freedom at all. Likewise, some begin by denying God so that man may be properly exalted. Man, they think, cannot be the greatest being, if there is a God. Is man not free, autonomous, unbounded by law or limit or even condition? One thinks of Dostoyevsky's troubled character Ivan Karamazov

242

here: "If there is no God, then everything is permitted." Once God has been denied, they deny that man has any soul. And yet the soul knows it did not make itself, and it knows that it desires to know more than itself, and feels that it is destined to something more than this world of material things. In order that man may not have such immortal aspirations, which point beyond himself (God forbid!), he must be conceived soulless, a random swarm of atomic particles, without spirit, or will, or finally, freedom. So Dostoyevsky thought it out for us in Russia, a century and more ago.

Although the attack on the public role of religion opened with a handful of specific Supreme Court decisions, it now reaches deeply into the public mind. Even some pious Americans think that any public decision that conforms with a religious teaching might be un-American. If some judge, teacher, or public official cries out "violation of the First Amendment," many good Americans are at a loss how to answer him.

Living the Declaration

We Americans today sense that something is wrong, deeply wrong. All our recent trends, our "liberation" from religion, our materialism and relativism, our sexual license, seem not to have made us happy. We are proud of our prosperity and our might in the world, unmatched in the long history of the civiliza-

Alan Keyes, Ambassador to the U.N., candidate for president and for the Senate, speaks and writes on enduring American political issues.

tions earth has seen pass away. Yet, when we defend liberty and innocent life abroad, we are uncomfortably aware that we kill the unborn and practice a slavish license at home. We had thought of ourselves as the beacon of liberty, a "city on a hill." And the world had sometimes echoed that sentiment. Now, faced with the promotion of the false face of freedom by our own citizens, some of us are speechless, incapable of giving reasons, silent, and ashamed of our silence, but not, of course, contented. But we are not altogether lost as a people. We have only to recall what made us a people, and to make it shine in our speech, in our deeds, and in all our lives.

In order to become worthy of our freedom, worthy of our national might, and worthy of the burden of responsibility that that surpassing might places upon us, in a world filled with the poor, the vulnerable, and the innocent, we need only once again live by the Declaration of Independence.

We began this book asking you to take the Declaration to heart. In recent years, the legislature of New Jersey debated a law asking for public school children to commit a bit of the Declaration to memory, and to recite it each day in their classrooms. Here is what a contemporary statesman wrote in defense of this law:

> If anything can be certain in history, it is that without the civic creed summarized in the opening of the Declaration, the United States would not exist as a free country. The Declaration gives the reasons for which the War of Independence was fought and expresses the motivation that enabled that war to be won. Since that day, the Declaration has been an indispensable foundation for a series of important struggles for justice in America, including of course the abolition of slavery. Without the Declaration, I believe, these struggles would not have been won.
>
> How can a single document be so decisive in the practical affairs of men? This really shouldn't surprise us. While crude wielders of power may think otherwise, ideas are far from impotent in the struggles of life. Ideas, and the words that express them, are actually the dominant force in shaping the destiny of human beings.
>
> How were uncountable masses of people held enthralled by handfuls of people through most of history and in most places in the world? It was not, typically, by the use of overwhelming force. Small groups of people never have enough force to overwhelm the masses. Masters succeed only when they enchain the minds and spirits of those subject to them.
>
> Around the Jefferson Memorial is inscribed a famous quote of Jefferson's: "I swear eternal enmity against every form of tyranny over the mind of man." This recognizes the crucial insight into the real source of enslavement, that slavery is not a matter of physical shackles, but of spiritual, mental, and psychological chains...
>
> Nothing in the course of human history has proved to be harder than actually establishing and preserving a society based on a practical acknowledgment of our equal human nature under God. This nation represents one of the great fruits of that struggle but it will not survive if we don't remember the moral principle that has been our strength.

244

Are we still raising young people who will be emboldened by the truth of human equality to fight for their liberty? Will they resist the temptation to give in to the cowardly behavior that allows tyrants to reign? Will they have the courage to resist tyranny particularly when it offers the kind of comfortable servitude that our era of material abundance makes possible?

If we intend to keep alive in our children the knowledge of the true source of their dignity, we must be sure that their minds are formed in the light of the Declaration. Recitation of the key passages of the Declaration is a simple—and, one might even say self evident—step toward this goal. . .

Contained in the Declaration are the seeds of an ethic of responsibility, for its acknowledgment of our obligations to God leads to the acknowledgment of our obligation to one another. The doctrine of dignified human equality under God provides the basis, therefore, for shaping character in our civic culture in such a way that we eschew being serfs and subjects but at the same time refuse to be bullies and despots. A generation raised on the Declaration will insist we owe to our fellow citizen the same respect that we demand from him.

The Declaration is not merely a powerful tool for spiritual and moral motivation it is probably an irreplaceable one. . .

The schoolchild who reads the Declaration, thinks about it and is moved to give it his assent in however simple a form, is a symbol of the American citizen of any age or intelligence. The full life of citizenship in America is a life lived in reflection on the truths of our founding, continued assent to those truths and continued resolve to act in light of them.

This is the challenge of liberty.

—Ambassador Alan Keyes, May 27, 2000

The legislation did not pass.
What should we, the citizens, do now?

Bibliography

The California Civil Rights Initiative: Restoring Equality Under the Law, 1996 (Assembly Republican Caucus, Office of Policy Research, Sacramento, California).

The Constitution of the United States of America and the Constitution of the State of California, 1997 (California Legislature Assembly).

Declaration of the Immediate Causes Which Induce and Justify the Secession of South Carolina from the Federal Union, 1860 (South Carolina).

Inaugural Addresses of the Presidents of the United States, 1961 (United States Government Printing Office, Washington, D.C.).

Adams, James Truslow, *The March of Democracy: A History of the United States*, 1933 (Charles Scribner's Sons).

Adler, Mortimer J., ed., *The Annals of America*, 1987 (Encyclopaedia Britannica).

Amos, Gary T., *Defending the Declaration*, 1989 (Wolgemuth & Hyatt, Brentwood, Tennessee).

Anderson, Nancy Scott, and Dwight Anderson, *The Generals: Ulysses S. Grant and Robert E. Lee*, 1988 (Alfred A Knopf, New York).

Bailyn, Bernard, *The Ideological Origins of the American Revolution*, 1967 (Belknap Press of Harvard University Press, Cambridge, Massachusetts).

Basler, Roy P., ed., *Abraham Lincoln: His Speeches and Writings*, 2001 (Da Capo Press, Cleveland).

Bruckberger, R. L., *Image of America*, 1959 (The Viking Press, New York).

247

Budziszewski, J., *Written on the Heart: The Case for Natural Law*, 1997 (InterVarsity Press, Downers Grove, Illinois).

Carson, Clarence B., *The Rebirth of Liberty: The Founding of the American Republic 1760–1800*, 1976 (The Foundation for Economic Education, Inc., Irvington-on-Hudson, New York).

Chapman, John Jay, *The Selected Writings of John Jay Chapman*, 1959 (Doubleday Anchor Books).

Coolidge, Calvin, *The Price of Freedom: Speeches and Addresses*, 1924 (Charles Scribner's Sons, New York).

———, *Foundations of the Republic: Speeches and Addresses*, 1926 (Charles Scribner's Sons, New York).

Corwin, Edward S., *The "Higher Law" Background of American Constitutional Law*, 1971 (Cornell University Press, Ithaca).

Cruden, Robert, *The Negro in Reconstruction*, 1969 (Prentice-Hall, Inc., Englewood Cliffs, New Jersey).

Diamond, Martin, *The Founding of the Democratic Republic*, 1981 (F.E. Peacock Publishers, Inc., Itasca, Illinois).

Erik Brunn, Jay Crosby, ed., *Our Nation's Archive, the History of the United States in Documents*, 1999 (Black Dog and Leventhal Publishers, Inc.).

Foner, Eric, *Reconstruction: America's Unfinished Revolution, 1863-1877*, 2002 (Harper Perennial Modern Classics).

Franklin, John Hope, *Reconstruction: After the Civil War*, 1961 (The University of Chicago Press, Chicago).

———, *From Slavery to Freedom: A History of Negro Americans*, 1969 (Vintage Books, New York).

Grob, Gerald N., and Robert N. Beck, eds., *American Ideas: Source Readings in the Intellectual History of the United States*, 1963 (The Free Press, New York).

Hamilton, Alexander, John Jay, and James Madison, *The Federalist*, 1937 (The Modern Library, New York).

248

Hickok, Eugene W., ed., *The Bill of Rights, Original Meaning and Current Understanding*, 1991 (University Press of Virginia, Charlottesville).

Holmes, Leon, *What Shall We Be? A Study of the Political Thought of Three Black Americans*, Ph.D. thesis, 1980, Duke University.

Horwitz, Robert H., ed., *The Moral Foundations of the American Republic*, 1979 (University Press of Virginia, Charlottesville).

Howe, Hezekiah, *Reports on the Course of Instruction in Yale College*, 1828 (Committee of the Corporation and the Academical Faculty).

Hyneman, Charles S., and Donald S. Lutz, *American Political Writing during the Founding Era*, 1983 (Liberty Fund).

Jaffa, Harry V., *Equality and Liberty, Theory and Practice in American Politics*, 1965 (Oxford University Press, New York).

———, *Crisis of the House Divided: An Interpretation of the Issues in the Lincoln-Douglas Debates*, 1973 (University of Washington Press, Seattle).

———, *A New Birth of Freedom: Abraham Lincoln and the Coming of the Civil War*, 2004 (Rowman & Littlefield Publishers).

Jefferson, Thomas, *Writings*, 1984 (Literary Classics of the United States, New York).

Keyes, Alan L, *Masters of the Dream: The Strength and Betrayal of Black America*, 1995 (Quill, William Morrow, New York).

Lincoln, Abraham, and Stephen A. Douglas, *Political Debates Between Hon. Abraham Lincoln and Hon. Stephen A. Douglas, in the Celebrated Campaign of 1858, in Illinois; Including the Preceding speeches of each, at Chicago, Springfield, etc.; also, the Two Great Speeches of Mr. Lincoln in Ohio, in 1859, as Carefully Prepared by the Reporters of each Party, and Published at the Times of Their Delivery*, 1860 (Follett, Foster and Company, Columbus).

———, *The Lincoln-Douglas Debates of 1858*, 1965 (Oxford University Press, New York).

Link, Arthur S., *Woodrow Wilson and the Progressive Era, 1910-1917*, 1954 (Harper Torchbooks, Harper & Row, New York).

Locke, John, *The Second Treatise of Government*, 1952 (Bobbs-Merrill Educational Publishing, Indianapolis).

Lutz, Donald S., *The Origins of American Constitutionalism*, 1988 (Louisiana State University Press, Baton Rouge).

Madison, James, *The Complete Madison, His Basic Writings*, 1953 (Harper & Brothers, New York).

Maier, Pauline, *American Scripture: The Making of the Declaration of Independence*, 1998 (Vintage Books).

Malone, Dumas, *The Story of the Declaration of Independence*, 1954 (Oxford University Press, New York).

Mayer, Henry, *All on Fire, William Lloyd Garrison*, 1998 (St. Martin's Press).

McDonald, Forrest, *Novus Ordo Seclorum, The Intellectual Origins of the Constitution*, 1985 (University Press of Kansas, Lawrence, Kansas).

McPherson, James M., *Battle Cry of Freedom: The Civil War Era*, 1988 (Oxford University Press).

Miller, William Lee, *Arguing About Slavery: John Quincy Adams and the Great Battle in the United States Congress*, 1998 (Vintage Books).

———, *Lincoln's Virtues: An Ethical Biography*, 2003 (Vintage Books).

Montesquieu, Charles de, *The Spirit of the Laws*, 1989 (Cambridge University Press).

Morison, Samuel Eliot, *The Oxford History of the American People*, 1965 (Oxford University Press, New York).

Morris, Richard B., ed., *Significant Documents in United States History*, 1969 (Van Nostrand Reinhold Company, New York).

O'Connor, Karen, and Larry J. Sabato, *American Government: Roots and Reform*, 1993 (Macmillan Pub Co).